To, Carol,

my friend and family

Zanzibar

A Memoir

Mehboob Qureshi

I hope this book will give you a window into my childhood.

Copyright © 2014 Mehboob Qureshi
All rights reserved.

ISBN: 1500912921
ISBN 13: 9781500912925
Library of Congress Control Number: 2014915421
CreateSpace Independent Publishing Platform
North Charleston, South Carolina

Acknowledgement.

Aunty Sharifah

Without her persistent prodding, this book would still be in my head.

Grandma

Without who's editing, this book would be illegible.

Dedication

This book is dedicated to you—my grandchildren. I wrote it for the day you wonder;

"Who am I?"

Mia, Nick, Luke,
Jake, Morgan,
Sam.

Preface

Where is home?

Home is where childhood memories were made.

For me, Home = Zanzibar.

Since I retired, I have had the luxury of time. Time to indulge in activities I did not have time for, while I was preoccupied with making a living. One of the projects I indulged in was converting my memories of home into words

For you, my children, Monroe, Wisconsin will always be your home.

That is the reason Mom and I chose two lots at the periphery of a cemetery on a hill in Monroe. No matter where life takes you, some day when you visit us there, you will also be able to see the house where you were raised—your home.

When you do, the view will bring back memories of your childhood and inspire you to put them into words for your grandchildren.

Love,

Daddy.

Home sweet home.

2702, 22nd Avenue, Monroe. WI. 53566

CHAPTER ONE

Our Roots

On my very first day in Mecca, Saudi Arabia, I witnessed an Arab man in his early thirties, crying and pleading his innocence vociferously, while he was dragged to a chopping block by five fierce policemen. All it took was three witnesses to accuse him of stealing and within six minutes of the accusation, the punishment was executed.

With one disgusting thud, the young man's right hand bounced off the chopping block and dropped on the ground. A couple of spurts of bright blood were followed by oozing of dark blood from the severed hand which turned pale slowly as the fingers relaxed to the accompanied by heart rending wails which still haunt me.

From that moment on, I lived in a constant terror of a false accusation. Only after the wheels of my plane departing from Saudi Arabia were safely tucked into the wheel wells with a thump and the doors to the wells shut with a clank of relief that my obsessing terror began to abate.

It was then that I realized how naïve I was.

I was raised a Muslim in Zanzibar, an Islamic country ruled by an Arab sultan. I was smug. I believed I knew Islam.

It was a surprise to discover that my life in Zanzibar did not prepare me for the Islam as practiced in the realm of the ibn Saud dynasty.

I watched in disbelief as the police enforced on everyone, adherence to prayers five times a day. I was having my first course at a restaurant when an *azaan*[1] blared out of minarets. Even before the *azaan* was over, the waiter rushed over and pleaded with me to leave immediately and to return for the second course after the prayer.

As soon as the Muezzin's call to prayer is heard, customers are hurried out of all places of businesses, doors are shut and soon after that, the police are out patrolling the streets, to make sure that all businesses and customers are obeying the law. If not, the policeman has the authority to met out a penalty, that he considers appropriate, right there and then.

I was told that a policeman has the authority to jail anyone who in his view has broken a law that deserves such a sojourn. Moreover, only the policeman who put a person in jail can get him out of it. If for some reason, the policeman is on a vacation or gave up his job and went back to his country of origin,

---

[1] A call to prayers

The Ka'aba

the prisoner ends up in a limbo for the rest of his earthly life.

The first day we were in Mecca, uncle Munir and I went to the Haram-el-Sharif. By the main gate there is an area where you can borrow wheelchairs. *Daadeeamma*² was too weak to do the *Tawaaf*³ on her own. So, we decided to borrow a wheelchair and help her finish the *Tawaaf* in a wheel chair.

The picture on this page shows the flat roof top, at the periphery of the *Harum*₃ where disabled persons can do the Tawaaf in a wheelchair. It is an honor and truck loads of grace comes to the child who pushes his parent in a wheelchair for the *Tawaaf*. Naturally, all the brothers vied for the job, but I got it.

I did not bully or bribe to get the job.

I pulled rank.

I am the eldest in our family.

In most places, it is customary that you leave some form of ID as a security and your ID is given back to you upon return of

---

² My mother
³ Circumambulation of the Kaaba

the borrowed object. I gave the attendant, an Arab wearing a typical Saudi jubbah and a kofia, my US driver's license.

He looked at my picture, and my name, and his expression turned from boredom to puzzlement. After intensely scrutinizing my driver's license, he asked me in an accusatory tone; "What is a Qureshi?"

I was taken aback. I could not guess what response he expected from me. I looked at him to see if his facial expression or body language would give me a clue as to what answer would satisfy him and while I was still figuring out the best answer to give him, he asked again—this time impatiently;

"Is it the name of a river, an occupation or an American town?"

I thought, "Oh my God!" as my heart dropped to my feet and my sweaty hands trembled. Some information on my driver's license has offended this judge, jury and executioner of the land of instant justice.

As calmly as I could, I sputtered; "Ya sheikh, Qureshi is my surname. I am a descendent of a tribe in Saudi Arabia—Mecca, to be precise."

The puzzled face slowly turned into an expression of comprehension and then into a broad smile. He came towards me with his arms open and outstretched, hugged me, kissed me first on one cheek then on the other. With his hands on my shoulders, he stepped back, and said,

"Welcome home."

From that moment on, at every visit to the Haram, Uncle Munir and I were treated as VIP's

On my last day in Mecca, I thanked him for all his help, wished him goodbye, and asked him to look me up if he ever came to the USA. Then, we exchanged calling cards.

His card said; "Ahmed ibn Saleh El Quraysh."

This story tells us who we are. We are descended from the El Quraysh tribe in Mecca, in what is now Saudi Arabia.

The most prestigious lineage among Muslims is that of Sayyid, the descendants of the prophet's daughter, Fatima. The prophet's only son died during childhood. Those who carry the prophet's surname trace their lineage to the prophet's paternal uncles.

During the expansion of the Islamic empire the Arabs spread out far and wide to spread their religion. They "burned their bridges" behind them so that they could live the rest of their lives in their new countries of adoption. Since armies are made up of only men, the Arabs married local women. This is why you will see the surname "Qureshi", in its vernacular version, in all the lands between and including Spain and Russia.

While I was in Zanzibar, I met a Mr. Munshi. He was a third or fourth cousin of *Abbajaan*[4]. They may even have a gone to grade school together. For a while he taught at a school in Dhandhuka. His family lived in an area called Qureshiwada. A "*Wada*" in Gujrati, is an area where people of a certain common

---

[4] My father.

tie live together. Since everyone in his "Wada" was a Qureshi he distinguished himself by the name *"Munshi"*, a teacher

While still a young man, he left India for Africa, married an African Lady and settled in Lilongwe in what was then Nyasaland and now Malawi. From what he told us, he made a fortune as a building contractor, although he had no formal training in civil engineering, nor could he speak or write English. I have a hard time visualizing him with a trowel in his hand or seeing his exposed skin covered with dirt. It is not what a well brought up Indian stoops to. In India, manual labor is for the low cast. A real Qureshi would never be caught dead doing manual labor.

When I was about eight or nine years old, we did not have Skype, greeting cards or even long distant telephone communications. We wrote letters. That process took an unpredictably long time to get to the addressee, if ever. To ensure that an urgent message got to a recipient within twenty four hours, we used the telegraph service.

Seeing a telegram delivery man in our neighborhood, during festive occasions, was a happy sight. At all other times, it was alarming. It usually signified that a relative of the recipient had expired, in a distant land.

For deaths in Zanzibar, we had a professional crier. His name was Muallim. In his deep, booming, somber voice, he would announce the name of the deceased and the time and place of the funeral, while riding his bicycle through our streets. The language he used was Kutchi, but would switch to Urdu, Gujrati or Kiswahili depending upon the predominant language of that particular neighborhood.

By necessity, all Zanzibari's are multilingual.

I remember, going to the local Cable and Wireless office to send out telegrams to friends and relatives, wishing them a happy Idd[2]. Mr. Munshi was among those that Abbajaan[1] sent a telegram to every Idd.

In the early 1950's, Mr. Munshi visited us in Zanzibar. He was on his way to Hajj. Mr. Munshi was a very entertaining conversationalist. He was also a historian and could quote with confidence, the exact date of events in the history of India.

---

[1] My father

[2] A Muslim festival.

He asked me if I knew who a *Peer* [1] is.

I did. The word means almost the same as the word "saint."

Since there is no interdiction in Islam, there is no place in Islam for a saint. But that has not prevented Muslims from inventing a similar entity—a *Peer*. Unlike saints, *Peers* do not perform miracles. But, they claim to have the ability to make your wish come true.

When Emperor Akbar, the great was in despair because he could not have a son, *Peer* Salim Chishti assured him that he will have one soon and Akber did. So records Indian history

Mr. Munshi told me, that there is a mausoleum to a *Peer,* with the surname of Qureshi, just outside Dhandhuka and that the Qureshi in Dhandhuka trace their ancestry to this saint. As a historian, like a Gerod, the oral historians of West Africa, he was able to name all my predecessors, and according to his calculations, I am the 13th generation descendent of *Peer*$_1$ Qureshi.

So, that makes all of you—my children, my nieces and nephews—fourteenth generation descendent of the *Peer,* who is a well-documented descendent of the father of our Prophet, Muhammad, Abdullah El Quraysh.

---

[1] A saint

Chapter Two
Dhandhuka

The story of the Qureshi's begins here, when time began.

In places where ancient civilizations have existed, archaeologists often find evidence of layers of three or more civilizations that had once thrived at the same spot. A natural catastrophe, like a flood, a fire or an earthquake destroys a civilization; then nature claims it back and covers it with a forest. Because the site has some geographic advantage, like the confluence of two rivers, a deep natural harbor along a trade route, or a spot strategically easier to defend against an enemy attack, a new civilization begins at the same spot and over thousands of years, the cycle repeats itself several times.

Dhandhuka is such a place.

Even to this day, an Indian does not believe in paper money or banks. If he is fortunate enough to have a good harvest, and there is a little money left over, he converts it into gold and his wife wears it. Indians are also, unpretentious. A stranger cannot tell apart, a multimillionaire from a pauper as they all dress alike and have about the same amount of jewelry on them. So what do you do, if you're extremely fortunate and you have saved more gold then your wife can wear at one time, without appearing to be a show off?

You bury it.

The floors in the homes of villages are made of a layer of cow dung, which needs replacing only once or twice a year. It is odorless, economical, and provides a smooth soft surface that stays warm in winter and cool in summer.

One of the ways to hide gold from neighbors and your family is to dig a hole in the floor of one of the rooms, bury your gold in it and then cover the entire floor with a fresh layer of dung. Dung, dries quickly. Even members of your family who walk into that room a few hours later, will not notice any difference in the floor.

An ingenious plan.

Unfortunately, no plan is perfect. The person who buried the treasure must never allow a slip of the tongue to give a clue as to where he buried it. He must not write down the location of it in case the piece of paper falls into wrong hands. That secret must remain in a dark infrequently approached recess of his mind, till it is time to retrieve it for an expected event like the wedding of a daughter or a crop failure due to a drought. There are years when the Monsoon skips India.

At times even the best laid plan fails.

The person carrying the secret becomes senile and cannot access his remote memory or death claims the person unexpectedly.

DHANDHUKA

Like everyone else in Dhandhuka, my paternal grandparents lived almost all of their lives, in Dhandhuka. They built their only home soon, after they got married. All her life, my grandmother had heard about pots of gold being found while digging a trench for the foundation of a house. So, she told the builder to dig a trench as deep as her funds would allow, hoping to find a pot of gold to build a taller house then she had planned for. Unfortunately, luck was not on her side and she ended up with a house with the same square footage as she had contracted for.

The only difference from the original blueprints is that, the house has an unusually deep foundation.

Tiles are the most expensive roofing material. It is permanent and seldom needs repair or replacement. The roof of my grandparents' house is made of tiles.

I did not know that.

I learned that during my first "*Utraan*", a kite festival held all over India on the 14th of January.

The day before and the day after *Utraan*, the sky is just like any other day of the year. But on the morning of this festival, it is almost obscured by kites flown by everyone, while snacking on foods traditionally served on this day—*undhiyoon*[1] and *Jalebi*[2].

The kites are as elaborate and as big as your pockets would allow and you fly it by day and by night during the 24 hour window.

---

[1] A baked mixed vegetable dish.
[2] A desert.

On that night, the sky apparently has too many stars; some stationary, some shooting. The ones that are moving is an illusion caused by Chinese lanterns tied to a kite string about five feet from a kite. The lantern is to help the kite flyer to locate his kite.

The flyers launch a squadron with its identifying color and design from a strategic site within their neighbor hood

The string used to fly a kite with, is coated with brightly colored glue mixed with ground glass. The exact formula for this ammo is a closely guarded secret held by kite accessory makers. The day after *Utran,* it is easy to pick out the kite veterans—their thumbs and index fingers have band aids on them.

Remote piloting a kite is fun. Winning a kite battle is a fantasy fulfilled. The fleeting looks of awe and envy from all the eyes in the village are for the victor to bask in, till the next *Utraan.*

Manfred von Richthofen—the red baron—the first ace, who wrote the first book on dog fighting, disdained his anonymity while flying in a formation in his squadron of identically colored fighters.

He painted his plane red to let the enemy know who and where he was.

The Barons of India do the same on *Utraan.*

As in all warfare, there is a code of conduct in kite battles. An honorable kite fighter will not harm kites flown by women and children.

An Ace ignores challenges from rookies from the neighborhood squadron. He will not risk exhaustion or compromise his kite's agility from battle wounds.

He will just relax and enjoy the flight while he waits for the champion from the enemy's squadron to break out of formation and fly to the designated battle air space.

This is the slap in the face with a glove.

The commander of the opposing team considers the best strategy. He mulls over the best fighter for the maneuver. He signals thumbs up to the best acrobat at the chosen strategy. The champion gets into a steep climb to get above and between the enemy and the sun.

In the rest of the sky, the kites throttle back and enter a holding pattern outside the battle air space. A hush descends on the entire village. All vehicles halt. All villagers stop whatever they are doing. All eyes are on the sky

And a duel to death is on.

Volumes have been written about strategy. A fighter choses the manoeuver his kite was aerodynamically designed for. A common trick is to loop you're kite over the string of your opponent's kite and then, you either jerk on the string the way a fisherman sets his hook into a fish or put your kite into a steep dive and let go of the string and let the string come out of the reel at its maximum speed.

The strategy is to use whatever maneuver it takes, to cut the string of the other kite, to the cheers, drum beats and jumps of joy in the neighborhood of the victor and watch in triumph, as your enemy's kite, now totally out of control, zigs and zags down to earth ignominiously, like a falling leaf in a turbulent autumn breeze.

As the kite gets closer to the roof tops, it is chased by a crowd of children, each hoping to be the one to catch and keep the kite and the attached string.

One "Utraan", a beautiful kite landed on the roof of my grandfather's house. I now know for certain, that it was a tile roof because when I got on the roof and walked towards the kite to retrieve it, every sinking step made a crunching sound.

I knew full well my grandfather's bad temper and could anticipate accurately his reaction when he discovers what I had done. That year, I was glad to be in Zanzibar before the next monsoon, when every tile I stepped on, was bound to leak.

Another memory of Dhandhuka is waking up to an unusual sound. On looking out from my window in the second story, I saw a flock of peacocks. A bird we did not have in Zanzibar, but were familiar with from seeing pictures in our story books.

This show was brought to us by the compliment of my grandmother, who throughout the year put birdseeds on the roof so that when we came from Africa, we would have peacocks visiting us every morning.

My grandmother woke us up early one morning to watch another entertainment. While rubbing our eyes, we looked down from the second-story balcony into our courtyard and saw an African, with his two daughters. They looked just like the Africans back home. Till that day, every African I had met spoke Kiswahili. I was confused when all I got was a vacant stare from them, when I greeted them in Kiswahili.

That day, my brothers and I, were treated to a performance of the Peacock dance in the Kathakali tradition.

India does have a small number of "*Siddi*"—descendants of African slaves. African slaves in the USA, South America and the Caribbean came from West Africa. The ones in India came from East Africa. They were bought by the Portuguese, most probably from the Slave market in Zanzibar, to work their farms in Goa. Goa was a Portuguese colony on the west coast of India, ruled from Lisbon, Portugal. Goa was annexed by India a few years after India became independent from British rule in 1947.

The *Siddi* lost their mother tongues, generations ago. But for their African facial features they are indistinguishable in the language they speak, the clothing they wear, the religion they follow or the customs they have, from the communities that they have settled in.

A Siddi lady.

On the left is a Siddi lady. The *tilak*[3] on her forehead makes her a Hindu. It is a generic *tilak*. Some are unique to the god they worship. Widows do not wear a tilak or clothes with color. She could be single but at her age, probably married. Indians marry young. She has a ring on her fourth left finger which is not helpful. Indians do not wear wedding rings. The saree is too formal for everyday wear. It is red, an auspicious color for

---
[3] The red mark between her eye brows.

festive occasions. The saree is draped over the left shoulder. Traditionally, Gujratis drape the saree over the right shoulder and Maharashtrians on the left. She is grating a coconut. That places her on one of the two coasts of India. Coconuts grow only within ten miles of an ocean.

My guess is, this Siddi lady from the Malabar Coast is preparing a wedding feast.

In Zanzibar we had a lady who made a living entertaining at hen parties singing while accompanied by her *Dholuk*[4]. Her name was *"Saru"*, (Sarah), *"Lungee"*, (an entertainer.) She too was a *"Siddi"* who did a reverse migration to Zanzibar, from the Indian State of *Cutch*.

Dhandhuka is divided into waadas—a neighborhood of inhabitants with a common tie.

My grandparents' home was in Qureshiwaada. The word waada implies that all the inhabitants of this particular waada are Qureshi's—descendants of Peer Qureshi.

Peer Qureshi has held his descendants in Dhandhuka, the way a magnet holds iron filings in its magnetic field.

Even if one of the Qureshi's was adventurous enough to contemplate moving out of Dhandhuka, local customs made it impossible to leave. Boys were groomed to help out dad on his farm. Girls were in a worse predicament.

---

[4] A two headed drum.

A very odd local custom dictated that girls from Dhandhuka must marry a boy from Dhandhuka, from a family of at least equal and preferably of a higher social standing. Only girls with a reputation of dubious virtue, married outside Dhandhuka because their reputation precluded them from ever finding a husband in Dhandhuka. This made it very difficult for Qureshi girls to get married. To marry a boy outside Dhandhuka carried the stigma of "something wrong with her"—morally, intellectually or physically.

They had to get married in Dhandhuka to a Qureshi or better yet, a *Sayyid,* a descended of *Fatima,* the prophet's daughter.

The boy had to be of the same age, or preferably, a little older. If she had any education, the boy had to have more education than her. All these restrictions, severely limited her choice of boys.

Odds are very good, that my brothers, my sister and I and all our offspring's would still be living in the Qureshi waada of Dhandhuka, were it not for my father, Mustafamian Amirmian Kureshi.

In Dhandhuka, the suffix "mian" is added to a first name to indicate a prestigious lineage.

Ahmedmian was the eldest son. Abbajaan was the second son and he had two younger brothers and an only younger sister. Although he was not the eldest, he took on the mantle of the eldest in the family. My grandparents did not think much of my oldest uncle, Ahmedmian, and in particular, could not get along with his wife.

A disliked daughter-in-law invariably causes a rift in a family. In time, the daughter-in-law will get her husband to view the situation from her perspective and gradually, the son and his family drift away. This happened to Ahmedmian and his family

By default, Ahmedmian's responsibilities fell upon Abbajaan, and he became the surrogate eldest brother.

Abbajaan was ambitious. He was aware that without a unique skill his future in Dhandhuka was bound to be dismal. He made a decision that shook Dhandhuka like a scale seven Richter earthquake.

He decided to go to college.

This was during the mid-1920's. At that time, even in the USA, the percentage of high school graduates who went on to college was in the single digits. In Dhandhuka it was unheard of.

His parents did not have much money, but one of his uncles, Shekhanmian, owned several farms, and a soap factory. Somehow, my father talked this uncle into lending him money so that he and his older brother Ahmedmian could go to college in the university town of Poona, in the state of Maharashtra.

This uncle of his did not believe in education, so none of his children went to school. He put all of them to work on his farms and his soap factory. His motto was; "The way to keep your family under control is to keep them dependent on you. If you educate children, they leave home. Then you have no choice but to hire help, which of course, cuts deeply into profits"

I'm not sure what approach my father used, but this uncle, despite his anti-education philosophy, agreed to loan him money. It must have been very little, even by the standard of living in those days.

Abbajaan taught in an evening school, while still enrolled full-time at a Civil Engineering College to earn a little money and in exchange for used college text books, he helped his professor's grade school children with their homework.

His college life was tough and Spartan.

Abbajaan never mentioned any of this to us. My parents were married during my father's second year in college. My mother spent some time with him during his last year in college. While we were growing up, my mother would tell us about the hardships my father went through to get the education he had. It served a dual function. It was bragging about her husband and at the same time, instilling in us a thirst for education.

The two brothers, rented a room and had a distant widowed aunt, come to stay with them to cook and do the usual household chores, in return for room and board. When the two brothers finished their training, they returned home to look for jobs, and the aunt returned to her hometown of Limdee.

In the early 1940s, I recall meeting her. I was excited to visit the town so that upon my return to Zanzibar, I could boast to my friends that I had been to Limdee. Limdee's claim to fame is a sentence in Gujarati that reads the same backwards as it does forwards:

'Limdee gamae gaadee malee"

It is a sentence like, "Able was I ere I saw Elba". "Kalee Dadee", which literally means 'Black Grandma", met us at that famous railroad station, immortalized in that Gujarati sentence.

I can visualize her waiting for us at the railroad station. And when she saw us come off the train she was filled with joy. We took a *"Tanga",* a two-wheeled horse carriage through the Main Street. It was a long straight Main Street with a clock tower in the center of it. I used the word "straight" in my last sentence, because it was the striking feature of Limdee. It was a well-planned city. In Indian cities, which were built before the invention of the automobile, the streets are anything but straight. Houses pop up randomly like mushrooms in a lawn and you have to meander your way through unmarked streets.

This was in the early 1940s when the British still ruled India. At that time, about 25% of the total Indian population, was ruled by and were citizens of 562 princely states.

The rulers had colorful titles like *Nawab, Maharaja, Sawahi, Chhatrapati, Maharana, Durbar* and the unique title of, His Exalted Highness, which was reserved for the *Nizam*—the ruler of Hyderabad.

Some, like the state of Hydrabad, were as large as mainland Britain and some were just tiny dots on the map, perhaps no larger than the principality of Monaco. There was even a small state by the name of *Zanjeera* that was ruled by a descendant of African slaves.

DHANDHUKA

The British did not directly rule the states, but British "paramountcey" was acknowledged by them, and the British provided defense, communication and foreign-policy. The Indians in the rest of India were "British subjects". The citizens of the princely states were subjects of the states ruler and were legally "British protected persons".

Limdee's Maharaja was a benevolent ruler. He had built complexes, where widows could live in single room apartments on a tiny pension from the Maharaja.

We visited her in one of those apartments. When it was time to leave, she gave *Phupejaan*[5] the only thing of value she had; a gold ring. *Phupejaan* demurred, as was expected of her, but *Kalee Dadee* insisted that she take it. "If you don't, upon my death, the *Durbar* will. I would rather see you enjoy wearing it and remember me by".

Phupejaan took it.

When Kalee Dadee volunteered to keep house for Abbajaan and Ahmedmian while in college, the brothers could not pay her anything. Abbajaan had promised her, that in return for her unpaid services, as soon as he had a job, he will send her twenty shillings a month.

Till the day we received a letter from Dhandhuka informing us of her demise, I remember going to the post office every month, to mail to her Abbajaan's check for twenty shillings.

After graduation, it was time to repay the loan. The older brother had only excuses for not paying his share of the loan.

---

[5] My sister.

To Abbajaan, repaying the loan was a matter of keeping your word and upholding the good name of his family. He paid off the entire loan by himself.

After graduation, in the fall of 1934, Abbajaan was on a train from Poona to Dhandhuka, when an advertisement in a newspaper aroused his curiosity. It was for a person with Abbajaan's qualification and teaching experience to start a high school in Zanzibar, a city somewhere in British East Africa.

More out of curiosity then interest, he responded to the advertisement and forgot the incident. In the early nineteen thirties, mail went by trains and steam boats and it took weeks for letters to reach their destination.

That was the year, my grandfather's only daughter *Khairoon* became a teenager.

In India, the window of opportunity for eligible girls is small. After puberty, every year that goes by without getting married, reduces its chances, exponentially. Getting Khairoon married as soon as possible, was the families obsession.

In India, a daughter's wedding is the largest expense a family anticipates. Most parents start saving for it, the day a girl is born. My mother started earmarking gold jewelry, expensive saris, top rated kitchen utensils, furniture and even foot wear, for my only sister Safiyun's wedding, even before she could stand up and walk on her own.

When a bride leaves *Babul*[6], she must not be in want of anything that a home requires.

The most important articles are those made of gold. The number of pieces of jewelry is insignificant. Jewelry is only a way to make gold portable and useful. The figure the groom's family is most interested in is the ounces of gold that come with her. Marriages have been cancelled on the morning of the wedding, when a bride's family cannot display the promised ounces of gold, for weighing and appraisal by an independent goldsmith.

In a culture where "face saving" is paramount, fathers of single girls dread this event.

My grandfather had retired from a thirty five year career as a *Talaati*— a farm tax assessor. He rode his horse and inspected the crops on the farms in his county, every spring, summer and fall and determined the taxes owed on the crops. It was a poorly paid job. He was able to feed and clothe his family but could not put aside money for his daughter's wedding.

In 1935, India's economy was in a slump. Jobs in civil engineering were nonexistent and Abbajaan could not find <u>any</u> job. A payment on the principle of the loan for college expenses of the Qureshi brothers was due and both brothers were unemployed. My two youngest uncles, Peermian and Hussainmian, were still in school. Grandfather's meager pension was the only cash inflow.

The Qureshi family of Dhandhuka was in a financial predicament. The home was as somber as a funeral parlor.

---

[6] A bride's parent's home.

There was a knock on the door.

My Grandmother opened the door.

It was the mailman.

"Salaam alaikum," greeted Ismail.

"Wa alaikum salaam, Ismail." responded my grandmother.

"You have a letter—from overseas."

Grandmother was surprised. She could not think of anyone who lived "overseas."

"Oh! For whom?"

"Mustafamian."

"Mustafamian? Hum. Thank you. Khuda hafiz"

"Khuda hafiz"

By the time my grandmother shut the door the entire family was tantalized by the content of the letter and they all gathered in the porch. This is where the family gathered for family discussions. Each of them had a certain place they sat at. My grandparents sat on a swing, Aunty Khairoon and uncles Peermian and Hussainmian sat on a *Sutrangee*[7].

Abbajaan stood in front of his parents with the letter. It had an eye catching stamp of Zanzibar with a sketch of the Sultan and the denomination written in Arabic and English.

---

[7] A rug.

The envelope's return address was:

His Highness's Services,

Department of Education,

Mambo Msiige,

Zanzibar.

British East Africa.

"Ah! Now I remember what this is all about. It is in response to my request for more information about a job offer."

He opened the envelope excitedly and pulled out a type written letter and a money order.

He looked at the money order first.

The figures on the money order made him gasp audibly. In his hand, he held more money than his middle class Dhandhuka home was worth.

He then read the letter.

He read the first sentence with deliberation. With each subsequent sentence his excitement and the speed at which he read, increased.

The letter quivered in his right hand.

He steadied it by using both his hands.

When he reached the end of the letter, he took in a deep breath and he exhaled;

"*Alhamdulillah.*"[8]

He looked at his curious family and said;

"It is a job offer from Africa."

"Africa!" my grandmother responded. "Isn't that where the lions and cannibals roam?"

"Yes. But I will live in a city called Zanzibar, a city ten times larger than Dhandhuka, with several grade schools and I will start the first High School in that city."

"That is too far" said my grandfather. "Be patient. You will find a job right here." My grandfather had no idea of what a civil engineer does. Even today, I doubt if there is a position for a civil engineer in Dhandhuka.

Abbajaan was Khairoon's favorite brother. She too wanted him around and said;

"We may not see you for years."

"Not so. The letter says I will be home for six months every three years. I have been to college for months at a time. This will not be any different, only a little longer"

"No." said grandmother. "Three years is not the same as three months. Besides you have a wife and a child. Think of their safety."

"You are right. It may be unsafe for my wife and especially for the baby. I will go alone and send for them if I find the place to be safe for them. If not I can always come back"

---

[8] Thanks, Allah.

"No. What makes you think it will be safe place, even if you went by yourself? It is a dark continent you are going to. No mother can sleep well if her son is in Africa."

"Mother, I told you. I will not live in a cave or in a tree in a forest. I will live in a city with better amenities then Dhandhuka. Like Ahmedabad, it has paved streets, cars, water and even electricity."

While waving it, he said; "Look at this money order. I can travel first class all the way to Zanzibar. I even have an advance on my first month's salary—five hundred Rupees! I can live like a prince on that salary and still save money for Khairoon's wedding and pay off my college debts in just three years. Even if I did get a job here, can you guess how long will it take to make that much money? Certainly, a lot longer than three years. Even ten may not achieve our goal. Three years will go by in a hurry and I shall return with all our financial woes behind us."

Grandmother sobbed softly. She realized that Abbajaan had found a way to pay for Khairoon's imminent wedding, but as a mother she had to satisfy herself that his basic needs will be met.

Grandmother sobbed softly; "You can't cook. You will starve to death before your three years are up"

"No I won't. The letter says that I will also teach Gujrati as a second language. Over 50% of the students will be Gujratis. There must be lots of Gujrati families in Zanzibar. I will room and board with one of them."

The two young uncles were silent. The topic was too heavy for them to participate in.

Khairoon's shoulders were crushing with guilt. It was her wedding expenses that were sending her favorite brother into exile in some god forsaken country of men eating men and men eating animals

"Think about how I will feel if something happens to you out there?

"No" said grandfather, in a tone that meant the discussion was over and his decision was final.

Grandmother was shaking her head from side to side, while gazing at the floor

Abbajaan was frustrated at the unanimous opposition of his family.

For the first time he hesitated and wondered if everyone is right and he is the one who is wrong.

For the umpteenth time he mentally calculated the Rupees it would take to pay for the anticipated expenses. The total still was the same. Again, he reviewed all his options. Again, Zanzibar was the best. His math and logic was not convincing his family.

He will have to use a different approach.

In Gujrat, proverbs carry more weight than quotations from scriptures do in other cultures. The language matured over thousands of years and distilled centuries of wisdom and advice in succinct proverbs.

An apt proverb defies a rebuttal.

With glistening eyes and in a measured choking voice he announced;

"*Dahyo deekro deshawer jaeh*"[9]

He looked around the room for a retort.

There was none.

Grandfather quickly reviewed his past confrontations with this son. When this one made up his mind, there was nothing he could do or say to make this adamant son of his change his mind. Besides, he had the only plausible plan. He did not like seeing his son leave Dhandhuka. He liked less the prospect of having a spinster for a daughter. Dejected, he slumped in the swing, stared at the floor and spoke no more.

Grandmother sat cross legged with her elbows on her knees and the palms of her hands supporting her cheeks—sobbing and shaking her head from side to side in disbelief at the prospect of her first chick leaving her nest. This never happened in Dhandhuka where multiple generations of a family live in the same house.

The two young uncles just sat there. Stunned into muteness, by the gravity of the discussion.

In a desperate attempt to prevent her brother from leaving, auntie Khairoon got up, ran towards her brother, embraced him with all her might and buried her face in his chest.

---

[9] "A good son goes abroad to support his family"

The rest of the family averted their eyes to allow them privacy and fixed their gaze on the floor.

Oblivious of the rest of the family, the siblings took their time bidding goodbye, in sobs, tears and to Khairoon's repeated whispers of;

"Don't go *Bhai*.[10] Please, don't go. I beg of you, please don't go"

This is the moment, which broke *Peer* Qureshi's spell.

This is the moment, that cut the umbilical cord that had tethered the Qureshi's to Dhandhuka.

This is the moment, when the Qureshi diaspora began.

---

[10] Brother

CHAPTER THREE

Mr. Boyd

I was startled by bells of different notes, ringing in a slow, somber rhythm. It was a sound I had heard only a few of times before that. I looked northwards in the direction of the sound.

From the second story of our home, we have an unobstructed view of the steeple with a cross on top of it, high vaulted roof and the tops of the stained glass windows of the Cathedral Church of Christ in Africa.

The sound was coming from the steeple of the cathedral.

Cathedral Church of Christ in Africa,
Kibokoni, Zanzibar.

With a sigh, I realized that the bells were tolling for our neighbor, Mr. Boyd.

At the age of ten, the symbolism of the cross on the steeple was a mystery to me. But, it always reminded me of a symbol we used in boy scouting when we went hiking in the woods. We marked a fork or a crossroad in a trail to help us get back to our camp. We used sticks, stones or whatever else that was available—after all, we were boy scouts—to make a straight line with a shorter line crossing the long line perpendicularly near the top of the straight line.

In Boy Scouting, that symbol stands for, "This way home."

The cathedral was built by an organization founded by Dr. Livingstone, a Scottish missionary, an abolitionist and an explorer of Africa[11].

Newspapers in England and the United States reported his adventures in Africa. The articles were widely read and subsequent ones eagerly looked forwards to. When an unusually long duration had passed without hearing from him, the newspapers and its readers became anxious. The New York Times decided to send one of its reporters, Henry Morton Stanley, to find out whether or not he was still alive.

Stanley, as had all the other explorers before him, stopped in Zanzibar—the Gateway to Africa. Zanzibar city had merchants experienced in outfitting such expeditions and could also recommend porters and professional guides to take explorers into, what was then called, "Dark Africa". After a long journey, Stanley was able to track down Livingstone in

---

[11] Discovered and named Victoria Falls, at the border between Zambia and Zimbabwe.

Ujiji, a little village on the eastern shore of Lake Tanganyika. A family link we have to this lake is Tao[12] Sam's brother, Simon who is an international authority on the fish in this lake. Odds are pretty high, that a cichlid you see in a fresh water aquarium came from this lake, now renamed Lake Malawi.

When Stanley met Livingstone for the first time, Livingstone was lying in bed outside his round thatched hut, too weak from an illness to sit up to greet his visitor. A newspaper sketch of the meeting, show Stanley approaching Livingstone with his pith helmet tucked under his left armpit and his right hand extended in anticipation of a handshake. It is said, that it was at this moment that Stanley uttered the immortal and oft repeated phrase;

"Dr. Livingstone, I presume."

"Swahili" the root word, is derived from the Arabic word *"Sahil,"* "the Coast". Hence, the people of the coast are called *Waswahili* or *Swahilis* (*Mswahili,* Singular) and their language *Kiswahili.* The language has a Bantu base and grammar with about thirty percent of words assimilated from Arabic.

When I was a child, the Waswahilis wrote Kiswahili in the Arabic alphabet. All Muslim children can read the Qur'an before they start Kindergarten. The children either go to a Qur'an school, or as was the case in my family, a Qur'an tutor comes to the children's homes to instruct them.

---

[12] Spanish for "Uncle." Sam is married to my daughter Sharifah.

It takes several weeks to learn the Arabic alphabet and several more to construct words with it. When they can read the first sentence in the Qur'an, parents invite friends and neighbors to their home. The host announces that the party is about to begin.

The guests stop chatting.

The well-dressed child takes his place on a carpet behind a Qur'an holder. He picks up the Qur'an, kisses it, opens it and finds the first page.

The gathering is hushed.

Proudly but haltingly, the child reads the first sentence;

Bis—me—lah-----he-rahman—nee-----ra--him.

Everyone cheers and claps and the "Bismillah" party is on.

Writing your mother tongue in the Arabic alphabet is a natural progression for Muslims. Kiswahili was written in Arabic alphabet when I was child.

About the time I started grade school; several schools were built in distant villages of Zanzibar. Although the students were proficient in the Arabic alphabet they were taught and then instructed in the Latin alphabet. Now Latin is the alphabet that Kiswahili is written in.

As the word *Kiswahili* implies, the language is spoken along the coast of East Africa—and Oman—and understood by all the tribes in East and Central Africa.

MR. BOYD

Two of our closest neighbors were Mr. and Mrs. Boyd who lived on the first floor of the house we lived in. Mr. Boyd was a Mswahili. He was liked by the children in our neighborhood.

Now, that is a compliment any person should be proud of. As adults, when we move into a new neighborhood, even after a year or two, we know our neighbors by sight and engage in the usual greetings and small talks with them and that is the extent of our knowledge of most of our neighbors. If you are interested in getting a concise and accurate evaluation of your new neighbor's personality, take your child, between the ages of five and ten "Trick or treating." Let the child choose and avoid the doors to knock on. The doors the child knocks on are the neighbors worthy of getting to know better.

Mr. Boyd was such a neighbor. He was of average height and a stocky frame. He was definitely obese by Waswahili standards. His crinkly hair and a heavy moustache were sprinkled with *umvi,* gray "wisdom" hairs. His facial features were similar to those of the other Swahili's—a flat nose, large lips and jet black cheeks. He was of pure African descent.

The Waswahili with Arab blood in them, have a complexion that fall into one of the shades of brown. Interestingly, we also have *Washirazee,* "people from Shiraz". The Shirazes claim to hail from Shiraz—a famous city in Iran. The color of their skin and their facial features are certainly a little different from that of the *Waswahili.* Their skin is lighter with a reddish tint. Although their claim seems farfetched, there is good historical evidence to back up their claim.

There is a mosque in *Kizimkazi*, which was constructed by a Persian colony. The *Kufic*[13], inscription on the *Mihrab*[14] is dated "ah 500"[15], which corresponds to 1107AD. The island of Tumbatu just off Mkokotoni has ruins of Persian architecture built in 1400AD.

The most convincing evidence of Iranian presence in Zanzibar is the Kiswahili language itself. Linguists have identified over a hundred and fifty Kiswahili words which are of *Farsi*[16] origin. Common Kiswahili words like, *Kaka, Dada and Nanga* are Farsi words. A Mswahili who recently visited an Iranian port on the Persian Gulf told me that he met Iranian sailors there who spoke fluent Kiswahili.

Like the Portuguese, the Iranians too left their footprints in Zanzibar. The village of Kizimkazi celebrates *"Mwaka Koga"* on the same day that the Iranians celebrate *"Nawroz"*—the most important celebration on the Iranian calendar.

Cloves are the main export of Zanzibar and the season for picking it is short. Zanzibar has always needed extra hands during the harvest season. This demand resulted in an interesting seasonal migration of clove pickers from as far west as the Congo. They were well compensated for their help, and during years when labor supply was short, they were allowed to keep and sell as much as 50% of the cloves they picked.

---

[13] An ancient, angular, Arabic alphabet developed in *Kufa*, a city south of Baghdad.
[14] A prayer nich.
[15] Al hijra. The date when the Islamic calendar began.
[16] The language spoken in Iran

This annual migration familiarized us with the "main land" Africans. A Zanzibari can always spot a non-Swahili African and be able to identify the tribe the African belongs to just by his facial features and body habitus. Of course, when they spoke Kiswahili, their accent left no doubt that they were foreigners.

The Waswahili are modest and self-effacing. Not so, the main landers—we referred to all Africans who came from the continent of Africa as "Main landers." Towards the end of the clove picking season, when the pockets of the main lander clove pickers were heavy with cash, it was amusing to watch a *Mndegereko* in his brand new gaudy mismatched clothes, yellow sunglasses and a cow boy hat, strutting by awkwardly in his squeaky new shoes.

The *Waconde*[1] were industrious and during a lull in picking cloves, they kept themselves busy by whittling away and creating African curious like the ones you see in gift shops all over the world.

Mr. Boyd was not one of those Africans. He was not a "real" Mswahili either; by which I mean, he was definitely different from the Waswahili born in Zanzibar. He only looked like a *Mswahili* because he was born on the coast of East Africa.

When he had to, he spoke in pigeon Kiswahili. With his neighbors he conversed in fluent Urdu. For relaxation, he read to his wife Sunder, novels in "*Marathi*— the language of the state of Maharashtra. To top it all off, if all that I have mentioned is not incongruous enough, they were Christians; the only Christian family in Kibokoni.[17]

Sunder was a pure Maharashtrian[18]. Her features were similar to ours but her skin was a little darker as she was from an area, a little south of Gujarat, India, where my parents and I were born.

Indians from Kashmir are light skinned and with blue eyes. As you travel south, the hair and skin and eyes get darker. By the time you reach the tip of India, the skin is darker than that of equatorial Africans.

.Mr. Boyd made a living as a carpenter. The two room apartment they lived in did not have electricity. I fancy myself as an amateur woodworker and almost all my tools are electric—including my screwdriver.

Mr. Boyd made furniture—unique works of art—using only hand tools. I can still picture him at work. He made intricate joints using only chisels, square saws, mallets and his eyes. When he was satisfied with the way the mating sides looked, he wiped the contagious edges with *"Surus[19]"*. Then, with a gentle tap of his mallet, the joints came together perfectly as if that is how they grew on a tree.

Mr. Boyd had no use for nails or screws.

The lumber he used came from local trees and *"Fu"* was the preferred one by local furniture makers. His hand plane glided

---

[17] The neighborhood we lived in
[18] The Indian state of Maharashtra
[19] Hot glue used by Indian carpenters

over the uneven wood like a skier gliding over moguls. A barely audible grunt accentuated the end of each rhythmic pass. Unlike a skier, at each run, Mr. Boyd shaved off a razor thin slice off the top of each mogul and they shot out of a hole on the top and in front of the plane handle, in tiny pig's tails, filling the room with the scent of *Jozanee*—the forest where it grew.

Result: a silky smooth piece of wood of perfectly even width, length and depth and grains that always evoked gasps of admiration.

Mr. Boyd was born on the east coast of Africa. I never found out exactly where, but from his facial features, my guess is, it was along the coast of either Kenya or Tanganyika. One day, at age seven or so, he was engrossed in fishing off the beach near his home, when he was surprised by a gang of *Mangas* who had sneaked up on him. They overpowered him, shackled him and put him in their dhow[20] along with other children, men and women that they had captured or bought, before him.

When the dhow had a full load of "cargo" it sailed up the east coast of Africa towards the Arabian Sea. There to sell its cargo, in the slave markets of the Middle East.

In 1872, Seyyid Barghash, the greatest ruler of the El Busaidi dynasty and my favorite sultan of Zanzibar, almost overnight became highly vulnerable and naked to his enemies by the confluence of two unpredictable and highly unusual natural disasters. I have drawn heavily from the works of Abdul

---

[20] A ship with a triangular sail. Usually seen along the East coast of Africa and the Nile.

Sheriff, professor of history at the University of Dar–es-salaam, Tanzania, for the historical details that follow.

During that era, an Arab's wealth was directly related to the acres of arable land he owned and whether or not he had enough slaves to farm it. By those standards, Seyyid Barghash was an extremely wealthy monarch.

The first catastrophe was a cholera epidemic which killed most of his slaves. No sooner had he recovered from the shock of that loss in manpower, then the only recorded hurricane in East Africa, swept across the southern tip of Pemba and pummeled the Island of Zanzibar in 1872.

On that day, the harbor was crammed to its capacity with dhows fully loaded with merchandise. The crews were just waiting for the trade winds to reverse its direction and blow northwards. The Sultans navy too was in the harbor and was battered mercilessly.

Within a few minutes, the precious cargoes on which the Sultan's annual revenue depended, either sank to the bottom or became worthless flotsam. Fragments of the navy began their slow motion descent to the deep, dark and deaf waters of the harbor, trailing behind a stream of bubbles, which burst upon reaching the surface, One after another, the fragments, upon reaching the ocean floor bounced off the ocean floor. The lighter ones bounced just once. The heavier ones more than once, with each bounce getting progressive smaller, and after the final bounce the pieces settled gently on the ocean bed in a comfortable position.

The once awe inspiring Sultan's navy, was reduced to a man-made fish habitat.

The huts all over the island stood no chance at all. They were sucked up, like confetti by a vacuum cleaner and scattered miles away from the villages. The homes in the stone town area of Zanzibar crumbled and collapsed into heaps of rubble.

The coconut trees with their high leverage, snapped like dry kindling. The squat clove trees cling to the ground as long as they could, but they too were uprooted as easily as weeds from a vegetable patch, after a soaking rain.

Cloves were the main cash crop of Zanzibar. It takes over eight years for a clove seedling to bear its first fruit. Seyyid Barghash could not even fall back on coconuts, his secondary source of income.

The freak hurricane that had never occurred before nor has it occurred since then, not only tore huge holes in a his pockets, leaving the richest man south of the equator, penniless, but it also knocked out all but one of his teeth. The only ship in his navy that survived in Zanzibar harbor was his latest purchase; the American Civil War Confederate cruiser, the *"Shenandoah"*. The *Shenandoah*, made it through the hurricane, but soon succumbed and sank from the mortal injuries it had sustained, leaving Barghash with only one naval vessel that happened to be in Mombasa on that infamous day.

Seyyid Barghash, as a Midwest saying goes, was "shot by both barrels"

The British Empire was thrust upon the English. They just happened to be trading there, when once mighty empires were temporarily vulnerable

They came. They saw. They took.

True to their pattern of conquest, the British chose this very moment to "request" Seyyid Barghash to abolish slavery in his domain. They followed a standard British procedure and the "request" was reinforced by the dispatch of three British Navy Frigates to emphasize the "request".

Profit from the slave trade was Seyyid Bargash's least lucrative source of income but after the hurricane of 1872, it was his only source.

The Americans in Zanzibar and the French Bishop of Reunion saw through this smoke screen of "abolition" and declared that the righteous British indignation was more out of a plot to destroy Seyyid Barghash and take over his realm, rather than out of concern for the plight of the slaves.

After conferring with his advisors regarding the British "request", and having weighed all his options—including fighting the British with France as his ally—Seyyid Barghash is quoted as saying;

"A spear is held at each of my eyes.

With which one, shall I choose to be pierced?"

He chose to have his non-dominant eye pierced.

On June 5th, 1872, he signed a treaty with the British abolishing slavery in the lands and waters of his Sultanate. The sultanate in addition to the islands of Zanzibar and Pemba, included parts of Kenya and Tanganyika. When I went to college in Kenya in the early 1950's, the port of Mombasa flew the flag of Zanzibar, as the ten mile deep coastal strip of Kenya was legally a part of Zanzibar's sultanate.

The slave market in Zanzibar closed its door for the last time and the British Navy began patrolling the Indian Ocean to enforce the abolishment.

In the waters off the west coast of India, a British naval ship spotted the *dhow* that Mr. Boyd was in and gave it a chase. The dhow's captain dumped the illegal "cargo" into the ocean, to get rid of the evidence and also to pick up speed so that he could outrun the frigate.

Mr. Boyd was rescued by the naval vessel in pursuit. I don't know how that chase ended and whether or not the dhow's crew was brought to justice, but I do know that Mr. Boyd was taken to an orphanage in India, in the state of Maharashtra.

The institution was run by an Anglican mission, headed by a Mr. Boyd. As is customary in missions, our neighbor was given a Christian identity; the last name "Boyd." Apparently, so was everyone else in that orphanage. I hope, to prevent confusion, Mr. Boyd Sr. gave the children different first names.

I believe George Foreman, the former world heavy weight boxing champion, named all his sons George. Despite having a large family of boys all named George Foreman; I am told that George Forman Sr had a tolerable family life.

I do not know Mr. Boyd's first name. Even if I knew it, Zanzibari culture would not have allowed me to address him by his first name. To everyone younger then him, he was Bwana[21] Boyd.

Mr. Boyd was raised an Anglican. He did not flaunt it—we were under English rule with all the privileges an Anglican was entitled to. He did not conceal it either—he did not have to.

He was in an Islamic country.

He did not proselytize—as a product of a Missionary orphanage, you would expect him to. His values blended well with where he was. He was one of us.

He was, a Zanzibari.

While in an orphanage, he was taught to read and write Marathi and received training in the skills of carpentry.

I am not sure why he decided to leave India and go back "home".

Perhaps, like a salmon at spawning time, he was overcome by an instinct to return to where he came from. As a freed slave, he chose to return to Africa. Not just Africa, but East Africa. Not just East Africa, but Zanzibar. Not just Zanzibar, but Zanzibar City. Not just Zanzibar City but Kibokoni—the home of the largest slave market on the East coast of Africa.

Just a coincidence?

Not likely.

---

[21] Sir.

MR. BOYD

Mr. Boyd's return to his roots is not an isolated incidence. The whole country of Liberia, West Africa, was founded by slaves freed by the Civil War in the USA.

One of them had a malfunction in his homing equipment and ended up in Zanzibar. He practiced law and earned the reputation of being so good at it, that he could get all his clients acquitted of murder, even if they were caught red handed at the scene of the crime.

Furniture making was not a lucrative profession. I recall Mr. Boyd borrowing a suit from my father so that he could attend a church service on Christmas. On days when we saw Mr. and Mrs. Boyd walking to the cathedral in their best (borrowed) clothes, we knew that it had to be an important Christian holiday. Another annual clue was a shortage of eggs. The Christians, in spite of an exorbitant price demanded, had bought out all the eggs the industrious hens of Zanzibar had produced, so that they could bake their "Chrismiss cakes."

Every Sunday my mother made an omelet with onions and lots of green chilies which we scooped up in our parathas for breakfast.—except at *Chrismiss* time, for lack of eggs. Then we had *mandazi*[22] and *mbazi* [23]accompanied by my mother's apology and a remainder that it was *Chrismiss* time. Because of this traumatic childhood deprivation, I suffer from an intense aversion to '*chrismiss cake*"; although to this day, I do not know what it is.

---

[22] Flat triangular doughnuts.
[23] Peas cooked in coconut milk.

The steeple of the Anglican Church has a clock with four faces, each one facing a cardinal direction—a gift from Seyyid Barghash.

As a child, I could not understand why an absolute monarch of a nation with over ninety nine percent Muslims would allow a church to be built, let alone make a gift of a clock to it. Wasn't the Muslim citizenry offended? Why didn't the Muslim clerics object to a place of worship for infidels amidst the true believers?

Before we moved to Pewaukee, Wisconsin, a Jewish community wanted to build a synagogue in our vicinity. Backed by a transparent pretext, the city fathers turned their thumbs down to that request.

Not allowing practitioners of the "wrong" faith to gain a foothold and perhaps prosper and proselytize in the midst of a community belonging to the "right" faith, is an understandable concern.

In my sixth decade of life, I realized that the gift of a clock to the Anglican Church was consistent with the spirit of Islam. Islam allows and protects other religions. The Muslim citizens of Zanzibar were not offended. The clerics actually welcomed the decision. The building of this church was followed by the erection of another one, a Catholic one this time, followed by the building of Hindu temples, a Buddhist temple and finally, an impressive Zoroastrian *Agiyari*[24].

---

[24] Place of worship.

Seyyid Barghash (Sultan; 1870-1888) was cordial in his approval of such places of worship. The only restriction he subtly hinted at was that the spire of the church not exceed the height of his palace—the *Beit-el-Ajaib*.

Skeptics probably see a sinister implied symbolism in the request. I cannot imagine a reasonable one. None of the mosques or minarets in Zanzibar are higher than the Cathedral.

No. No. No.

The explanation lies in the personality of *Seyyid Barghash*. He was a builder who was proud of what he built and almost vain about the B*eit-el Ajaib*. If anywhere in his realm, a structure had gone up higher than the *Beit –el-Ajaib*—his pride and joy—he would have beheaded himself.

Morocco, gave sanctuary to the Jews fleeing from the Spanish inquisition, in the Kasbah of Rabat and were treated on par with the Muslims and the Protestants who had

Beit-el-Ajaib

fled from that Inquisition. When Jerusalem fell to the crusaders, they boasted that the streets of Jerusalem were ankle deep in Muslim blood. When the Muslims recaptured Jerusalem, not even a hair was hurt on a Christian or a Jewish head.

Islam is a tolerant religion[25].

Even when in power, it has had no problems co existing with other religions. Muslims believe that Allah sent innumerable prophets to spread his word. Jesus, Mary, Joseph, Abraham, Moses and David are all mentioned in the Koran as prophets of Allah and revered by Muslims. It is a sin to criticize any of the religions that preceded Islam, because some of the beliefs held by them are the true words of God. We just do not know which part of their book is authentic and which part has been adulterated. We have two choices. Throw out the baby with the bath water or treat it all with respect.

Muslims do the later.

Yes. Aurangzeb, the Emperor whose policies initiated the downfall of a great Mogul Empire in India, was intolerant of and cruel to all non-Muslims. He was an Emperor who claimed to be a Muslim but was not a Muslim Emperor.

Akbar the Great was a Muslim Emperor but not a Muslim. Akber repudiated Islam and founded *"Dinne Elahi"*, a religion that died with him.He raised the Mogul Empire to its zenith, by following the pragmatic Islamic principles of religious tolerance and the equality of all citizens in the blind folded eyes of the law.

Several of his chief ministers and advisers and Generals were Hindu's. He married *Jhoja*, a Rajput princess, who continued to practice Hinduism in his palace during her marriage to Akbar. That marriage was a brilliant political move. Their child, Salim,

---

[25] "Muhammad" Karen Armstrong.

ascended the mogul throne with 50/50, Hindu/Muslim blood flowing through his veins; making him an Emperor, acceptable to the followers of both of the predominant religions of India.

Mr. Boyd was not the only African in town who was a slave at one time. There were several other citizens of Zanzibar, now free, but who were once slaves. Several Arab families had former slaves, who after slavery was abolished, continued to live with them as free and equal members of the family and when they got old were taken care of and treated with respect. In Zanzibar old age is an asset. The elderly are revered because of the wisdom gained from longevity and their contribution to society. When unable to look after themselves their family took them in and looked after them. There are no nursing homes in Zanzibar.

I take that back. There is one. For cows.

The entrance to a farm in *Sateni* has a metal archway with *"Puribai gawshala*[26]*"* in Gujrati script. To Hindu's a cow is sacred. When cows owned by Hindus got old and feeble, they were enrolled in Puribai's school.

When we were growing up in Zanzibar, we were often warned by our parents to beware of the *"Mangas"*. The *"Mangas"* are Arab traders from the countries surrounding the Arabian Sea. For a few weeks in summer, they descended upon Zanzibar, like a swarm of locusts. For centuries, their dhows were blown to the east coast of Africa and back home again by the trade winds. At one time their cargo was mainly slaves. The ones who had captured Mr. Boyd were the *"Mangas."*.

---

[26] "Puribai's school for cows."

When the trade winds blew south towards Zanzibar bringing the *"Manga"* with it, our parents admonished us not to leave home alone, go to and return from school only with a group of classmates and never approach areas where the *"Mangas"* congregated. The reason for this admonishment was that, Zanzibari's still suspected the *"Mangas"* of stealing children and selling them as slaves, in the Middle East. Slavery is still legal in Saudi Arabia.

As a child, not only did I know of slaves, I also spent most of it in dread of becoming one.

The area we lived in and where Christ church is located is named *"Kibokoni."* A *"kiboko"*, in Kiswahili, is a hippo. A *kiboko* is also a whip, made out of a hippo's tail—a highly efficient pain inflicting weapon, used for disciplining slaves.

The neighborhood we lived in was dotted with little prisons built by slave traders for holding slaves till they were auctioned off at the slave market. Every one of these structures, in addition to cells, had a whipping post; hence the name, *Kibokoni*, the place of whipping posts.

Mr. Boyd was in his usual state of health and in his early sixties. We were surprised to hear that a doctor was sent for as Mr. Boyd had intractable vomiting.

The doctor came over promptly, riding his bicycle with his black bag strapped on the back seat

He asked several health related questions. Then he began his examination. He paid particular attention and lingered quite a while, when he assessed the color of Mr. Boyd's pale lips and finger nail beds. He then listened to his heart and lungs, checked his ankles and his lower back for swelling by pushing his thumbs in those areas for a few seconds, then abruptly taking his thumb off the area and observing his thumb print. He then pulled a chair next to Mr. Boyd's bed and sat on it, with his hand he felt the belly. At first he felt gently all over the belly. Then with the weight of his body behind his palm he felt for the deeper abdominal organs. Once again, he stuck the ends of his stethoscope in his ears and listened to the four quadrants of his abdomen.

Having completed his examination, he pulled the stethoscope out of his ears and put them back in his black bag. It was time to find out what was wrong with Mr. Boyd. The air was still, silent, and saturated with apprehension. All breathing was slow and shallow. All eyes were fixed on the physician.

The usually calm caring face of the physician could not conceal that the possible diagnoses he was considering were all fatal. Like a drowning man reaching for a straw, he was hoping to grasp a disease he could treat.

After an eternity in deep thought, hoping against hope for a negative answer, he stepped forwards, put his hand over Mrs. Boyd's left shoulder and asked calmly;

"Was the vomitus black?"

In Zanzibar, it was common knowledge that a black vomitus was a herald of death. Mrs. Boyd's eyes widened and a strangling knot in her throat would not let her speak.

She replied by nodding.

Apprehensively.

Slowly.

Affirmatively.

The doctor's face fell. His last treatable diagnosis was dashed and his reassuring grip on her shoulder relaxed. His lips parted to utter words.

Not wanting to know what he had to say, Mrs. Boyd rushed towards him, embraced him with all her strength and wailed and wept over his shoulder.

The doctor returned her embrace, patted her back in a rhythm, while he stared vacantly at the ceiling and let her cry.

At least once a year, he made this dreaded diagnosis and suffered the agony of a helpless physician. There was nothing he could do for Mr. Boyd, but he certainly could allay Mrs. Boyd's guilt.

As she sobbed in his embrace, in a soft gentle voice he helped her calm down.

"In the years I have known you; you have been an ideal wife and a caretaker.

No one could have nursed him better then you did. You stayed up nights and followed my directions exactly as I gave them to you. You gave him the best possible care.

I am the one who is letting him down. Someday, doctors will know how to treat this problem but today we don't.

But as long as a person is breathing, there is always hope. I have several patients who survived this disease. So, will your husband.

Let us hope and pray"

Mrs. Boyd sobbed for a few more moments. She then forced herself to regain her composure. Wiped her cheeks, with the end of her sari, took one step back. A few seconds passed in silence. With eyes focused on the floor before her and in a soft voice she said;

"Thank you for seeing my husband."

After a brief pause, and with her eyes still focused on the floor, in a barely audible whisper she added;

"God bless you."

Mr. Boyd had a bleeding stomach ulcer. Today, a routine problem easily treated and almost always, without surgery. But in the early 1940,s Zanzibar, even if the doctor was smart enough to make the diagnosis, there was no blood banking or potent antacids. If the patient was going to recover, he had to do it on his own. Very few did.

Mr. Boyd passed away peacefully that night. He never was a man of means. Neighbors chipped in to pay for his funeral at the UMCA Anglican Church. It was Mr. Boyd's wish to have church bells tolled during his funeral. That entailed an extra expense to cover the bell ringer's fee. Mr. Boyd's neighbors came up with that too.

In 1998, Uncle Moin, Shahdia, Feisal, Sharifah, grandma and I were in Zanzibar for three days. After a long non-stop flight from London, we needed a break to recover from our flight, before flying to Arusha for a strenuous *safari*[27].

Among the places we visited in Zanzibar was Kibokoni, where a sign,

"Site of the former slave market"

caught our eyes. The sign had an arrow directing tourists to the main entrance to the Cathedral Church of Christ in Africa.

We decided it was worth a visit.

We had to wait a few minutes before the next group could start the tour.

While we waited at the entrance, the irony of the visit made me chuckle. I was raised in the shadow of this Cathedral, yet this was the first time I was entering it—as a tourist.

Our guide was a Mswahili in his mid-twenties. We had schools that were run by UMCA. He probably attended one of those schools. He spoke English well but with a strong Kiswahili accent. He wore trousers, a shirt, a black tie and a light weight jacket, attire Christians wore on formal occasions.

"Ladies and gentlemen, my name is Damianee.

---

[27] A jeep tour through a wild life preserve

Welcome to the Cathedral Church of Christ in Africa. This Church was completed in 1879 by UMCA. The letters UMCA stand for, the Universities Mission to Central Africa. The universities which sponsored the mission and built this cathedral were Oxford, Cambridge, Dublin and Durham."

He first led us to a dungeon. The steps to it were just wide enough for one (skinny) person and it led us to a tiny room no larger than an average bathroom with a square hole one foot square with inch thick bars for a window.

"Slaves with metal neck collars linked to other slave neck collars with a chain, stayed here for a night. They were the next day's auction inventory."

Even our small group of seven, were claustrophobic in that dark, damp musty space. Damianee, told us that sometimes over a dozen were crammed in this room, "like matchsticks in a match box."

I looked around. All faces were ashen.

Before he could finish his sentence, we bolted out of that place and up to the lobby to suck in fresh, cool, reviving air.

He then lead us to the alter. He stood with his back towards the alter and waited for everyone to catch up with him.

"We are standing where the main Slave market on the coast of East Africa, used to be. We chose the slave markets whipping post for our altar's location and built the church around it".

ZANZIBAR

"Where you stand now is the place we place caskets of members of our congregation for a funeral service.

Can any one name a famous member of our congregation whose casket laid here for a funeral service?"

No one could.

I knew one. Mr. Boyd. His casket must have been placed here, but he was not a famous person, so I did not volunteer that information.

Statue of Livingstone in Zambia

"It was Dr. David Livingstone, a UMCA missionary and an explorer of Africa. We performed his funeral service here.

With his right hand above his shoulder, in a fist with his thumb pointing behind him, Damianee proudly pointed to a cross above the alter.

"This cross has an interesting history."

We looked at it. It is an unimpressive wooden cross. No striking workmanship. No awe inspiring carving. No embedded precious stones. No gold. Small.

"When Dr. Livingstone died in 1873, we followed his wishes. During his final illness he spent hours in the shade of his favorite tree outside his hut. According to his wishes, we buried his

MR. BOYD

heart under his favorite tree and brought his casket to Zanzibar for a funeral service and then shipped it to Scotland for burial.

"Decades later, we went back to the tree under which we had buried Dr. Livingstone's heart. We cut a branch off that tree and made a cross out of it"

Pumping his raised fist back and forth, with his thumb jutting backwards he ended the sentence with;

"And we hung it here."

We looked at the cross again.

This time, with reverence, at an icon made from a tree that was nourished by the heart of an abolitionist.

A plain icon.

A clear message.

As clear as the Boy Scout symbol for, "This way home"

This symbol was on that wall, the day bells pealed during Mr. Boyd's funeral.

It was there to guide an ex-slave home.

The home of the free.

Photograph of slave sanitation workers in
a Zanzibar street. Circa 1853

Chapter Four
Chhipawaad

My *"Naneeamma"* (maternal Grandmother,) used to recite a nursery rhyme, which narrates succinctly, the founding of Ahmedabad. The names of several cities in India have the suffix *"abad"*. It stands for "a prosperous place." The prefix of such a word is usually the name of the founder of the city.

"There was a Sultan." *Naneeamma* said. "And his name was Ahmed. One day, Sultan Ahmed was on a hunting trip with his entourage and his favorite hunting dog. The dog was the best in his entire kingdom and was bred specifically for the Sultan, for its size, strength, speed and especially for its ferocity.

During a hunt, the dog broke away from the hunting party, ran to a bush and started barking at a rabbit that was hiding in a bush.

Then, lo and behold, instead of running for his life, the rabbit got up on his hind legs, and confronted the dog in a menacing posture. The dog, startled by the size and belligerence of the rabbit, put his tail between his legs, turned around and whimpered back to his master for protection—from the rabbit.

Sultan Ahmed was amazed.

He had never even heard of such a confrontation. He dwelled on the incident for weeks and after consulting several experts in his realm, concluded that the only explanation for the incredible spectacle was that the local water had to be rich in healthy nutrients to nourish such a brave rabbit.

Having reached that decision, he decided to vacate his capital and moved it to the spot where the rabbit had scared away his dog.

And he named his new capital, *Ahmedabad.*"

Today, Ahmedabad is a sprawling metropolis which has engulfed the old capital but some evidence of his rule remains.

My favorite is *Jhool ta minara,* the swaying minarets.

There is a mosque in Ahmedabad which had two minarets. They were built of bricks but they swayed with the breeze. When a day is calm, you can climb up a flight of stairs to the top of the minarets, push on its wall and make it sway.

Abbajaan[28], a civil engineer, was always fascinated by the structure and could not even begin to explain why the minaret swayed. Neither could the engineers in the Ivory towers of England. They took the mystery as a challenge and since they ruled India they decided to take down one of the minarets to find out why it swayed. The minaret was taken down one brick at a time. Each brick was measured,

---

[28] My father.

weighed, labeled and placed at a different site to replicate the minaret.

The replica, built exactly like the original, stood solidly on the ground, like a minaret should. It did not sway. In disgust the English tore down the replica.

Fortunately for posterity, the English decided not to tear down the remaining minaret to find the answer to their question. I doubt if they would have become any wiser, had they done so.

Where once there were two, now there is just a lone, plain, unobtrusive minaret in a forest of beautiful ones.

But, every time there is a breeze, then and only then, she flaunts her uniqueness with a tantalizing sway, and dares her onlookers to make another attempt to make her divulge the secret of her sway.

Ahmedabad is called the "Manchester" of India. The Manchester it is compared to is the one in England. Like its English namesake, Ahmedabad has several cotton mills each employing thousands of people.

My uncle Peermian used to work as an electrician in one of these mills. I remember once stopping by his place of work. It was a huge building with hundreds of mechanical looms. Each loom was run by a person who was continuously busy fixing broken threads and replenishing empty bobbins. It was also a very noisy place. I remember Peermian *chacha*[29] showing us the buttons and switches in his office. He pointed to one

---

[29] Uncle.

orange push button, about an inch in diameter, and said, "99% of all the complaints I hear are when I am late pushing that one." When pushed, that button sounded a siren, which was a signal to the workers to shut down their looms and take a 10-minute tea break.

Sarabhai, one of the richest persons in India, owned this mill. He was a legend while he was alive. His attire and demeanor was so ordinary that even his employees mistook him for a coworker. Although blessed with material wealth, he had a cursed family life.

His only son was mentally and emotionally retarded. At times, he was docile, and even likable. But there were instances when he was fierce, violent and a mortal danger to anyone around him. Since those incidents were unpredictable, like a wild animal in a zoo, he lived in a cage in his home.

The implication of the second legend is that, there is no blessing better than having a healthy family. If he had a choice, Sarabhai would have gladly traded all his material wealth for a healthy son.

Most of my memories of Ahmedabad are of our days in Chhipawaad.

"*Chaap*" is to stamp. A "*chhipa*" is a stamper. The *Chhipas* are talented craftsman, who dye and stamp cloth. They speak *Marwadi*, a language Gujratis do not comprehend. When the cotton mills were built in Ahmedabad, their skills were in demand and thousands of Chhipas migrated from Rajasthan to Ahmedabad. The rolls of cloth that came out of the factories were white. Chhipas dyed them and hand stamped them into Sarees, bed sheets and table cloths.

Of all the uncles, the one we spent the most time with was Peermian, who lived on *Lambee Sheree*,[30] in the Chhippawaad of Ahmedabad.

My father and Peermian, his younger brother, got along well and of all the sisters, my mother got along best with Sakeena, the one I called *Khalabibi*[31], since she was younger than my mother. Khalabibi's children addressed my mother as "*Khalaamma*"[32], since my mother was the eldest in her family.

The majority of people living in this waada were *Chippas*.

Every time we left our *Chacha's*[33], house to go anywhere in Ahmedabad, we had to meander through *Laambi Sheree* which is occupied on both sides by the *Chippas* who work out of their homes.

With them they brought from Rajasthan, their taste for dazzling colors—and the swastika. In India, the swastika is a shield against evil spirits and ubiquitous on jewelry homes, cars, cradles and clothing.

Since childhood, I have associated the swastika with Chhippawaad, because of its abundance in this waada.

---

[30] Long street.
[31] Khala is an aunty. Bibi, pronounced "Bee Bee" is an honorific like the word" lady."
[32] Amma is a mother. Only the oldest aunt is addressed as "Amma."
[33] Uncle.

The *Chhipas* used the streets as an extension of their workshops. They had long narrow tables on which they unrolled reams of plain cloth. Each family had their own set of unique stamps carved out of wooden blocks about the size of a brick. All members of a family work together. With lightning speed, they dip the stamps in inkpads and then stamp the cloth with unerring accuracy. The result is a continuous pattern, at the borders of the cloth and in the medallions, which even on close scrutiny fail to show any break between the stampings.

The Gypsies of Europe are also well known for being talented. For centuries, they have made a living as musicians, dancers, fortune tellers and craftsman. In Ireland they are called "Tinkers" as tinsmithing is one of the crafts they are good at. They are very secretive, speak in a language of a non-European origin, and live in colorful horse drawn wagons with the Swastika and other hex signs painted on them.

The first time I saw a gypsy wagon was on a country road in County Wicklow, during my student days in Ireland. Of all the signs on the wagon, the one that caught my eye was the Swastika.

It is an ancient Aryan hex sign to ward off evil spirits. Anthropologically, Indians are Aryans so it is not surprising that it is a very common symbol in the Indian subcontinent. It is painted on the floors where a wedding will take place and swastika charms for bracelets are popular among Hindu women.

Hitler adopted the swastika as a symbol of the third Reich because he too claimed to be an Aryan. What I could not understand was why the Gypsies respected the swastika. It was not likely that they admired Hitler or shared his values. He did to them what he did to the Jews.

The United States also has Gypsies. Yul Bryner, the Hollywood actor who played the King in "Anna and the king of Siam" was one of them.

In 1967 and 1968, I worked as a staff physician at Emily P. Bissell Hospital, in Wilmington, Delaware. In those days, every state had a hospital dedicated to treating only patients with tuberculosis. The hospital was built in the center of a five acre lot, sold to the State of Delaware for one dollar by the DuPont family. Dr. Young, Chairman of the medical staff, told me that soon after he was hired, he admitted a gypsy patient to the hospital. When he came to work the next morning, all the parking spaces in the hospital were taken up by dozens of brightly colored covered wagons with Swastikas on them.

When it was time for patients to have visitor, dozens of men, women and children poured out of the wagons and came to the hospital. These were Gypsies who had come to the hospital to pay their respects to their king.

The Gypsies, all over the world, live a nomadic life. They stay at the outskirts of a village long enough to rest up and make enough money to replenish their food supply. Once that is done

A gypsy king

they pack their belongings in their wagons and off they go to the next village. They wear garbs of dazzling colors and speak a language that has no resemblance to any of the European languages. They are a mysterious people, and their anthropological roots an enigma.

The British too are fascinated by the Gypsies. George Barrows, an Englishman, infiltrated the gypsies, lived with them for years and wrote a book about them which made very interesting reading about the culture of the Gypsies but did not solve the mystery of whom they are or where they came from.

In 2003, an anthropologist in England did a DNA test on a Gypsy and— lo and behold—the DNA test establish that the Gypsies of Europe came from Rajasthan, India.

When I read that, it took me back to the day when I saw a swastika on a covered gypsy wagon in county Wicklow. It struck a familiar cord. And it puzzled me.

CHHIPAWAAD

I could not explain why the swastika, the gypsy's talent for arts and craft, their use of bright colors and their strange language seemed so familiar and yet I could not think of where I had seen it before.

Now I can.

I saw that in Chhipawaad.

Gypsy dancers in Bollywood costumes.

CHAPTER FIVE

A Day At The Market

Early in the mornings, from the ocean, a siren like sound wafts into coastal villages of Zanzibar.

The sound is shorter than a siren but is repeated irregularly and multiple times.

Scanning the ocean reveals no source of the sound. But the villagers know it well, unhurriedly they finish up whatever they are doing and head for the beach.

The sound is from fishing boats, which are still over the horizon. They blow on a conch to announce that they are on their way home with the day's catch.

If you cut off the small pointed tip of a conch, you are left with a passage which gets progressively larger with each spiraling turn, till it reaches the wide end—a natural wind instrument, of limited notes but of an astounding range.

Villagers walk in sand, by the fish laid in rows, in front of each fishing boat and shop. If the number of unsold fish is small, the fisherman will dry it by an open fire that evening, for future meals. If the quantity of unsold fish is worth a lot more than the extra cost of transportation to Zanzibar City, the fisherman will pack them in a basket and carry it on his head to the village bus stop. Sooner or later (usually later) a bus shows up at the stop.

The "Bus" is the chassis of an English lorry, over which a local carpenter has built a personalized body, from local lumber. It is a glue and nail job without any devices of suspension. Riding the bus makes you aware of not only the beautiful Zanzibar scenery, but also the presence of every pebble the wheels ride over.

Baskets of fish, chickens, fruit, cassava, vegetables and coconuts destined for the market in Zanzibar City, are hoisted to the top of the bus and secured with ropes. Finally, the passengers take their seats. We used to spend several weeks every year in Jambiani. Whenever we ran out of supplies, I joined the passengers.

After a warning hoot to let the village know that the bus was leaving, the ancient bus would lurch forwards, and then slowly meander across the road to avoid pot holes, bounce over the uneven areas and surprisingly arrive intact at the main market in Zanzibar City.

We had three separate markets.

The Chicken Market.

The northern most building was the chicken market. It was filled with cages of live chickens, clucking away, on either side of the smelly aisles. Point to the chicken you have selected and the seller will slaughter it, pluck it, carve it, wrap it and hand it to you, while you wait.

A DAY AT THE MARKET

In the countries that I am familiar with, the most expensive and the most prestigious meat served only on special occasions, is—chicken.

During a break from our medical studies, Nicholas Senketuka and I were reminiscing about foods back home. It was close to lunch time and we were hungry—that explains why this particular topic was discussed.

Nicholas was a *Muganda*. His home was in Buganda, a subnational kingdom in Uganda, East Africa, ruled by a king—the *Kabaka*.

The current Kabaka

ZANZIBAR

In Uganda, as in India, a family rolls out a red carpet for a son –in-law's visit. Every villager in both the countries, own chickens fed

on free range. No matter how prosperous a villager is, the number of chickens he owns is of course, finite.

He quoted to me a proverb in his mother tongue, *Luganda*:

"A son-in-law should not visit his in-laws oftener then the number of chickens his in-laws own"

I laughed.

His proverb reminded me of a chicken proverb the English have, I quoted it and we both had a hearty laugh.

In between waves of laughter, we worked on combining the two proverbs and came up with a multilingual, transcontinental proverb;

"Never count the chickens,

before they are hatched,

but always do so,

as you leave your in-laws."

When in a Muslim country, it is important to know the words, "Halal." and "Zabiya"

"Halal" is Arabic word which mean "permissible" or lawful". The adjective, is used with the nouns of foods, beverages, cosmetics and even pickles. A halal food may be consumed but only when it is Zabiya—another Arabic word, which means flesh from a halal animal that, was slaughtered in an Islamic or a Jewish sacrificial ritual. Chicken is halal but should not be consumed if it is not Zabiya.

The concept is similar to "Kosher" and most probably derived from it. "Kosher" meat from a Jewish butcher is "Halal" for Muslims and pork, no matter which butcher it comes from, is *"Harram"*, "Forbidden". It is a one way ticket to hell, for Jews and Muslims.

Essentially, it is the practice of good hygiene. For example, in both cultures, the flesh of an animal that died naturally is forbidden. It is halal but not Zabiya

A Jewish doctor gave me the most plausible explanation for the practice of Zabiya.

All animals (including humans!) have more microbes living in and on them then the total number of cells in the body. However, while alive, the body and the bugs live happily in symbiosis. Upon death, the body loses its defensive mechanisms; the bugs enter the blood stream and during the terminal heart beats, spread to and infect every cell in the body.

Consume such flesh and it will ruin the rest of your last day.

The essentials of Zabiya are:

> 1. Use a sharp knife—and be quick about it. (A good humane advice.)

ZANZIBAR

> 2. Severe arteries and veins but not the spine. (A good idea if you prefer not getting "Mad Cow disease" or "Chronic wasting disease" of the deer.)
>
> 3. Drain the veins quickly, by suspending the carcass. (Read the last paragraph again.)

You must wonder, how do you make a halal fish, "Zabiya"? A fish can only live so long after it is out of water. They are all dead by the time they arrive at the beach and most certainly by the time they arrive at the fish market.

The official answer is that the fish was "Zabiyed[34]", before the fisherman reeled it in!

Ask any Muslim; "Why is a dead fish Zabiya?" and you will hear the following story.

Abraham was only a millisecond away from sacrificing his son, when God told him;

"Stop."

With relief and bursting with joy, he shouted, "Whoopee" as he raised his right arm and flung his knife in the air. The sharp aerodynamic knife flew quite far and landed in the

---

[34] Do not bother reaching for a dictionary. You will not find it there--or anywhere else.

(Mediterranean?) sea. As the knife was sinking towards the ocean floor, it slit the neck of a fish. What we call the gills in a fish, is the slit Abraham made.

Whereas, the knife was sharp.

Whereas, It was a swift slash.

Whereas, the fish was alive when that happened.

Now therefore, a fish is "Zabiya"—if it has gills.

I would love to claim this story as my own, if only I can explain how the knife descending through the water; slit the fish on both sides.

The *Bohoras*[35] do not believe this story and will not eat a fish unless it was made Zabiya by them. That requirement restricts them to consuming only fish they caught and made Zabiya and no Bohora wants to do that as fishing is not a lucrative profession in Zanzibar. Fortunately , there is a species that stays alive long after it is out of water. If an early bird Bohora meets a fisherman as soon as the fisherman returns to his village, he may find a live fish of that species to make it Zabiya. The *Kiswahili* word for that species—as you may have guessed it correctly—is, "*Samaki ya wa Bohora*"[36]

The Fish Market

The next building north is the fish market. It is odorless, as fresh fish has no smell. Grandma almost fainted from

---

[35] A sect of Shia Muslims from India.
[36] The Bohora fish

the stink, the first time she stepped inside the fish market in Ahmedabad, India. Those fish were caught in the same ocean as the one Zanzibar is in, but were caught at least 24 hours ago and were transported without refrigeration. As the interval between catching it and eating it increases, the stink increases and the flavor deteriorates exponentially. Even today, Ahmedabad or for that matter any place further than 25 miles from the ocean is not a good place to spend your money on fish.

This explains why the cuisine of Gujarat and other inland states of India have no fish and the cuisine along the coast of India is mainly fish, cooked in Coconut milk, just like the way the Zanzibari's do.

At the fish market in Zanzibar, after you have selected your fish and before you start bargaining, make sure it is fresh. You do that by lifting the slit in its neck to inspect the color of the gills. The color should be bright pink. Any shade darker than that and particularly the lighter hues of brown, should make you walk away from the fish, having saved yourself the time you would have wasted bargaining for it.

The mind accepts the familiar as normal—how things just are and should be— never questioning it, till it is exposed to the unfamiliar.

Not till I was in my mid-fifties, that it dawned on me that there was something odd about the seafood preference of the Waswahili.

A DAY AT THE MARKET

We were in the Bahamas, in the Caribbean and I noticed that Bahamians of African descent ate conch—a shell fish. Back home, the Waswahili never did.

With disgust, a Mswahili fisherman, would toss back into the sea, any crustacean, including lobsters, that were inadvertently caught in their nets or traps. These foods, I learned later, are an expensive delicacy in other parts of the world.

I do not have an explanation, only a guess.

The Waswahili were converted to Islam by Omani Arabs. Oman is in the Arabian Peninsula, in the same body of water that Zanzibar is in. Omani's are Sunnis, a sect of Islam, which prohibits eating sea food without gills.

Almost all dietary prohibitions, in all cultures are a distillation of knowledge gained from centuries of trial and error with foods that are locally available. The same process admonishes the Europeans against consuming shell fish in months with an "R" in it.

As a child, I vividly remember a much discussed tragedy, in the village of Chwaka. A large turtle was sold in the local fish market and within days, most of the villagers who had consumed it, died of ptomaine poisoning.

Is it any wonder then, that in addition to shell fish, the inhabitants of Chwaka do not eat turtle?

If this dietary avoidance persists for a few generations, the true reason for the avoidance will be forgotten. In a couple of centuries after that, a Chwaka Mullah will misinterpret a passage in the Holy Koran, making the avoidance of turtle, a commandment of Allah. Most Muslims in Chwaka will practice the prohibition. The ultraorthodox will pointedly avoid eating turtle in public, to impress those present, with their piety.

The goat market,

This building was north of the Fish market.

Goat is the most popular meat in Zanzibar. Kids were exported live from Somalia for slaughter in Zanzibar. In my part of the world, the word "Kid" is used for a young goat.

Unlike the chicken market, the goats were all dead, skinned, gutted and hung by their hoofs on a hook from the ceiling, in stalls on either side of a central aisle. As you enter the market, all the butchers try to catch your attention by waving and shouting a welcome greeting to you. I always ignored the rest and headed straight for the stall of Salum, as my mother was satisfied by what he sent home with me. As long as he did not send with me inedible parts of the goats anatomy, the meat was satisfactory to my mother.

In Zanzibar, as in most African and Asian countries, you do not specify the cut of meat you want. If you do, you will get a vacant stare from a very confused butcher. The kind thing to do is to tell him only how many pounds you want and leave the rest up to him.

A talented butcher can thrill you by his moves; the way a ballerina does.

Salum had several carcasses slung in front of him in several stages of butchering; from an untouched carcass, to a skeleton with barely any meat still attached to it.

He would lunge and separate a muscle by its fascial plane, like a master surgeon. Then, with a thud, hack off a hunk here. With a flourish, shave off a slice of a long muscle off a bone there. In the blink of an eye, he could extract a piece of meat from an irregularly shaped body cavity and with his free hand, toss the piece on the scale, while monitoring the progress of its pointer through his peripheral vision.

As the scale pointer approached the numeral representing the pounds you ordered, for good measure, he would toss in a "treat" like a kidney and / or a slice of liver, to bring the scale pointer just past the target numeral.

The contents in the tray on the scale were then slid into a bag and he told me the price as he handed the bag to me.

In a land where bargaining is the norm, I did not bargain with Salum. We had an undiscussed understanding. I had several butchers to choose from but bought meat exclusively from him and to make sure I returned to him, he provide me with the best meat he had and to quote to me the lowest price he could afford to sell it at.

The Beef Market

This was in the northernmost part of the market complex. Zanzibar did not have beef cattle. We had only milk cows. The meat market was the last stop in a cow's life journey, soon after the quantity of its milk had diminished to an unprofitable level.

I would like to narrate the interior of the beef market but I cannot, as I have never been in it.

In Zanzibar, beef was a poor man's meat.

We did not eat beef.

We were middle class.

Zanzibar is a fertile island. Because it is a tropical island, you do not keep a garbage can close to living quarters. It is usually kept, on dirt, by a door leading out of the back porch. By the end of the second week of our vacations in *Jambiani*[37], one of the children's chores was to pull out six inch tall tomato, cucumber and melon plants which had grown from seeds that had missed the garbage can.

Naturally we had all the indigenous vegetables. Because we had a large Indian population, some of them strict vegetarians, we also had vegetables that Indians like. In India, it is easy to be a vegetarian. The variety of vegetables are endless and the cuisine so delicious that when in Gujarat, I seldom miss meat.

The Indians and Arabs of Zanzibar incorporated the indigenous foods into their cuisine. We often ate the ubiquitous cassava, better known in the USA as tapioca. Fresh cassava is cooked in coconut milk with a pinch of salt and a chopped green chilly.

---

[37] One of the seaside villages that we vacationed at.

Fish or meat can be added to it for a main dish—delicious. The cassava tastes like scalloped potatoes. During school recess, venders had roasted cassava, with a sprinkle of salt and red chili powder. It tastes like a roasted potato with a zing to it. Cassava that cannot be consumed right away, is died and then with a mortar and pestle ponded into a powder—*"Ugaree"*—that can be stored at room temperature. Add a tablespoonful of *Ugaree* to a bowl of hot water and presto, you have oatmeal, only better tasting, by far, than Quaker Oats.

For desert, *Ammajaan* cooked *"Mkono ya tembo"*, elephants trunk. It is a ripe plantain that is at least eighteen inches long. It is simmered in coconut milk with a teaspoon of sugar and a cardamom pod. It is served hot. It can also be battered and deep fried in coconut oil the way Cuban restaurants do it.

Among my heroes is Seyyid Barghash, a Sultan of Zanzibar.

While a prince of Zanzibar, he went to school in India and there he tasted a mango for the first time. It must have left an indelible mark on his mind, for years later, when he ascended the throne of Zanzibar, one of his first acts was to send the royal ship to India to bring back mango seedlings that he planted in several spots in Zanzibar, including, the Murhubi palace and fortunately it has flourished.

Mango was the favorite fruit of Ghalib, my favorite Urdu poet, the Mogul emperors and Sultan Barghash.

Zanzibar was not lacking in any sensual delights, but to bring Zanzibar closer to paradise, Seyyid Barghash, added the gustatory delight of the Mango—a fruit that truly belongs in heaven—and in Zanzibar.

Return home

By midafternoon, all the selling and shopping is done and the villagers gather by their particular bus stops. There was no time table for the bus. The driver knew how many of his villagers he came with and when all of them were back, it was time to return home.

The bus, now much lighter than its market bound weight, would begin its slow journey back home, continuing the same gyrations only of larger amplitude as it was much lighter

The shaken up passengers, happily spill out of the bus when they reach their destination into the arms of their waiting wives and children The children wondering what surprises Daddy purchased for them while in the *Mjeenee*.[38]

Jussa, the driver and owner of the bus was the last one to get out of the bus after he had dropped off his last passenger and parked his bus behind his House/store.

Jussa's family was a typical Indian family in Africa; a sole Indian family living and running a general store in an African village.

The daily routine for all bread earners is the same all over the world. Have breakfast. Put in a day at work. Eat dinner with your family. Spend an hour or so watching TV. Go to bed. Wake up swearing at the alarm clock. Repeat the same the next day.

---

[38] The City of Zanzibar.

A DAY AT THE MARKET

Jussa's usual day was almost the same, with one exception; He did not have an alarm clock. He did not need one.

It was the sound of the conch that woke him up —startled, in disgust and temporarily profane.

Chapter Six
Fatimabibi

At lunch one day, my father was unusually quiet and engrossed in a problem. As soon as lunch was over, he told all my siblings to take our daily nap and told me to accompany him to an important "appointment."

I prepared myself to confront a serious situation.

On our way, he was preoccupied and from his lip movements, I could tell that he was saying the rosary. About ten minutes into our walk, I could no longer hold back my curiosity and asked;

"Where are we going?"

"To see an astrologer." was his curt reply and he resumed mumbling his rosary.

An astrologer? Why?

Skipping a nap and allowing me to do the same, had never happened before. Now I too became worried, but did not dare to interrupt him again from his muttering of the rosary.

We were the only Qureshi family in Zanzibar and I just had lunch with all of them and had not noticed anything unusual with any of them.

At that time, he was considering giving up his job and moving our family to Dar-es-Salaam[39] to accept a highly lucrative partnership in a civil engineering firm. The dilemma was that he had worked 23 years in Zanzibar and in another seven years he would be eligible for a pension and live a comfortable retirement. If he accepted the offer from Dar-es-Salaam, he would have to kiss goodbye to his pension and take on the unknown risks that the future may hold. Perhaps he needed some guidance from an astrologer. I was with him because only my mother and I were in on the discussion about this offer. My younger siblings were too young to grasp the ramifications of uprooting ourselves from Zanzibar.

In silence, we walked the rest of the way to *Kiponda*.

The houses in Kiponda, like most of the houses in the Stone Town area of Zanzibar City, were built by Arabs well over a century ago.

The first stories of the houses are the income producers and are used by the owner of the house or rented out, as stores or offices. That floor is avoided as living quarters as people walking by could sneak- a - peak at the female occupants of the house. The highest stories are living quarters, where several generations of a family live together. Those stories had an abundance of windows to let sunlight in and for cross ventilation, but all of them had curtains and / or grills to allow the women to look out without being seen by those outside. The women from such homes usually wore a "Bui Bui[40]" when on the streets.

---

[39] The largest city in and the capital of, Tanganyika.
[40] A veil. A Burkha. A chador.

The main entrance to the first story usually has a huge door that Zanzibar is famous for. When an Arab decides to build a house, the lion's share of his budget goes towards buying a door. The door is as large, with as much intricate carvings, as he can afford. After the door is in place, the rest of the house is built around it. The number of stories, rooms, and the size of the building depended on what was left over, after purchasing the "Zanzibar door."

Zanzibar and India have been in contact for centuries. The brass spikes on the doors, is an Indian influence on Zanzibari culture.

Over 300 years ago, a thick high wall with a door large enough to let elephants and chariots in and out, encircled Indian towns and even villages. If an enemy came to invade, the citizens withdrew within the wall and shut the doors. The invading armies always had elephants in addition to cavalry, and infantry. One way to end a siege was to ride the elephants to the door and have the elephants ram down the door with their heads.

To discourage that, brass spikes were placed on the door. I am certain that at least doing recorded history; there have never been any elephants roaming in Zanzibar or Oman. The beautiful shining brass spikes on the doors are not there to deter them. It is an embellishment.

When we reached the house in Kiponda, the "Zanzibar door" to the house was open. We stepped inside and looked around the foyer, which was dimly illuminated by sunlight, but no one was in sight. So, according to Zanzibar custom, we said, "*Hodee, Hodee.*" The expression roughly translates into

A Zanzibar Door.

"Hello! Anyone home?" Our host came out to greet us at the door with the appropriate response of *"Kareebu, Kareebu"*, "Welcome, Welcome."

The person we came to see was man in his mid-fifties, dressed like a *Mullah*. He took us to a room with only rugs to sit on. He sat cross legged behind a writing desk about the height and size of a coffee table and beckoned us to sit in front of him. He talked to us in fluent *Urdu*, a language preferred by Mullahs and Islamic scholars of India no matter which state they were raised in.

Tea was served by a servant, during the initial customary small talk. While sipping his tea, he asked us what he could do for us.

My father told him of the disturbing news about my paternal grandmother's health that he was receiving in the letters from India. My father could not leave for India right away as another teacher was already in India and if my father went to India now; his school would be unacceptably short staffed. The earliest he could leave would be in about three months from now. Was it possible that he could see his mother if he waited three months?

I was stunned.

"Oh no! Not Dadee amma![41]" Of all the relatives we had in India, the one I loved the most was my Dadee amma.

My earliest recollection of Fatimabibi, my paternal grandmother, is when she was in her late sixties. She was short, about five foot four, a little plump, had a slight hunchback, and had a pretty round face. She had a soft voice and her singing was sweet and soothing.

She was one of those persons who take their time doing everything. Every movement was slow and deliberate. Every sentence was spoken slowly, with each word pronounced with deliberation and with long pauses between them. One of those persons that always make me wonder if their thyroid level needed boosting. They don't. Their skin, heart rate and mentation are normal. Physiologically they are normal. They just do everything slowly.

She seldom got angry but when she did, she erupted like Vesuvius did. On one occasion, she was annoyed at her husband and she lashed out at the Qureshi clan in very unflattering terms.

When Indians get angry, they do not insult the person they are angry at. Instead, they insult the person's family. If they are really angry, they will insult the person's uncles, and if they're furious, they will insult the person's father. That is about as far as they go, unless they want the argument to degenerate into a fistfight, in which case they insult the person's sisters. The ultimate insult, which leads to a fight to death, is insulting the person's mother.

---

[41] Paternal grandmother.

Having made her point that the Qureshi lacked intelligence and sophistication, she would rub in the fact that <u>she</u> was not a Qureshi. She was a **Chauhan.** (The emphasis on the word "Chauhan" is hers.)

Maharana Pratap—a Chauhan.

In India, surnames convey a lot. Her surname tells you that she is not descended from the Arabs, but from Hindu converts. Chauhan is a name that one can justly be proud of. During its years of glory, the state of Rajasthan was ruled by the Chauhan dynasty. Grade school textbooks in Gujarati literature have stories about the heroic exploits of famous *Ranas,* like *Maharana*[42] *Pratap.*

Soldiers were called *Rajput,* which literally means "Sons of the Kingdom". The stories are about absolute loyalty and fighting fearlessly to death to uphold the honor of King and Country. Mothers sent off their sons to battles, with the admonishment of never ruining the family's reputation; by dying from or

---

[42] Maha means great. A Rana is a king.

returning home with, wounds in the back. If death comes to a Rajput, it comes only from wounds, sustained while facing the enemy.

Every grade school child has heard this historically accurate story, about how fierce a Rajput's loyalty is. There was a coup in Rajasthan, during which the royal family was slaughtered. The nursemaid who took care of the crown prince made it out of the palace unnoticed and took the crown prince to her home in a distant village. As long as the crown prince was alive, the insurgent's goal would remain unfinished. So, they sent out a passé to finish off the crown Prince. The passé went to the nursemaid's village, found her hut, stabbed to death the crown prince in his crib, and returned home jubilantly.

Then begins a story within a story about how corrupt and ruthless the usurper was.

After two decades of misrule, every citizen in the state had had enough and the unuttered prayer on the lips of every *subject* was for a savior. Just when the situation could not possibly get any worse, the crown prince returned with an army, defeated the usurper, reclaimed the throne, married his childhood sweetheart and the couple lived happily ever after.

The children listening to this story with rapt fascination never interrupt the storyteller with questions. The appropriate time for questions and clarifications is at the end of the story. Everyone knows that.

At the end of the story, one or more children invariably say something like, "But you said, that the prince was killed in his crib when he was an infant. The ending of your story makes no sense"

The storyteller would feign embarrassment; offer some unconvincing explanation for the oversight and with perfect timing would complete the story with a jaw dropping addendum:

"Sorry, I forgot to tell you that the nursemaid did not take the crown prince into her hut. She hid him in bushes outside her hut. After that, she went into her hut, dressed her own son in the crown prince's clothing and put her son in the crib."

No wonder my *Dadee amma* was proud of her heritage.

My grandmother was a great storyteller. This was in the days before TV, cinema, radio and the gramophone. The days before electricity came to Dhandhuka, oil lamps lit the streets. A municipal worker would come at dusk, trim the wick, replenish the oil if necessary, light the lamp, replace the glass chimney and shut the door to the lamp and latch it. He would then climb down his ladder, walk to the next streetlight and repeat the same routine again. He returned at dawn to put out the lamps. This was his daily routine, except on nights when there was adequate moonlight.

After supper, the adult males would go off and do their thing, the daughter-in-laws would clean up the kitchen, bathe the babies and put them to bed and Grandmothers took their grandchildren in the backyard patio to tell them bedtime stories.

This is the way things were in Zanzibar as well. After supper, children in our block would go up to the *Agaasee,* the flat roof of the house, for bedtime stories. It was so in the *mainland* as well.

In the mid-1950s, a friend of mine and I visited a *Surtee*[43] family, in a remote village in Tanganyika. That family ran a general store and was the only Indians around for hundreds of miles.

This was *Wakonde* territory. The *Wakonde,* even to this day, make the bulk of their living by wood carving. Walk into a store anywhere in USA that sells souvenirs from Africa and you will see the handiwork of the *Wakonde.* In summer, the *Wakonde* guard their crops from birds with a sling, from a platform, similar to the one deer hunters' use in this country. When there are no birds threatening the crop, they keep themselves busy, by whittling. When they had enough carvings to sell, they sell them to travelers when a train stops at the nearest railroad station.

After supper, the host and his children took us out to a little clearing in the village center. It had a little bonfire in the middle, and there was a crowd of Africans sitting in a circle around it. Without any cajoling, one of the Africans would get in the middle of the circle and tell a joke, sing a song, or do a skit.

A young African boy got in the middle of the circle. He wore his hat jauntily. A small twig, representing a pipe, stuck out of his mouth. He strutted to the center of the circle, the way only an arrogant English colonialist can. The crowd chuckled at

---

[43] A family from the state of Surat.

his grotesque gait. His sidekick played the part of a Makonde carver selling his wares at a railroad station. The bargaining started at a leisurely pace till the train whistle blew. Then the tempos of the bargaining speeded up and lead into a comedy of errors. At the second and final train whistle, the "Englishman" grabbed the carvings he had purchased, threw his money at the carver and ran for the train. The carver then yelled at the running Englishman and made the spectators laugh heartily.

He yelled, "Don't forget who has the best deal on this railroad station. Next time you go by, ask for me by name. My English customers call me; "Youbloodyfool"

Before electricity, all cultures created their evening entertainment.

Unlike the African evening entertainment of a variety show, Fatimabibi's entertainment was just stories. Her stories, like the stories of all the grandmothers in those days, were like the Indian movies. There is something in the Indian psych that likes this format of entertainment. It seems to appeal to Indian listeners of all ages. Even their plays are over three hours. I was fortunate enough to get tickets to a very popular Gujrati play while we were in Ahmedabad. It was cleverly crafted and entertaining, but it went on for over five hours. The five hours was in addition to the fifteen-minute "tea break intervals" after each of the five acts. It did not end till after 2 a.m. In the last act, the King was at center stage delivering a soliloquy. His army was supposed to be standing, at attention behind him. Most of them had fallen asleep leaning on their spears!

All grandma stories begin with the same introductory sentence:

"Ek thaa Rajah, aur ek thee Ranee."

"There was a King and there was a Queen."

At appropriate intervals, the storyteller breaks out into a song and just like in the Indian movies, there are at least 10 songs interspersed in the story. The songs are a marker of the end of a chapter, like the little symbols at the end of an article in magazines. It also gives the listeners a little relief from the intense concentration that the stories demand.

To my knowledge, no Indian movie has ever departed from this format. No Indian movie is shorter than three hours. A movie can be dull to the point of boring you to tears. It can have unknown actors. It can have songs that jar your eardrums, but that movie will make a profit as long as it's not less than three hours.

The duration of the movies are linked to an Indian's concept of value. You are not getting your *Rupee's*, worth if the movie is under three hours long.

What my grandmother spun, were spells.

The stories have been handed down the generations. The feedback from the listeners has modified and polished them to perfection. No matter how tired, we were, none of us ever fell asleep during a story and when it ended, we always insisted on listening to another one. If we were unsuccessful, we would settle for a "short one". Sometimes we heard a short story. Quite often, we did not as it was way past our bedtime by the time the first story ended. Then, when all our pleading were ignored and our excuses were exhausted, we went to bed—reluctantly.

Life in Zanzibar was leisurely. Schools and government offices were closed on Christmas day, Boxing Day (December 26th), New Year's Day, the Queen's birthday and the birthday of His Highness the Sultan of Zanzibar. Since the population was 99% Muslims, we also had a Holiday on Idd, and had the whole month of *Ramadan*[44] off.

Ashura was also a public holiday, but only in Zanzibar. The rest of East Africa did not celebrate it. The word is derived from *Ashara, the* Arabic word for ten. *Ashura* is the tenth day of the month of *Muhharrum*—the most important date on the *Shia* calendar. The day Imam Hussain, the grandson of Prophet Muhammad, was martyred in a battle in Karbala, Iraq.

The *Shias* were a tiny minority. The Sultan of Zanzibar was not one of them. It seemed strange to me that *Ashura* was a public holiday, and only in Zanzibar. I mentioned that to my father and he had a fascinating explanation for the holiday.

The richest person in town, during the First World War, was a Shia. The government of Zanzibar was insolvent and could not come up with the payroll of the government workers and the government turned to this businessman for a short-term loan.

Not only did he agree, but offered the loan interest-free in return for a favor. The "interest free" clause was an inedible icing on the cake. Accepting interest is a sin in Islam. His community

---

[44] The holy month of fasting.

would have ostracized him if he had accepted interest. But, the clause made the loan very attractive to the English.

The favor he asked was that Zanzibar declare *Ashura* a public holiday in perpetuity.

Just before I left for medical school, I went to a friend's business to say goodbye to him. As I entered his store, a striking customer walked out of the store. He had a stocky stature, a round face a closely trimmed beard and a mustache. He was bald with a narrow rim of salt and pepper hair. He did not have any footwear. His clothes were cheap and well-worn but they were freshly laundered. As we passed each other in the doorway he flashed a faint smile at me. His demeanor radiated dignity.

"Who was that man?" I asked Bakr.

"That" said Bakr "is the hero of our Shi'ite community. He made His Highness's Government declare *ashura* a public holiday." Since my puzzled expression did not subside completely, he went on, "Yes, he is now penniless. Some of his major business deals backfired. When you discuss business with him, his judgment is as shrewd as it ever was, but he has no capital to start all over again."

Abbajaan was employed by the British Colonial Services. In addition to the holidays I have mentioned before, teachers in high school, got an additional one months' vacation every year; the "short leave". We spent those in rented homes on a beach in a village like Jambiani.

Every three years, my father had six months off as his "long leave". It was during those "long leaves" that we used to spend six months in India. The English spent those months in England.

It was during one of our visits to India in the mid-1940s that I really got to know my grandmother well and became very fond of her. I would go along with her on her errands, and also when she went to visit her friends.

I still remember vividly one of the most disturbing moments of my life. We were in my grandmother's house. In a very casual manner, she mentioned to me that she had lived long enough and was ready to die!

The thought shocked me.

Here was one relative who was very nice to me and I wanted her to be a part of the rest of my life. As a child, humor was the defense I used to get myself out of unpleasant situations. I told her jokingly, "It is easy to say that now. When death looks you in the face, you will change your mind." I wanted her to spend more time with me. I wanted her to live forever.

She looked at me and smiled condescendingly. She thought the whole conversation amusing and much to my embarrassment and in my presence, she repeated the "cute" discussion to her friends.

While in the house of the Mullah in Kiponda, all these memories streamed by me in a split second and I was jolted back into the room by the Mullah asking my father his and my grandmother's dates of birth.

He then looked into a reference astrology book, took a piece of paper and with a pencil scribbled an astrological equation.

This was the first time that I became aware that my father believed in Astrology. Later, we discussed astrology, and he told me that he did believe in astrology, but as a Muslim, he would not resort to it except under "extreme circumstances".

As a Muslim, you do not try to find out what tomorrow holds. That, you leave up to *Allah*. As the Waswahili say *"Kesho Mungu"*.[45]

That is why you were taught to add *"Inshallah"*,[46] to any future commitments. No matter what sort of a day He gives you; accept it thankfully, knowing in your heart, that He picks the best choice for those who leave the choice up to him.

Yes, there will be some tomorrows of peaches and cream but there will also be tomorrows filled with pain and sorrow. It's OK to feel sad at a loss. After all, we are human. But, while your heart is heavy with grief and the tears are rolling down your cheeks, your lips must only say *"Alhamdulillah."* (Thanks be to Allah.) Because, He chose the best outcome for you.

We waited patiently and quietly for several minutes for the *Mullah* to give us his prediction. With a sigh, the *Mullah* looked up from the sheet that he was doing his calculations on, looked first at me then at my father and said; "Your star and your mother's star are moving away from each other in

---

[45] " Tomorrow is up to God"
[46] "God willing"

the galaxy. I am afraid you have seen your mother for the last time."

Fortune telling is the second oldest profession. The Hindu cast of "Joshi" makes living reading palms. These are astute psychologists. Your hand, which the palmist is holding in his hand, is not to decipher the lines in your palm. It is there for him to feel the tone in your muscles. He knows the trail is getting cold when your hand tenses up and the skin gets dry. He does not need you to verbalize your hopes and fears; your body language conveys that to him with better eloquence. Through years of practice and experience, your body vibes steer him to the answer you wish to hear. With your anxieties allayed, you pay him willingly and walk away happy.

Astrology has survived millennia because it provides a human need—hope.

The astrologer, who confidently predicted the loss of my grandmother, told us what we did <u>not</u> want to hear. That, made me doubt my disbelief in astrology.

And the doubt deepened, when his prediction came true.

CHAPTER SEVEN
Mahatma Gandhi

Mahatma Gandhi

Mohandas Karamchand Gandhi was born on the second of October, 1869, in Porbunder, a city on the Arabian Sea in Saurashtra, a state adjacent to Gujarat. Culturally, the two states are similar and share Gujarati as a common language.

Mohandas was his Hindu first name. Indians do not have middle names. But, the English do. Unsatisfied with just two, the

English adopt at least three more. Loaded with names, they cannot understand how anyone can go through life with just one.

When presented with a document for approval, a blank space where a second name has to be sends the English into an acute anxiety attack and they reject the entire document before even proceeding to the last name.

To survive in British bureaucracy, Indian siblings use the same middle names—their father's first name.

Karamchand was not the Mahatma's middle name. It was his father's first name.

Gandhi is not a Hindu surname. It is a Gujarati word for a merchant who deals with medicinal herbs. Indira Gandhi was not related to him. She was the daughter of India's first Prime Minister, Pundit Jawaharlal Nehru and married a Parsee whose last name happened to be Gandhi.

When we were children, my mother made hair oil for us. About once a year, my mother would send me to a Gandhi for the ingredients. The Gandhi I used to go to was Saleh Gandhi. To all the children of my age, he was "Saleh *Kaka*". Saleh is a Muslim first name. *Kaka* is an honorific. Literally, a *"Kaka"* is a paternal uncle. In Gujrati, when you address a male who is a lot older then you are, you always use the suffix *Kaka* and for a female, the suffix *Masee*—a maternal aunt.

Saleh *Kaka* was tall, scrawny and in his late sixties, with a sunken face, a long white flowing beard and a gravelly voice from talking to customers for over fourteen hours a day, seven days a week since he was twelve years old.

As most Indian merchants did in those days, he sat cross-legged on a thick rug in the middle of his store. A long cylindrical pillow lay behind him and two short cylindrical ones lay on each side of him. The walls behind and on his right and left were full of little drawers, like the walls in a safe-deposit vault of a bank.

Without taking his eyes of me, he would inquire about the health of my family and while carrying on a conversation, he would reach behind him, open a drawer, get a handful or a pinch of whatever was in it and put it in a bowl in front of him. He used both his arms and the one he used next, depended on whichever arm the next drawer was closest to. Watching Saleh kaka at work was like watching an octopus at feeding time.

With herbs from at least 20 different drawers, he compounded a pound of "hair oil *masala*[47]." The concoction had dried leaves, roots, bark, petals, seeds and several unidentifiable objects. It gives hair oil a pleasant fragrance, keeps your head cool in summer, warm in winter and of course, it is oh! so good for your hair, scalp and especially—your brain.

My mother threw the "hair oil masala" in a gallon of sesame seed oil and boiled it for several hours before letting it cool. She then strained a year's supply of hair oil.

The human mind needs gods.

---

[47] A mixture of spices.

Legends are today's gods. To their contemporaries, our legends were humans with frailties. Time has filtered out their vices and now their mention evokes only, their exaggerated virtues.

I was in grade school when Gandhi was at the peak of his popularity.

Lord Krishna's "Famous last words" were;

"Whenever there is injustice in the world, I shall return."

Some Hindus worshipped Mahatma Gandhi as an *avatar*[48] of Krishna. Unlike my Hindu classmates, my Muslim upbringing made me weigh him on a skeptic's scale.

I saw his strengths. I saw his weaknesses. I saw a great man.

His legacy to the world is *"Satyagraha*[49]*"*—a wand that makes the powerful powerless.

The police are trained and equipped to confront violence, not peace. Armed to their teeth and supported by armored vehicles and whirring helicopters above, they are bewildered by an unarmed passive crowd, knelt in a prayer or singing proudly;

> "God save our gracious King."

Upon their release, jailed protestors swell the ranks of heroes for the cause. Beating them up or shooting them in the presence of the press, creates sympathy and support of a watching world.

---

[48] Reincarnation.
[49] *Satya* =Truth. *Agraha* = obstinacy. Non-violent political resistance.

Without the Mahatma, India's independence would have been postponed for years, if not decades.

His charisma was incredible. He could mobilize a protest march of thousands whenever it was politically necessary. Whenever his little heart desired, he could paralyze government offices by asking Indians not to go to work. He lived Hinduism and the Hindus followed him unquestioningly on his nonviolent path towards India's independence.

He was an astute politician and a past master at manipulating the press.

He did a "fast to death" to stop the largest massacre of the Muslims by Hindu's and of Hindu's by Muslims in the city of Calcutta.

It worked.

When he was assured that peace had resumed, he broke his fast with a sip of orange juice.

While leaving the Goetz Cinema, after seeing David Attenborough's move "Gandhi," Buzz, the manager, stopped me and asked me if it was true that Mahatma Gandhi quelled a massacre in Calcutta just by threatening to die from a fast.

"Yes, it is true." I responded, "But don't ask me why it worked. Ask a Hindu my age"

Mahatma Gandhi objected to the creation of Pakistan but was not an anti-Muslim. His adamant platform of treating the Muslims as equals of Hindus was the reason he was assassinated by Nathuram Godse, a member of an extreme right – "Hindustan[50] is for Hindus only"— political party, which is still flourishing in today's India.

While in high school, I read *Atmakatha*[51], Mahatma Gandhi's autobiography in his mother tongue Gujarati. Unlike most political autobiographies, Mahatma Gandhi's autobiography is candid. He comes across as a kind, fair and a spiritual person. When I turned over the last page, I knew him as well as any of my friends.

One serendipitous trivia I had read in his autobiography was that he had stopped in Zanzibar. He was on his way to South Africa, where he practiced law. Hence this chapter about Mahatma Gandhi in a book about Zanzibar.

In South Africa he was confronted with the injustice of apartheid. Here, he tested and honed his *Satyagraha* against apartheid. Later, he took Satyagraha to India where that weapon was as awe inspiring as the explosion of the first atomic bomb.

The ship's captain decided that Gandhi's sexuality was thwarted by his virginity and took him to a brothel in Zanzibar to get rid of it.

The attempt backfired.

Gandhi emerged from that experience still a virgin and assured of total control over his "animal instincts". For the rest of his life, periodically, he retested his self-control by sharing his bed with a naked 16-year-old girl.

---

[50] An archaic name for India. It does not stand for "Land of Hindus" In Farsi, "Hindu" means "Black,"

[51] The story of my soul.

About 400 miles southeast of Delhi is *Khajuraho*, an area ruled by the *Chandela* dynasty between 900-1300 AD. The *Chandela's* are followers of the Tantric sect of Hinduism, which considers sexual pleasure as a divine gift to humanity and indulging in it a prayer. About 10% of the statues they carved are explicit.

The world was aghast when the Taliban blew up the ancient statues of Buddha in Bumian, Afghanistan in 2001. Gandhi almost did the same to the erotic statues at the temples of Khajuraho.

Guwmata, mother cow, is sacred in India. A cow is a Hindu's second mother. She nourishes him after his mother's breasts have dried up. Eccentric Mahatma Gandhi preferred goat's milk that he had milked himself and had a goat on a leash that followed him wherever he went.

Quaid -e- Azam[52] Muhammad Ali Jinnah, the founder of Pakistan, initially had the same goal as the Mahatma. Jinnah was one of the founders of the Indian Congress, the first political party to fight for Indian independence.

Nehru, Gandhi, Tilak, and Jinnah were the first patriots. Like the patriots, who founded our country, membership and in particular leadership of an organization with the goal of breaking away from the British Empire and establishing an independent country, carried certain risks—like getting hanged.

Mahatma Gandhi and thousands of members of the Congress party, both men and women, were beaten and jailed; some, multiple times.

---

[52] "The great leader"

The Quaid-e-Azam

Before the British, India was ruled for over 300 years by, a Muslim dynasty. Baber, the first Mogul, tore down a temple and built a mosque from the stones of the temple in *Ayodhya*, the city where Lord Rama was born.

Aurangzeb, who ruled during the decline of the Mogul dynasty, was a religious fanatic and cruel to the Hindus. He also beheaded a Sikh *Guru*—the equivalent of a Pope and earned the eternal hatred of the Sikhs.

The anger towards the Muslims, simmering in the hearts of the extreme Hindu fanatics reached a boiling point when independence was in sight. They were going to get even for the past sins of the Muslims and dreamed of modeling an Independent India after *Ashoka*, the Hindu emperor who ruled India before the Muslims.

Jinnah's support for Gandhi started waning when he heard speeches from the ultra-right firebrand Hindu politicians. He became concerned about retaliation of the Hindu majority (90%) against the Muslim minority and subsequent events proved his apprehension to be well founded.

A rift began between Gandhi and Jinnah and neither of them could stop and sew it up in it time. Jinnah broke away from the Indian Congress, started the Muslim League and campaigned for the partition of India into India, in areas where the Hindus were in a majority and Pakistan, where the Muslims were in a majority.

The partition of India in 1947 precipitated one of the worst carnages in modern history. Thousands, on both sides, died during the religious riots that started on the day the flags of India and Pakistan were raised for the first time on the morning of August the fifteenth.

Upon partition, Pakistan was made up of two parts, East Pakistan and West Pakistan and the two parts were separated by over 1000 miles of India.

Religion, as the sole unifying thread of Pakistan, has been a failure. When East Pakistan tried to break away from West Pakistan, the West Pakistani army butchered their "brothers in Islam", and raped their East Pakistani "sisters". East Pakistan, with the help of India, fought off West Pakistan and now is known as Bangladesh.

Today's Pakistan is over ninety percent Muslims. It is no more a Utopia for Muslims than Ireland is for Christians. Both countries have been in a perpetual violent clash between the sects of the same religion.

In retrospection, Jinnah's and Gandhi's initial platform of Hindus and Muslims living together in a single secular country was the best option.

I wish Gandhi and Jinnah had reached a compromise and had fought together for a united secular India. That would have avoided over six decades of continuous acrimony and three wars between the two countries, which now have nuclear missiles cocked and pointing at each other.

Gandhi preached nonviolence all his life. Ironically, an assassin's bullets ended it violently. The last word that came out of his lips as he lay dying at Birla House was; *"Hey, Ram"*.

Ram is the name by which god Vishnu, the protector and the preserver of the human race is known during his seventh incarnation.

When I heard of Mahatma Gandhi's last words, my mind went back to my Gujrati third grade class. Mr. Dave told us that you can always tell a person who has lived the good life. He leaves with name of the Lord on his lips. Gandhi certainly did both.

I have never met Gandhi in person. The closest I got to him was to view the urn his ashes were in. After his cremation, some of his ashes were brought to Zanzibar for the Indians to view it at the Hindu *Vyayamshala*[53], next to our home. From Zanzibar the ashes went to South Africa.

The Mahatma's life ended without glory. The champion of non-violence died a violent death. The India he hoped to keep united tore apart. So did his family.

Even his funeral did not go smoothly. Traditionally, the eldest son lights the funeral pyre. Harilal, his eldest son, refused the honor.

To hold ashes of a deceased is a sacrilege in Hinduism. The ideal site for its dispersal is the Holy Ganges and the appropriate time is immediately after the funeral.

---

[53] Gymnasium.

He wished his ashes scattered at the spot where the Ganges meets the Yamuna to become the Mighty Ganges, symbolically expressing his hope that the meandering tributaries of history will someday unite the Hindus and the Muslim to become a mighty nation.

Instead, his ashes became souvenirs. The number of urns with his ashes, held secretly by souvenir hunters, is unknown. The known sites are at the Lake Shrine Temple on Sunset Boulevard in Los Angeles and The Agakhan Palace in South India.

Rumors have it, that they have been dispersed over all the known rivers of the world including at the origin of the river Nile at Jinja, Uganda.

Known dispersals have occurred in the Indian Ocean in South Africa. These ashes were displayed in Zanzibar on its way to South Africa.

The ashes of Harilal, Gandhi's eldest son, were dispersed in the Indian Ocean by Bombay immediately after his cremation.

Gandhi's granddaughter, Nilamben Parekh had some of the Mahatma's ashes. In a well-publicized ceremony, she sprinkled them at that same site, to unite the souls of the Mahatma and her father, Gandhi's wayward son, Harilal.

Mahatma Gandhi was born in the right place and at the right time. History has credited him with a winning political tactic that made the mighty British relinquish and place at his feet, the jewel in the crown of the British Empire.

May all his ashes end up in the ocean. May his soul rest in peace. May the waves carry his message attached ashes, reach the shores of all the lands. And may that ring in, an era of;

"Satyagarah, not war"

CHAPTER EIGHT
Saabermati Ashram

One of the Hindu religious beliefs that Mahatma Gandhi tried to change was the caste system.

The caste system originated during the Vedic period (1200-900 BC). According to the Laws of Manu, *Brahma*, the god of creation, sacrificed *Purusha,* the stem cell of the universe. *Brahma* created the sky. It came from *Purusha's* head; the sun from his eyes, the moon from his soul, the *Brahmin,* the priests, from his mouth, the *Kshatriya* or noble warriors from his arms, the *Vaishya* or traders and farmers from his thighs, and the *Shudra* or servants, from his feet. The *Bhungee,* also called "the untouchables" belonged to the *Shudra* caste.

Like a multi layered cake, the casts are separated into layers. The Vedas make it clear that the lower castes pollute the higher ones, while the higher castes percolate purity to the lower castes. In order to avoid contamination of the upper castes, it is essential to keep the castes separate and secluded from each other, to marry only within their caste, to aspire to go only into professions destined for the caste and never step outside their prescribed social and geographic perimeters. I did not use the word "perimeter" figuratively. There is a real geographic one.

Of all the languages I am familiar with, Gujrati has the most proverbs. They are brief, colorful and often humorous. Invariably, there is one for every situation in life and an antithetical one to go with it.

"*Gaam hoy tnya Dhedwado hoy*".

Wherever there is a town, there is a *Dhedwada*.

Dhedwaada is *a Waada* where the *Dhed* live. The *Dhed* caste remove dead animals from farms. They eat the flesh and sell the hide. Even a small village, like Dhandhuka, had Waadas, where members of the "lower cast", like the *Bhungee,* and the *Dhed* lived, in a semi-quarantined isolation, about a mile from the periphery of Dhandhuka.

The Dhandhuka I knew had no flush toilets. There was a latrine in a corner of our house which could be accessed by a trapdoor on one of the outside walls. Every day a *Bhungee,* came to service it, in return for a couple of *rotis*[54].

When they entered Dhandhuka, it was only to perform the task they were incarnated to perform, and left town as soon as the task was done. While walking from one latrine to another, they keep enough distance from the villagers so that even their shadow does not fall upon the "upper class."

Such a catastrophe would defile a Hindu who has to go home right away, discard his clothes, scrub his body with soapy water

---

[54] Flat unlevened bread.

till his skin almost bleeds and then go through a "purification" ritual by a priest[55].

This custom still exists.

I believe that in the mist of ancient India, it started as a reasonable practice of hygiene. It makes sense not to get too close to or touch someone carrying an infectious substance. If my assumption is correct then the reason has been forgotten and an infallible divine explanation has replaced it.

Mahatma Gandhi, the humanitarian, became a champion of the *Bhungee*.

While he was in South Africa, he threw the first punch at apartheid and sanctimonious nations, especially India, supported him vociferously at the United Nations. In India, during his struggle for India's independence, he argued that as long as Indians do not treat one of their own equally, their objection to apartheid is hypocrisy.

He did not use the word *Bhungee*, and referred to them as *Harijuns*—people of *Hari. Hari* is the title of god *Vishnu*. Gandhi preached that members of all castes should have equal civil rights and opportunities for education, employment, housing and all the other good things in life that members of the higher casts have taken for granted as their exclusive privilege.

He had some success, mainly through legislation, which remains in the books. An effort to enforce them has met with resistance, like the riots in Ahmedabad, by members of the

---

[55] A Hindu priest is always from the Brahmin cast,

upper castes who resented an admission quota for the excluded members of the lower caste at *Gujarat Vidhyapit,* the University of Gujarat in Ahmedabad.

Mahatma Gandhi built his firs*t ashram* on the banks of the river *Saabermati,* which flows through Ahmedabad.

"*Ashram*" is a Sanskrit word for a secluded school, headed by a *guru*[56]. Way back in Indian history, an Indian boy's life was marked by "stages". The first stage was childhood. He spent that stage, with his parents and siblings. He spent the second stage of his life acquiring knowledge and education. During that stage, he left home and joined an *ashram*. To prevent distractions from civilization, the *ashrams* were situated deep inside forests. There at the feet of a *guru*, he morphed into a proper Hindu gent. There were no semesters, a curriculum or even an exam. He graduated when the guru said he had.

He then entered the next stage of his life which he spent earning a living and raising a family. That stage is followed by *Sunyas,* the last stage when he renounces this material world, finds an isolated spot in a forest, a mountain or the bank of a holy river and enhances his soul, through meditation and prayers, till it departs from his body,

During one of our stays in Ahmedabad, we visited Rasulmian, a cousin of Abbajaan, at Sabarmati ashram. Rasulmian was raised in a house next to the house my father grew up in.

---

[56] A teacher .He is addressed as *"Guru dev," god the teacher.*

I remember that house. A man in his eighties, dressed like my Grandfather, used to sit in the backyard of that house and smoked away his *hookah* for hours on end. I have been close to people smoking a *hookah* before. In Zanzibar, the *Washihiri,* Arabs from Hadhramaut, Yemen, used to smoke hookahs in their shops. The smoke from the *hookah* this old man smoked had an unfamiliar odor to it. I asked my grandmother about it and she told me that the man was smoking opium.

"Opium? Isn't that illegal?"

"Yes, now it is. It wasn't always so. Before the law went into effect, *Surkar*[57], issued permits to those who were addicted to it."

This neighbor had a permit that enabled him to go to any pharmacy and buy opium legally.

In the generations preceding mine, opium smoking was a status symbol. Since it was extremely expensive it was the indulgence of the elite and constipation, a side effect of opium, was a status complaint.

The neighbor's addiction is a vestige of Asia's colonial era. The reason for having colonies was to have a lucrative captive market. The sale of opium was legal in India because it was lucrative for the English.

Opium has changed the course of history in Asia. Our neighbor, China, had an "Opium war" from 1839 to 1842.

---

[57] The government.

To a school child today, the words "Opium war" should conjure up a vision of our Drug Enforcement Agency sending covert troops to a country like Afghanistan to burn poppy fields.

The "Opium war" in China, occurred because the Chinese Emperor banned the use of opium among his subjects when he became alarmed by the rise of opium addiction and all the associated social problems that go with it.

The English, who were making a hefty profit from the sale of opium, did not like the law. So, like a good colonialist, they went to war with the Emperor, defeated him and made him rescind that law.

That is what the "Opium war" was all about.

Rasulmian was the son of that old opium-smoking neighbor in Dhandhuka.

Rasulmian, had dedicated his life to *Satyagraha*, rose through the ranks of that movement and at the time I met him, he was Mahatma Gandhi's assistant *guru* at *Saabermati Ashram*—a pretty impressive position.

Obviously, Mahatma Gandhi liked him and was impressed by Rasulmian's dedication to *Satyagraha* and had honored him by attending the wedding of one of his daughters.

Rasulmian greeted us at his Villa in the *Ashram* in a *Khadee*[58] *Sulwar Kameez*[59]. His wife wore a *Khadee* Sari. This was just a

---

[58] Homespun cotton cloth.
[59] A comfortable apparel similar to a pair of pajamas,

few years before India became independent. Mahatma Gandhi was at the peak of his popularity. *Satyagraha,* "clinging to the truth", a campaign better known outside India as "civil disobedience" or "nonviolent confrontation" was in full swing. This approach was so successful that decades later, among others, it was adopted by Dr. Martin Luther King in our country with similar success.

The first flag of India that Mahatma Gandhi had proposed had a *Churkha,* a spinning wheel, in the center of the flag. In several of his pictures and video clips, you will see Mahatma Gandhi sitting cross legged on a floor, turning the wheel of a *Churkha,* with his left hand and pulling a ball of cotton into a string with his right hand. He and his followers spent several hours a day at a *Churkha* and were proud to be seen and photographed at this patriotic activity. The *Churkha* was symbolic of Mahatma Gandhi's attempt to hurt the British economically.

Cotton grown in India was shipped to Manchester, England, where cloth was made, then exported to India and sold at exorbitant prices. This provided jobs for the merchant seamen, dockworkers, railroad workers and factory workers in England at the expense of the Indian workers. Gandhi wanted Indians to boycott imported English cloth made out of Indian cotton and instead use a *"Churkha"* to make thread, weave it into a *Khadee* and wear it defiantly.

"Salt march" was another act of his defiance. The subcontinent of India juts into the Indian Ocean like a peninsula and has thousands of miles of coastline but India could not make its own table salt. It had to be imported from England.

Mahatma Gandhi brought the world's attention to this irony by organizing a march. Thousands of his followers marched behind him to the Indian Ocean to make salt. At the Ocean, the police confronted the marchers, and beat them up with *Lathee*—a long truncheon.

The marchers did not retaliate. They did not flee. They kept marching on till their injuries made them collapse.

Mahatma Gandhi got what he wanted out of the march—pictures of the bleeding collapsed salt marchers, splattered on the front page of newspapers of the world. The moral pressure from a world in horror of British atrocities in India, hastened India's independence.

The visit to *Saabermati ashram* was the usual visit to a relative. The usual pleasantries were followed by a sumptuous dinner. Something about this meal seemed to be out of place. I sensed the surprise that the Qureshi's felt at the dinner but I could not put my finger on the reason for it. I did notice that the servants looked different. They wore the same plain *Khadee* sari. the same like our hostess, but they were darker and had an accent. The meal was a delicious Gujrati vegetarian meal.

On our way home, I overheard my parents and uncles, discussing the staff at the *ashram* and I realized that the meal was grown, cooked and served by *Bhangees*. The first time any of us had seen that.

We should have expected that. We were in an ashram. Not any old ashram, but an *ashram* that was founded by Mahatma Gandhi, the champion of the *Harijans*.

I was elated.

I saw a seed of Mahatma Gandhi's equality of all humans, sprout.

I wondered when I will see a second seed sprout.

I haven't—yet.

CHAPTER NINE

Cloves

The island I grew up in is also known as the "Spice Island," as almost all spices grow here. Mariners in the eighteenth and the nineteenth century have recorded that they could smell spices even when Zanzibar was still over the horizon and they let their noses guide them the rest of the way to Zanzibar.

Spices made it possible for my father to make a living, made my diet appetizing, cured me of maladies and made my life's course a meander.

I would be in India today had it not been for a spice –cloves to be more precise—that made my father settle in Zanzibar.

Cloves are indigenous to the islands of Tidore and Ternate in Indonesia.[60] Although jealously guarded, in 1770 a French diplomat smuggled clove seedlings from Indonesia to the East African French island colony of Mauritius and from there it spread to the East coast of Africa and to the islands of Pemba and Zanzibar.

The credit for usurping Indonesian dominance in clove trade must go to my favorite Sultan of Zanzibar, Seyyid Barghash.

---

[60] Napoleon's buttons. Penny Le Couteur & Jay Burreson. ISBN 1-58542-220-7

Seyyid Barghash bin Said Al-Busaid.
1837-1888

Although the climate of Zanzibar is suitable for growing almost all spices, cloves are the least labor intensive. Seyyid Barghash decided to concentrate on cloves to the exclusion of the other spices and the current cash crop of coconuts. Farmers knew and were comfortable with coconuts and were reluctant to try a new crop that takes at least eight years to mature and bear its first fruit.

Barghash, the absolute monarch, proclaimed:

"From this day on, we will plant two clove trees for every coconut tree we plant"

He did not have to add, "Or else…" Absolute monarchy has its advantages.

To determine what the demand of any commodity will be in eight years is at best a speculation. Bargash's gamble paid off and when I was there, Zanzibar produced 80% of the world's cloves and monopolized its trade.

Prosperity reigned in Zanzibar, the Sultan was Seyyid Sir Khalifah bin Haroub Al Busaidi and the King was cloves.

Today, there is a hardly a home in Europe that does not have a black pepper shaker; it is ubiquitous and cheap.

But, it was not always so.

In the 15th Century, spices were more precious than jewels. To impress their guests, wealthy European families, dramatically opened their safe door to dazzle their guests with a display of their spice rack.

The vine of black pepper, *Piper nigrum,* is indigenous to the state of Kerala, on the south west coast of India. The lands and the seas between Europe and India were uncharted and the bulk of the markup in the price in Europe was due to "shipping and handling".

Spices were shipped from India to Baghdad via the Red sea, then to Istanbul and from there across the Mediterranean to Venice, which reached its height of prosperity mainly through its monopoly of the European spice trade.

All powerful nations are built with profits from commerce.

The two superpowers of the day were Spain and Portugal. Both of them realized that the first rival to wrest the spice trade from Venice, will become the undisputed European superpower.

The middleman in the Middle East were literally in the middle and each hand over doubled the price of spices. It made good business sense to eliminate the middle man and multiply several folds, the margin of profit which was huge to begin with.

One way to eliminate the middle man was to send out an army and defeat every nation between Europe and India. The other option was to circumvent the middleman by going to India by sea. The second option was the pragmatic one and simultaneously Spain and Portugal decided to become the first to find a sea route to India.

And the race for wealth and spices was on.

My father taught Alhaj[61] Aboud Jumbe and he taught me when I was in High school. Later he became the second president of Zanzibar and the Vice president of Tanzania. When Uncle Moy, Faisal, Aunties Shahdia and Sharifah, grandma and I were in Dar-es-salaam in 1998, we had the honor of visiting him. I cherish that visit and his autographed book, "The Partnership" that he gave to me as a memento.

During that visit, uncle Moin spent the better part of a day in the American Embassy in Dar-es-salaam filling out an application for

---

[61] An Arabic synonym for Hajji. A person who has performed the Hajj.

a visa for a relative of aunty Rukia. On the 7th of August, 1998 that embassy was bombed by El Qaida and over two hundred persons including twelve Americas died in that blast. If uncle Moy had delayed his visit to that embassy by a couple of days, he would have become the thirteenth American to die in that bombing.

During a history lesson, Mr. Aboud Jumbe, drew a vertical line through Rome on a map of Europe, to demonstrate the boundary that the Papal bull created. The Bull gave Spain franchise to the world west of the line and to Portugal everything east of that line. This explains the diametrically opposite directions Columbus and da Gama took to get to India.

Spain sent Columbus westwards.

When he spotted some islands that he thought were only a few knots west of India, he named them West Indies. Even when he did find America, he refused to believe that he had not found India. The skin color of Native Americans must have been enough of an oddity to raise some doubt that these may not be inhabitants of India, but he persisted in his delusion and named them "Red Indians."

Columbus failed in his mission. His "successes" were due to serendipity.

Ironically, the most expensive piece of real estate in the continent he discovered was later traded for spices.

The Dutch East India Company wanted total control over nutmegs, which at that time, grew only in the Banda Islands in Indonesia. The Dutch owned all the Banda islands except the island of Run, which was colonized by the English. In 1667, the Dutch chased the English out of Run and in a treaty, gladly traded the Dutch island of New Amsterdam for the island of Run. Today, the island of New Amsterdam is better known as Manhattan, N.Y.

Portugal sent Vasco da Gama eastwards. Prior Portuguese sailors had charted the route up to the Cape of Good Hope. da Gama was the first to chart the route from there to Malindi, the port on the east coast of Africa where Aunty Zarina[62] was raised.

Malindi is southeast of and has the same language and ambience as Zanzibar. There is some doubt whether the first pilgrim actually landed where Plymouth Rock is but there is no doubt that a monument marking where da Gama landed in Malindi is authentic.

Vasco da Gama is falsely credited for discovering the route from Malindi to India. That route was well known to Arab and Indian sailors for thousands of years before da Gama was born. The identity of the pilot is unclear. Some credit an Arab, ibn Majid. Two points make it unlikely that he was the pilot who steered da Gama to India. Arabs did not sail to India, they sailed to Arabia. Also, ibn Majid is recorded to be elsewhere at that time. In school I was taught that the pilot who steered his ship from Malindi to Calicut,[63] India was an Indian sailor from the province of Kutch.

---

[62] My brother Munir's wife.
[63] Calicut. Population: 400,000. SW of Bangalore, on the Malabar Coast. Calcutta, now renamed Kolkata, is in the Ganges delta on the NE and in the 1950's was the most populous city in the world.

CLOVES

In 1498, when Vasco Da Gama sighted India, he had achieved his goal for wealth through spices but like all colonialist, he exclaimed:

"*Christ e espiciarias*[64]"

The king of Calicut was interested in trading with da Gama but da Gama was a soldier not a businessman. He had a better idea of how to get the spices more cheaply. He returned to Calicut five years later with more ships, guns and men, sacked Calicut, helped himself to the spices and began five centuries of Portuguese colonization of Africa, India and the Far East.

To remind us of that era, India had Goa, a province that was governed by the Portuguese till the 1950's. The natives in Mozambique on the East coast of Africa speak Portuguese. Mombasa has Fort Jesus and Zanzibar has the Portuguese fort. Kiswahili has Portuguese words like *Kasha* and *Bendera* and Zanzibar's sister island Pemba, holds bullfights under Portuguese rules—the bull's life is spared.

From Brazil, they brought to the coast of East Africa, *maize*[65], pineapple and what is now Zanzibar's staple food--*muhogo*[66].

I have often wondered what people ate in the Twelfth century.

The Waswahili did not have *muhogo,* the Irish did not have potatoes, the Italians did not have tomatoes and the Indians

---

[64] For Christ and spices.
[65] Corn
[66] Cassava. Tapioca .

did not have chilies. These were introduced to the "old world" from the "new world" after Columbus set his sails for India.

The law of supply and demand works in both directions. The discovery of a sea route, increase in production and finally the advent of refrigeration plummeted spices to its present unglamorous status.

So, what is it about spices that once inspired incredible voyages of discoveries, caused wars between nations separated by a continent, hatched fascinating intrigues, brought immense wealth not just to a few merchants but to entire nations and changed the course of history?

It is because spices are primarily a food preservative.

This is why the hotter the climate of a region, the spicier is the region's cuisine. The cuisine in south India is HOT. As you travel north, it gets milder and milder and by the time you reach Kashmir, the food is as bland as Cantonese food.

With the advent of refrigeration, most left overs can be safely consumed till at least the next meal. But the fear of getting sick from rancid food is still so strong that even the poorest of the poor in Gujarat, for the lack of a refrigerator, throw away all leftovers even though they are spice protected.

When Europe learned from retuning crusaders that a dish with black pepper remains edible longer then the same dish without it, the equation:

Price = demand/supply, became demand heavy and the price of spices soared.

What makes spices a food preservative is the deterrent spice plants use to protect themselves from predators. Like the puffer fish and the cobra, spice plants use poisons to retaliate against insects, fungi and bacteria. This is the characteristic that retards colonization and proliferation of microbes in foods and prevents "food poisoning."

The pharmacological effects of most poisons are dose related. At low concentration they are lethal to microbes (the way antibiotics are.) but are harmless to humans with healthy livers and kidneys.

Can the detoxifying capability of humans be overwhelmed by a massive dose of spices?

Yes, it can.

Even staple foods can be fatal. A few years ago, several children in a boarding school in Indonesia died after eating cassava. The skin of cassava is thick and dark brown. Just under it, is a green layer. The thickness of the green layer varies with different varieties and it gets thinner as the root ripens. A good cook always whittles off this layer till the cassava is all white. The green layer has a precursor of hydrogen cyanide.

Solanum tuberosum, the potato, also has a poisonous green layer. When out of the soil and exposed to sunlight, it protects itself from predators by rapidly thickening the green layer which has the toxin *Solanine*—the last factor is why potatoes are stored in dark basements. Eating the green layer In potatoes or inhaling fumes from rotting potatoes has resulted in deaths.

The second reason for using spices is for the enhancement of flavor. Spices are what make the difference between eating to live and living to eat.

Even with the minimal and infrequent use of spices in European foods, is it possible to feel satiated with fried eggs without crushed black pepper on it? An Easter ham without cloves in it? A slice of apple pie without cinnamon in it? Or a pumpkin pie without nutmeg in it?

I don't.

Spices make nourishment appetizing mainly through the aroma they add to it. The tongue can identify only: sweet, sour, salt, bitter and *umami*[67]. This becomes evident when the sense of smell is dulled by a "cold." A blind folded person with a viral rhinitis cannot distinguish between a potato and an onion.

To encourage hydration, hot *"Kadhi"* [68]works better than IV fluids. There is warmth in the fluid which is soothing to the throat. The spices float up your nasopharynx to shrink and restore aroma to entice you to increase fluid intake.

The other subtle attributes of a cuisine is perceived by our eyes and by our other senses—hot, smooth, crunchy, sharp etc.

The most important organ that determines what our favorite foods are is the brain. We associate turkey with Thanksgiving and hot dogs with ball parks. They taste best on those occasions.

---

[67] A Japanese word for the taste of beef broth.
[68] A Gujrati soup.

CLOVES

In my case the most delicious food in the world is what my Mamma cooked. Even her sister's cooking was not as good.

The proper use of spices is an art.

I find Mexican cuisine boring. The chilies are so overwhelming that at its best, the experience is like listening to a loud solo instrument. Other cuisines which dabble in multiple spices are an irritating noise.

Over several thousands of years, India has evolved recipes which determine the choice of the right spices, their correct proportions and the sequence in which they are added to a particular food, to create a symphony for your senses. So highly are the maestros respected, that a chef in India is addressed as *"Maharaj"*—"Your Majesty."

Another use of spices is as a dye. Anyone who has cooked an Indian meal is aware that you handle turmeric with care. If you stain your clothing with it, the stains will never come off. For hand woven oriental carpets, the same chemical reaction is used for dying wool yellow. I understand that horse urine works well for yellows too. But, who will pray on a rug dyed with urine? When buying a hand woven oriental carpet with yellow in it, always ask how it was dyed.

I have heard of the use of mint for dying wool dark green and saffron for red. Red wine is a cheaper alternative to saffron but has a different hue.

Ultraorthodox Muslims, the laughing stock of poets, consider consuming alcohol a mortal sin. Any activity associated with it, like printing a label for a bottle of wine, is as sinful as consuming it.

If a drop of alcohol falls on you, you must peel off that part of your skin—immediately—before it contaminates your soul.

The mother of all sins is to bring alcohol in, on or with you in a mosque.

"Piety and moral goodness have naught to do with ecstasy;

Stain your prayer rug with wine!"

Hafiz.

Hafiz, a Persian poet, is poking fun at Muslims who believe that carrying into a mosque, alcohol or even something stained by it is sacrilegious.

The rug does not contain any alcohol. The alcohol portion of the wine evaporated a long time ago. It did not stain the wool as it is not a dye. The stain was caused by the skin of the red grapes. Therefore, carrying a prayer rug into a mosque that was "stained by wine" is not a sin. Grape juice has never been *haram*[69].

If carrying alcohol into a mosque is a sacrilege, then the carrier of the rug is the one committing that sin. Since the day he was born, he has entered mosques with several ounces of alcohol in him. All humans, whether they consume alcohol or not, manufacture alcohol in their guts, by a process similar to what happens inside yeasts after it has consumed sugar.

---

[69] Forbidden.

In Urdu, *Najawaab,* is an unanswerable question. Next, is my favorite *Najawaab* couplet;

"Let me blatantly drink alcohol, in a mosque crowded,

Or, direct me to where, God cannot watch me drink"

Ghalib?

The versatile spice also has medicinal uses. The Greeks used it for medicinal purposes in 5th century BC. Ayurveda medicine, which utilizes only herbs and spices, was founded in India thousands of years ago and still is the branch of medicine that most Indians trust.

When I was in Nairobi, Champak, my roommate, woke up one night with an excruciating toothache. I gave him a few cloves and told him to chew them with the tooth that hurt. He slept the rest of the night like a baby. He is the first patient that I treated—successfully.

As a Zanzibari, I was familiar with that trick which my mother used on us. Dentists in Zanzibar use the same trick to postpone an emergency tooth extraction in the middle of the night. We had a factory in Zanzibar that extracted and exported clove oil. Later, when I studied biochemistry, I learned that cloves have *eugenol,* a powerful topical anesthetic.

The ancient Chinese used it as a breath freshener as cloves are also bactericidal.

Some expensive brands of cigarettes, like "Craven A," mix cloves in their tobacco to give the drag a cool sensation. During our teens, we achieved the same result by poking in a clove in the tobacco end of a cheap filter cigarette.

Kizimbani has an experimental farm run by Zanzibar's agriculture department. The last time we were there, our tour guide sent a boy up a nutmeg tree to pick a ripe one. With his pocket knife, the guide separated the pulp from the nut.

"You know this?" he asked, as he began scraping towards its stem end, the stringy web like strands coating the nut. When no one volunteered even a guess, he provided the answer,

"Mace." Continuing in fractured English, he added, "One fruit, two spice."

He then told us in Kiswahili that since we Waswahili are "*Islamu*[70]", we do not consume alcohol.

"To get a high for an *Ngoma,*[71]......". He stopped in mid-sentence. Then, with the tip of his knife he pointed to the inside of a nutmeg that he had just halved and finished the sentence "... our women use this".

I too laughed with the rest of the tour group and dismissed the comment as just another Swahili old wives tale.

In retrospection, that story is too good not to be true. Nutmeg over dose does cause hallucinations. It is reasonable to assume that in low doses, nutmeg can cause euphoria.

---

[70] Muslim
[71] An impromptu gathering usually by a bonfire when men and women dance steps of their own improvisation , to the beat of a drum.

CLOVES

At the Monroe Country Club, the most popular cocktail was "Brandy Alexander ala an old secrete Swiss recipe." I did not have to probe for the secret ingredient. I could taste it. It is nutmeg. The cheap Swiss of Monroe got "more bang for their buck" by adding nutmeg to alcohol.

The last Qureshi to leave Zanzibar was the same one who got there first —my father. It was cloves that took him to Zanzibar and when he bid farewell to Zanzibar; he had in his ship's hull, several sacks of cloves.

After the 1963 revolution, as an incentive for Indians to leave Zanzibar, the new Government allowed Indians to leave Zanzibar with as much cloves as they could afford to buy. A onetime waiver of export tax was the incentive. The first ones to take advantage of that waiver did very well and retired in sweet comfort. My father was among the last ones to leave Zanzibar with cloves. By the time he reached India and put his cloves on the commodities market in Bombay, there was a glut in cloves and he took a loss. A bitter way to end a thirty year career.

The last time I was in Zanzibar was in 1998. We saw almost all the known spices flourishing –except cloves. Clove trees had died through neglect. Many were chopped down for firewood.

The tree that once made Zanzibar what it was, is near extinction in the island from where it dominated the world's clove market. The harvests have been steadily dwindling. In the 1990's it produced less than eight percent of the cloves and ranked an embarrassing third in the world, after Indonesia and Madagascar.

Friends, who had visited Zanzibar prior to my visit, had advised me not to return to Zanzibar, as the visit would be "disappointing." I went anyway hoping that they were wrong. They were wrong.

I was not disappointed. I was sad.

The Zanzibar I saw was not the Zanzibar I remembered. The house I grew up in is a lifeless, dilapidated warehouse. I hoped to run into neighbors I grew up with. I did not see any.

Stores that made families wealthy were empty and unoccupied. Only the firm's name carved in stone remain. Streets that once bustled with business activity are deserted and has an eerie ambience which hasten your steps out of there.

Every time I saw a storefront or a building that looked like a structure a doctor might practice out of, I walked up to it to take a closer look at the name of the occupant; hoping to read a familiar name.

I did not see such a sign.

When I was in Medical school, there were well over a dozen students from Zanzibar that I knew of, who hoped to return home to practice. Not one of them has. Far and wide they have been scattered, by unanticipated historical events. Like the Jews scattered all over the world, who hoped that someday they will return to Jerusalem, the exiles of Zanzibar kept a similar hope flickering in their breasts, while they practiced in Tanganyika, Kenya, Egypt, Oman, Libya, India, Pakistan, Ireland, England, Sweden, Holland, Germany, Australia, Canada and the USA.

Forty years later, they are retired and despondent. Unlike the Jews, they do not have a Jerusalem to return to. Nor do they hope to be buried with their loved ones, in their Mount of Olives.

During my youth, I used to spend my afternoons watching or playing cricket at Mnazi Moja. Almost every day, around 5.00 PM, a fire engine red Bentley, without license plates and a miniature red flag of Zanzibar fluttering off its hood ornament, drove by.

Traffic both ways stopped, the way it does here when we see flashing lights and hear the siren of a police car or an ambulance. Nannies pushing babies in perambulators[72] on sidewalks stopped and kicked in the brakes on their perambulators. People sitting on benches watching the games stood up and turned to face the car. Soccer, golf and cricket players stopped their games and stood still respectfully with their heads bowed towards the Bentley.

It was as though you were watching a video of the event and someone had pushed the "Pause" button on the DVD player. Everyone was frozen on "Pause"—except for the chauffeured Bentley, which drove by at a slow dignified pace. Sitting in the back seat was a benevolent elderly Arab with a heavy moustache and a long beard. He wore horn rimmed spectacles, a turban and a Jubbah. He turned his head from side to side, to the Zanzibari's' on both sides of the road and acknowledged their,

---

[72] An English word for a baby stroller. They were huge and built like a minitank.

"Salaam alaikum" by touching his forehead with his open right hand, then bowed gently and replied, "Wa alaikum Salaam".

The person in the Bentley was the Sultan of Zanzibar, Seyyid Sir Khalifah bin Haroub Al Busaidi, on his daily "constitutional".

Once the Bentley was out of sight, the "Pause" button was released and the scene picked up where it had left off.

On my last day in Zanzibar, as I pensively snaked through her streets, I happened to be at Mnazi Moja, around 5:00 PM.

The scene was just as I remembered. The sky was clear, the Pemba grass was emerald green and there was a gentle salty breeze blowing from the west. A few Waswahili boys were practicing soccer. There were nannies on the sidewalk, walking two abreast and chatting away while pushing babies in perambulators. On the roads surrounding Mnazi Moja, there was the familiar traffic of cars, cyclists, a donkey cart bringing produce to town and lots of pedestrians on their afternoon walk.

For a moment, I hoped the scene would be as complete as it used to be— Zanzibari's frozen in their activities and a fire engine red Bentley, without license plates and a miniature red flag of Zanzibar fluttering off its hood ornament, driving through it.

That bud of hope did not bloom.

My head had nipped it.

It was aware that the last Sultan of Zanzibar, Seyyid Jamshid bin Abdullah Al Busaidi, had fled from Zanzibar during the revolution of 1964.

CLOVES

My misty eyes did not see the car.

My head shook from side to side.

My lips let out a long sigh—then whispered;

Oh, Zanzibar.

My poor, Zanzibar.

My poor, little, Zanzibar.

Your children are in exile.

Your Sultan ran away from home.

And your King is dead.

Long live the King!

Chapter Ten

The Streets Of Zanzibar

A walk through the streets of Zanzibar is an exotic feast for the senses; for those who will allow a free rein to their curiosity.

Come with me. Together we will walk and experience the streets of Zanzibar.

Zanzibar is a city frozen in time, where one can live a day the way it was lived two centuries ago, when the history of the East coast of Africa was being made.

The Portuguese fort will make you wonder about the number of slave hours it must have taken to construct such a daunting structure.

The Beit–el-ajaib, when seen through a retro view lens, of the 19th century, will live up to its name, "The house of wonders."

Zanzibar doors will capture your attention with their elaborate carvings and tantalize you with the secrets behind them. The mansions pregnant with history will radiate dignity. Livingstone, Stanley, Burton Speke and Seyyid Barghash, just names in history books, will guide you as you walk in their footsteps and enter their homes.

If the streets in the Hollywood sets of; "The Thief of Baghdad" fascinated you, the tangible, colorful, and vivacious Zanzibar will awe you.

Zanzibar has narrow streets.

This phenomenon is not unique to Zanzibar. You will see the same in all ancient Arab cities. Countries where oil was found bulldozed old cities and built ultramodern cities over those sites. Cities like Zanzibar and Fez in Morocco have no oil, so the cities have remained undisturbed and are listed as sites of historic heritage by UNESCO.

Most of Zanzibar is inaccessible even by the tiny English cars—the mini's. Streets that are wide enough to allow minicars to pass through them are at the periphery of the city. There are some fingers at the periphery that poke in towards the city center, here and there, but in most of the city center, you either walk or ride a bicycle.

Let us study the picture of Zanzibar's "Main Street." It resembles a bottle. You are looking at the belly of the bottle with the Post Office with a car parked in front of it, on the left and a few of Zanzibar's high end stores on the right. Look north in the picture and you will see a bottle neck—only one car

The Main Street of Zanzibar.

THE STREETS OF ZANZIBAR

(small) at a time can go through it in either direction. When the car parked in front of the post office wishes to go northwards, it has to wait till a car heading south has cleared the neck.

This is not the end of my narration. Now, I have to tax your imagination. Clear from your mind the usual picture of a bottle.

Now imagine a picture of a bottle with two necks—one at each end. Pass a string through about three such bottles so that they are touching each other in series. You have now created a 3D model of Zanzibar's Main Street.

A car heading north from the Post office will enter the first bottle neck only to enter the belly of the first bottle and then has to contend with the next and the next and the next bottle neck. While in the bottle's belly, the car, like a train at a railway station, has to wait to allow a train in the desired track to come in and vacate the track. A Zanzibari driver has to go through this intricate choreography and without the benefit of a traffic sign or a traffic light.

It requires patience.

Those who have it are rewarded with plenty of opportunities to catch up on their reading.

Why are the streets narrow?

Two centuries ago, a street's width was considered ample, if an Arab could ride his donkey through it, without scraping the outside of his knees on the houses on either side of the street.

To explain why the streets are seldom straight for more than a block, let me give you a couple of reasons that I am aware of.

Houses were built close to the edge of a lot to maximize space for the backyard. This resulted in houses getting built close together. It was not to conserve heat. It was to create an aerodynamic effect called the venturi effect. A breeze going through a bottle neck picks up speed, which helps to cool the city.

The second reason is that Zanzibari's buried their dead in a family cemetery in their backyards. In compliance with this tradition, most of the deceased Sultans of Zanzibar were buried in the royal cemetery adjacent to the south outside wall of the Sultan's palace.

Graves in Arab countries are left undisturbed till *"Kayama"*—judgment day. It is sacrilegious to walk over a grave and no street or house can be built over it. When asked where he was building his new house, an unamused Englishmen complained: "By George, the best lots in Zanzibar are occupied by the bloody dead."

Then there are trees to contend with. Look at the picture of a baobab tree. Only an insane Arab would attempt to chop this tree down. A wise Arab leaves the tree alone and lets the streets bypass the tree, the best was they can.

A baobab tree

As time goes by, more houses spring up around the tree. The neighborhood then is identified by the tree it surrounds and becomes, "*Mbuyunee*", "The neighborhood around the *Mbuyu* tree." "*Membeni*," the mango tree neighborhood" and "*Mzambraunee*" "neighbors by the *Zambarau* tree"

Now you see why Zanzibar has streets that are not only narrow but lead into unpredictable directions.

You will hardly have walked a block or two before you are struck by sights, smells and taste you are familiar with; only now, the same experiences will be perceived with increased intensity and with added dimensions.

The expensive annuals you bought in Wisconsin for their bright flowers are perennial weeds here. The Hibiscus is huge and luxuriant. Its branches droop with the weight of its blossoms which unlike back home are not just bright—they are vibrant. The color of leaves, flowers and fruit are dazzling.

This observation is not due to the unleashed imagination of a mind in a vacation mode. The difference is real.

Imagine the globe of the world. The tropical lands are nearer the sun, and the sun's rays are closer together when they strike the earth here. This phenomenon imparts a larger "volume" of heat and sunshine to the equatorial earth. The heat makes plants grow faster and healthier. In other areas of the world leaves have a dull surface to absorb all the sunshine they can possibly collect. Here, the leaves get more sunshine then they need, so they develop a shiny upper surface to reflect the excess sunshine, and hence, the leaves sparkle.

Sun light is made up of all the colors of a rainbow put together. When it strikes a flower, the flower absorbs rays from a certain portion of the spectrum and reflects the rest. What the flower reflects is what we perceive as its color. In the tropics the same flower reflects the same spectrum of light as in Wisconsin, except that in the tropics, it has a lot more of it to reflect. That's what makes all the colors in the tropics brilliant.

When an object is seen as black, it is because it absorbs all of the sunlight that strikes it. That is why a black car parked in a summer sun is hotter than a white car. In Zanzibar, all houses are white for the opposite reason. It keeps them cool.

The houses are not painted. About once a year they are white washed.

In the hinterland of Zanzibar City, lime stones Calcium carbonate ($CaCO_3$), is burnt on a bonfire to convert it into a white powder of Calcium oxide. The powder is sold to whitewashers who dissolve it in water, to make it into Calcium hydroxide. Calcium Hydroxide is a clear watery solution. The whitewashers brush this solution on walls with wide brushes. There is no skill involved. The whitewasher has to make sure that the entire wall is smeared with the solution.

Whitewashing is an unforgettable demonstration of a chemical reaction. When applied, the coat of Calcium hydroxide is transparent and through it, you can clearly see the grime and graffiti. Let a few hours go by for Carbon dioxide in the air to react with the white wash and the grime and graffiti gradually begins to fade away and ultimately it is totally obscured by an opaque, egg shell thin layer of gleaming white, Calcium carbonate.

Multiethnic Zanzibari's, wear their traditional garments. An Arab with his black Jubbah with patterns embroidered with gold threads. A Sikh gentleman with his colorful turban. A Comorian lady in her black *Bui Bui*[73]. A Hindu lady in her gay *Sari*. A Mswahili girl wrapped in her multicolored *Khangas*. The waist coat and a *Shuka* on an Arab from the Gulf States.

The splendid colors of these garments are the brush strokes on the canvas of the streets of Zanzibar and the sight will raise your spirits; the way an occasional sunshine does, during our long dreary, depressing winters. You will wonder, if a Genie had caught a rainbow, crushed it in his hand and then, gently sprinkled it over Zanzibar.

Our walk, at times will entail walking around some trees that are in the middle of a street or which make a blind alley, but you will be glad that they are there.

The Langi Langi tree is huge. It can reach over three stories in height and its flowers with long thin petals cover an entire neighborhood with its sweet fruity fragrance. During one of our visits with Aunty Sameena and Uncle Tim when they lived in St. Louis, Missouri, Grandma and I were in a bath and body shop, when I spotted a bottle of perfume with the name Langi Langi misspelled "Lang Lang" on it. The sales girl described correctly

---

[73] A Burkha .A veil.

the tree and the flower but placed the tree in Madagascar. She did not even mention Zanzibar.

I was offended. So would anyone who has even an ounce of pride in his hometown. So, I prodded her with more information and it turned out that she had never been to Madagascar or Zanzibar. She was merely repeating the sales pitch of the marketing department of the manufacturer of the perfume. "Madagascar" does have a ring of a faraway romantic island.

When she finished parroting her pitch, I told her that I am from Zanzibar and the tree is indigenous to Zanzibar. Very nicely, I advised her to change her pitch to;

"It is a flower that is indigenous to Zanzibar and perhaps also to Madagascar".

The ubiquitous Jasmin bush gives out its fragrance all day and increases its output of fragrance by several notches, after the sun goes down. To me, the fragrance of Jasmine invariably transports me back home, where the flower not only adorns the landscape but also the hair, wrists and the necks of our women.

If you have never been to a tropical island before, you will be astonished to discover that fruit has fragrance. The tropical fruit back home were picked when the fruit was still in its unripe, odorless stage of growth. A tree ripened fruit has a characteristic fragrance with a slight variation of the fragrance between the varieties. Locals can tell which variety of a banana bunch is hanging in a fruit stall just by its fragrance.

You will see banana bunches in different shades of yellows and reds and ripe bananas with green peels.

The size will vary from a pinky sized *"Sucari"* [74] to ones as long as your arm, called *"Mkono ya tembo*[75]*"*.

The mangoes too vary in size and color. There is a small golden yellow one grown specifically for drinking. You squeeze the banana till the pulp is as soft as possible, then you bite off the stem and drink the juice from that pit as you squeeze out the juice with your right hand.

When in Africa and Asia, always use your right hand for everything— especially for eating and drinking. If you are unable to use your right hand because it is in a cast—and I cannot think of another good reason for breaking this rule—always say;

"Forgive me for using my left hand".

Break this rule and in some countries, you will be deported immediately or something even worse will happen to you.

The reason is simple. As usual, the reason is the practice of good hygiene. These are the cultures where they wash themselves after defecating and they use the left hand and only the left hand for the washing. In at least one aspect of their life, these countries have evolved to a paperless status.

---

[74] Sugar
[75] An elephants' trunk.

Not all fruit is universally liked. Some are despised. A good example is the Durian. My brothers and I have an incurable craving for it. The rest of my family hates it. If we wanted to eat it, we were not allowed to do so in our home. We had to split it and eat it on our balcony. It is similar in taste and fragrance to Limburger cheese. It is smooth, creamy, with a strong, long lasting after taste and an intense fragrance that, within minutes, permeates an entire house and all the fabrics in it.

Unlike a wildflower that squanders its fragrance indiscriminately, the noble durian saves its favors for the few. The few with their palates honed on multiethnic cuisine. The few with a discerning nose. The few with a mind open to untried adventures.

Lunch is the largest meal of the day and if you are in a street at that time, you will be exposed to appetizing aromas. The heavy fattening smell of *Ghee* from frying parathas; the unique smell of cassava cooking in coconut oil; the pungent smell of frying fish; the multi octave smells of Indian spices and the soothing soft sound of simmering basmati rice. These new smells, will assail your nostrils like a symphony of aromas from an orchestra of exotic musical instruments.

Even the taste of the mundane banana will astound you. Yes, the sunshine is better here. But that is not the sole reason.

Bananas we eat in Wisconsin were picked when they were green. Like premature babies, their development was arrested before reaching its full potential. They "ripen" on their way and in the warehouses before they make it to the grocery stores. At times the "ripening" is hastened by artificial means. For these reasons, there are dimensions to tropical fruit that cannot be experienced in Wisconsin.

Can you differentiate varieties of bananas by their fragrance?

Were you even aware that bananas have a fragrance?

They do.

On a tree, a fruit starts out as a green odorless nubbin which gradually grows in size, improves in color and matures in taste as it ages; reaching its peak of perfection when it is about to fall off a tree on its own. The color and flavor is to induce birds, animals (and humans) to carry the seed as far away as possible from the parent tree so that its propagation spreads.

In Zanzibar, we wait to pick the fruit till it is fully ripened on the tree and fulfill the trees mission. The tree in return, rewards our patience with a fruit with the best color, aroma and flavor that it can produce.

You will hear at least six different languages spoken on the streets. As you walk by stores you will hear broadcasts and song in Kiswahili, Arabic, English, Hindi, Gujrati and Urdu.

Coming from behind you, will be sounds from bicycle bells and the words. "Hatari[76]" and "Nipishe[77]". Step away from the

---

[76] Danger
[77] Let me pass.

sources of these sounds. There is a bicycle or a donkey cart about to run over you.

From either side of the street, shop keepers will beckon you to step into their stores with "*Karibu, Karibu*[78]."

From any direction, you may hear the squawk of a "Zanzibar" parrot. The adjective "Zanzibar," is a misnomer. The parrots are not indigenous to Zanzibar. Their home is the Congo.

The only creature that is indigenous to and exists only in Zanzibar is the red colobus monkey. As a child I had one of these as a pet and he rode with me on my bicycle handle bar, when I ran errands for my mother.

Colobus kirkii

Most monkeys are omnivorous and all monkeys steal food from homes and food stalls. The red colobus monkeys cannot digest simple sugars and restrict their diet to leaves and unripe berries. But they too steal—they steal charcoal—the only species observed to do that. Presumably, they eat charcoal to reduce the discomfort from flatulence

---

[78] Welcome.Welcome.

due to their diet and to abate the noise and stink associated with the relief of flatulence.

There are some sounds you will hear from hawkers who may be out of sight.

"Wacha mchezo kulla Makai" is the cry of a tall Mswahili with a limp, wearing a khanzu, a kofia and sandals made from discarded tires by a local cobbler. He pushes a smoky cart. His cry means;

"Stop playing. Eat roasted sweet corn" [Self-explanatory.]

You may run into another Mswahili carrying *"Kichwa ya Mnazi"*. His cry, which can be heard at least a quarter of a mile away is *"Chooee. Chooee."*

[No meaning. Just a catchy hawkers cry.]

He sells the tip of the top of a coconut tree where the embryonic fruit, flowers and leaves are. It is white, crunchy and slightly sweet, like coconut water. A refreshing snack.

The one you will find interesting is the local witchdoctor. He wears a colorful turban a waist coat over his khanzu and since he is well to do, wears imported leather sandals. He carries a box with potions and his cry is;

"Hareeree. Hareeree. Dawa tumbo mshipa"

This cry will require a lengthy translation. Hareree is the name of the "medicine" he is peddling. It will cure your "Tumbo"—the stomach. So he claims and that may be true. Furthermore, he states that it will cure maladies of the "Mshipa". The Oxford dictionary of Kiswahili defines it as a "A muscle or a vein" but in Zanzibar, I have heard the word used nonspecifically for pathologies of all the other organs of the body—a claim that stretches credibility.

One hallmark of quack cures is the claim of curing multiple unrelated illnesses. A cure that cures everything cures nothing.

The most mouthwatering sound in Zanzibar is;

"Ahh Nda Nda" [No translation possible. No such words.]

When you hear that, you know Ali Bageeya is within a hearing distance. His first name, indeed, is Ali. Bageeya is not his surname. Zanzibari's replace last names with the product the person sells. Omari "Tungule" sells tomatoes. Hamise "Machungwa" is the orange seller and Baniyani "Bunduki" is the Baniani (a Hindu) who is a gun smith.

Ali, a five foot three inches tall Arab from Hadhramaut, wore a sleeveless shirt over a stripped Mshuka, walked bare feet and carried a box on his head.

Carrying loads on your head is ergonomically correct. It was a common site in our neighborhood to see a Mswahili woman walking home with a glass bottle of cooking oil perched on her head.

Once, I read an article about training female models. One of the exercises that they had to do, was to walk with a book on their head. The claim is that it gives them a sexy gait. I do not recall seeing that benefit in Waswahili women. But then, it is hard to tell what sort of a gait a woman has when she is wearing a Burkha.

Ali was famous for his Bagea. A bean deep fried cake served with Chutney made of grated fresh coconuts, few diced green chilies, a pinch of salt and a squirt of fresh lemon juice. A snack to kill for without regret.

There is a sound that you will hear only on the streets of Zanzibar.

A coffee seller.

It sounds like a quarter turn made in a rapid succession on a high pitched rattle. The sound is generated by two coffee cups one inside the other held in a hawkers hand. The cups have vertical grooves on the outside. As he walks in the streets, he spins the inner cup. The rattling sound is made by the grooves of the twirling cup, inside the stationary one.

The sound alerts you to a coffee seller somewhere close.

On the ground on his right is a portable brazier full of burning charcoal. The coffee container in his left hand sits on top of the brazier while the seller is walking. The cylindrical brass can attached to the brazier is for water to rinse out used coffee cups.

For ten cents, you leisurely sip three cups of black unsweetened expresso Arabica coffee, while the seller discusses with you, the topic of your choice.

I hope I have whetted your appetite for walking through the streets of Zanzibar and to savor the sights, tastes, smells and sounds of my home town. Do so only with a guide. Navigating through the streets of Zanzibar without a guide is only for those born and raised in Zanzibar

In case you choose not to heed my advice, allow me to give you more reasons, why you should.

The streets of Zanzibar are a maze—the world's largest. There is no river for you to follow it out of the city; nor is there a tall land mark at the periphery of the city for you to weave your way towards. The inhabitants do not speak English. The streets have no names. The houses have no numbers. And the color of all the houses is the same.

White.

Chapter Eleven
My Mother's Remedies

My mother was the oldest in her family. Under her mother's supervision she raised her younger siblings and participated in nursing them when they were sick. By the time she had her own children, she was an astute clinician.

When I came home with sports injuries, she used to apply a warm paste of turmeric, salt and chilies and wrapped a bandage around it to keep the paste in place. It worked every time. The turmeric, like a warm brick, maintains heat longer and is an antiseptic for abrasions. The salt reduces swelling by osmosis and the chilies are a transdermal analgesic.

Today, physicians prescribe "Capocin" which is nothing more than an expensive chili paste. It is only one third as efficacious as my mother's recipe; the ingredients are readily available in all Indian homes, you do not have to make a trip to a drug store to get it and the ingredients in my mother's recipe cost next to nothing.

The same recipe minus chilies, made into a clear soup is a great gargle for sore throats. Table salt is also bacteriostatic especially for strep. We did not get unnecessary antibiotics or their side effects. Only now have the epidemiologists begun warning doctor's not to use antibiotics till it is indicated.

My mother was ahead of her time in her approach to the common cold, sore throats and the flu.

Her most impressive remedy was for an unproductive cough from a post nasal drip. The symptom of an unrelenting tickling sensation in the throat which keeps you up all night with bouts of a dry cough which fail to relieve the tickle. She roasted cloves, ground them up, and then stirred the powder into a spoonful of honey. She made us gargle it as long as we could. And *Walla*, the cough was gone. The effect was from the cloves that anaesthetize the pharynx and break the reflex arc of the cough. The honey makes the cloves stick to the pharynx.

She had an impressive repertoire of remedies for babies' ailments. For a colicky baby she advised young neighborhood mothers to use *ajwan*[79]. In Grocery stores in UK and Canada, I have noticed bottles of "Gripe Water". It smells and tastes like *ajwan*.

A Family Practitioner friend in Toronto swears by it. For calls from mothers of colicky babies in the middle of the night, he advises them to go to a 24 hour grocery store for "Gripe water" and give two teaspoons. With a grin, he says, "I never get a second call from those mothers."

Gripe water has *ajwaan* in it and *ajwan* has an atropine like substance in it that relieves bowel spasms.

---

[79] Fennel seed.

In Vuga, police inspector Ramesh Misra's parents had a *Dhatura* tree in their backyard. The generic name for this fig tree look alike is *Datura Stromnium*. I noticed that some of our neighbors, with the owner's permission, picked leaves that had fallen of that tree. In lush Zanzibar, picking fallen leaves is considered an activity of the insane. I learned later that my mother had sent them to pick the leaves. They were advised to dry the leaves, crush them, mix them with a little tobacco, wrap a pinch of the mixture in cigarette paper and smoke it to get over an acute asthma attack.

I practiced Pulmonary Medicine for over thirty years. It was only during the last five years of my practice that the FDA approved of the use of atropine inhalations to break the bronchospasm[80] of Emphysema, Chronic bronchitis and Asthma. The leaves of the *Dhatura tree* are loaded with atropine.

Folk medicine has evolved from centuries of trial and error. For centuries the Chinese have used herbs that contain ephedrine, to cure an asthma attack. Ephedrine is a drug I used a lot in my practice.

I remember well an elderly African American patient who complained of getting short of breath while in bed and only when he was in Northern Wisconsin during the deer hunting season. Even the patient considered his complaint bizarre. Grinning sheepishly he added; "I get up, drink a nice hot cup of coffee, Then I feel alright and can go to bed and sleep soundly the rest of the night"

---

[80] The constriction of the bronchial passages which cause wheezing and shortness of breath.

Pulmonary Function Tests proved that he was not going out of his mind. He had asthma. Deer hunting season is in fall when Northern Wisconsin is cold and he slept in an unheated cabin. He had an unusual asthma that occurs only on inhaling cold air.

Drinking coffee relieved his asthma as it has caffeine in it. For infants with wheezing, my mother's advice was giving the infant tea instead of milk in the feeding bottle. Tea also has caffeine, which is a first cousin of Aminophyllin, the prescription drug for asthma.

Like all good clinicians, my mother was aware of her limitations and was not embarrassed to defer to specialists when she felt uncomfortable with a case.

One of them was Khatu[81] Dadee[82]. Khatu Dadee was in her seventies. Lanky with long fingers and a voice louder than necessary, from Auditory nerve damage from exposure to her husband's loud occupational noise. Her husband spoke even louder than her. He was a part time carpenter. Artisans in Zanzibar never retire completely.

She was the Ear, Nose and Throat specialist. We went to her when mother diagnosed Acute Tonsillitis.

Like all good clinicians, she always took a History and did a Physical. She inspected the face and the neck. She then proceeded to palpation and felt for enlarged lymph nodes under the jaw and in the front of the neck. Finally, she made us open

---

[81] Acronym for Khadijah, the prophet's first wife,
[82] Paternal grandmother. All elderly females were addressed as "Dadee"

our mouths wide and say "Ahhh" and looked all over the inside. Then, if we had Tonsillitis, she said loudly;

"Yes. You have *Kankada*—HUGE ONES.".

That was a diagnosis we dreaded as it was invariably followed by her emergency surgery.

She went to her kitchen where she cooked on a wood fire. She returned with a thimble sized bowl full of ashes. She sat us down in a corner so that we had no room to wiggle. With the heel of her left hand on our foreheads, she pushed our heads into the corner to restrain it. After dipping her right index finger in the ash, that ash tipped extra-long finger, flew like an unerring nuclear tipped smart missile to penetrate and explode in the tonsil.

The ash was to create friction to keep the tip of her finger in the tonsillar bed and also to soak up the gushing, gory pus.

The finger felt like a red hot poker but the moment it was retracted, we were miraculously cured.

On one occasion I was in her "waiting room" waiting my turn for the surgery. To distract my mind, I struck up a conversation with her husband who kept rubbing his eyes which were blood shot, probably from an allergic conjunctivitis. As a child who hoped to be a doctor someday, I put in a plug for my future profession and told him that he did not have to put up with the discomfort which can be easily treated by a doctor. His response was unforgettable.

"Your eyes are the most precious and the most delicate part of your body." he said, pointing to both his eyes at the same time with a "V" he made with his index and middle fingers.

Never trust them to a doctor.

Always take care of them yourself."

He went on to tell me that, three times a day, he goes to his backyard, picks the tenderest leaves from a *Mortutho*[83] and squeezes its juice in his eyes.

The conversation ended there as it was my turn for "Surgery"

Another specialist I was referred to was a "Bone setter."

I was standing on the ledge of an open window and would not get down from it even after several "Get down this minute" from my father. In anger, he lifted me off the ledge by my right wrist and dislocated my right shoulder.

It hurt.

I was referred to a *"Sonara"*[84] in Hurumzi[85]. He made a living as a goldsmith. Bone setting was his side line. I do not believe he could have done it full time even if he wanted to. The incidences of dislocations in our community were too few and infrequent. The art of bone setting was a family skill passed down the generations via apprenticeship.

---

[83] Mint
[84] A gold smith.
[85] An area in Zanzibar,

He manipulated my shoulder and with a snap, put back the head of the humerus in its socket. Just like Khatu Dadee's treatment, the relief of pain was astounding and instantaneous.

Then, I had several daily sessions of massages. Tepid oil with multiple herbs in it was used to "strengthen" the joint.

During the massages, I watched the rest of the family work with gold—a fascinating skill.

On a block of wood, they placed a tiny chunk of gold. A lit oil lamp sat next to the block of wood. With a metal blow pipe, with its narrow tip bent at a right angle, they blew the flame over the gold to soften it. Then they worked on the gold with their Lilliputian tools, to transform chunks of gold into beautiful ornaments.

"A hundred strikes by a Goldsmith; One by a Blacksmith", a Gujrati proverb floated up my mind as I watched them at work.

The energy expended is the same. That is one interpretation. Another is that a Blacksmith's blow makes but an ugly dent. A hundred deliberate strikes delivered tenderly, create a thing of beauty. The proverb compares the end result of work by a plastic surgeon with that of a butcher.

When an Indian housewife gets sick of wearing an old-fashioned ornament, she takes it to a jeweler who melts it and recreates it in the latest vogue.

"The cost of labor exceeds the cost of gold," is a proverb we used when we felt that the cost of labor was exorbitant. It was a relevant proverb when I was a child. Now, with the skyrocketing increase in the cost of labor, the proverb has lost its impact and will be out of circulation when my grandchildren are adults.

A goldsmith is an artist first. I asked, Kassim, my masseuse, to draw the Beit-el Ajaib for me and after a brief flourish of a pencil on a piece of paper he presented to me an amazingly realistic sketch of the palace.

On the last day of my treatment, Kassim's father did a final check-up of my shoulder and discharged me with the admonishment;

"Be careful. It will take even less naughtiness to dislocate it again"

Wounded at being blamed for the dislocation, I told him how it happened in detail, complete with interruptions for sobs and rivulets of tears running down my cheeks.

The family listened to my account in empathy, silence and seriousness. Then the patriarch of the family broke the silence and somberly suggested;

"We should call the police and have your father put in jail."

I froze in horror. The tears turned off. The sobbing stopped. I was too choked up to utter anything, so I shook my head violently from side to side to convey my objection.

I would have forgotten this incident, if that sonofabitch patriarch had not run into my father and squealed on me.

I wished I had the ability to shrink myself into the size of an ant so that I could crawl under the living room carpet, when Abbajaan narrated that incidence to my giggling mother.

Folk medicine does cure minor ailments.

In villages too remote from a medical facility, it is the only care.

I am not aware of instances of harm from such remedies. Even those who prescribe or receive such care are aware of the limitations of such care and readily seek professional medical help,

Folk medicine is here to stay,

Chapter Twelve

Mr. Kanga

On my first day in grade school, I saw the most intimidating person in the whole world. He was the 4th grade teacher at the Sir Euan Smith Madresah.

His name was, Mr. Kanga.

Mr. Kanga had the presence of a colossus. He was at least 6 ft. tall and weighed well over 350 lbs. Looking at his face was like looking at the top of the Beit-el-Ajaib from the street in front of it. His face, full of fat, was globular, with three extra chins under it which rippled in sequence when he nodded. His huge pear shaped torso made his oversized extremities look stubby. His girth made it hard for him to clasp his hands in front of him. During award ceremonies, when he had to clap his hands in appreciation, he did so by clapping his hands above his head.

Of all his features, that one that subdued us all, were his huge eyes--like two oblong orifices with flames leaping out of them. Every thundering step he took caused the two story stone and mortar school to shudder. Though huge, he walked with the confidence and the grace of a bull elephant and he walked wherever he wished to, without fearing a challenge. He had about him an air of disdain that you see only in creatures at the top of the food chain. He was at his scariest when he trumpeted in anger.

Between my grade school and the Indian Ocean, was our playground. West of it and detached from the main school, was a one story student's W. C's. The structure was out of hearing range of teachers and a safe haven for students to vent their anger in. In that restroom, from day one in grade school, I learned about what my future held, from students senior to me. I heard frightening accounts, from those who had suffered a tongue lashing from Mr. Kanga. Almost every week, there was a more terrifying version to supersede the last one.

The only semi humorous comment I recall hearing was; "I have good news for those who have been wishing Mr. Kanga dead. Your prayers have been half answered. Mr. Kanga is going to India for a six month vacation."

I am certain that the sigh of relief that remark evoked, could be heard in the teachers' lounge in the main building.

I wanted to finish grade school but was apprehensive about having to go through the fourth grade -- Mr. Kanga's class. During the first three years of grade school, I kept telling myself; "There has to be a way of finishing grade school without going through the fourth grade."

Of course, there was no way. Like everyone else, I too ended up in his class. On our first day, we sat in his class, like a flock of turkeys in a coop on Thanks Giving Day, wondering which one of us will end up on Mr. Kanga's plate as dinner that day.

MR. KANGA

Like the final reincarnation of King Kong, Mr. Kanga slowly waddled into our classroom while huffing and puffing fire.

This is when I had my first close look at him. He was more than everything I had heard about him. In striking contrast to the rest of the teachers, he was fair skinned with green eyes and sandy hair.

People in northern India, particularly in Kashmir, have that dearth of pigmentation. But, they do not speak Gujrati. Mr. Kanga did; with an unmistakable accent and an inability to pronounce correctly a couple of letters of the Gujrati alphabet.

Put all these observations together and they spell just one word—*Parsee!*

At that age I recognized the Parsees but did not know them. I remember during one of our school breaks, cycling South of Zanzibar town with friends. South of the English golf course and west of the Sunni cemetery, the Parsees owned a few acres of secluded land.

In a high stone wall surrounding the *Agiyari*, the "Fire Temple", there were cracks you could peep through. We did. I could clearly see a well-tended garden with a domed structure in the middle of it. The structure was large enough for a sit down dinner for about three hundred people. The four walls were surrounded by a spacious covered veranda.

It did not look like a usual Zanzibari home converted into a place of worship or a typical small farm house. It had unusual features which convinced me that it was designed and built for a special use. The only similarity it had with most of the buildings in Zanzibar was that it was whitewashed.

In a hushed voice, Jussa, the oldest in our group, whispered;

"Trust me. I cannot divulge any more. If you cross this wall, the *Dastur,* Zoroastrian priest, will grab you, drive a spike through the top of your head and attach the spike to a hook in the center of that dome. At the bottom of that dome is a large shallow bowl, the same size as the dome and full of rice, to catch the blood dripping off your toes. For Parsee religious feasts, that is the only kind of rice the *Dastur* will bless before it is served to his congrigation"

Having learned more than I wanted to, I was glad when the gang decided that we were hungry and we hopped on our bikes and went to a safe and a serene site for a picnic--the Sunni Cemetery.

Well. Well. Well, I thought to myself. There is more to Mr. Kanga then what I knew so far. Oh my God! He is also a Parsee!

In all schools, the first order of business at the beginning of each year is the nomination of the class monitor. A monitor is a surrogate teacher and carries all the authority and some of the respect of the teacher. When the teacher is not present in the classroom, his duty is to maintain law and order in the class and keep down the noise so that it does not distract the students in the adjoining classes. He breaks up fights before they get out of hand and dutifully reports to the teacher, students who have broken class rules. Before the teacher arrives, it is the monitor who makes sure that the blackboard has been wiped clean. He could delegate this responsibility to another student but then the monitor runs the risk of getting an inferior result and erupting Mr. Kanga's displeasure. Most monitors thought it wise to do it themselves.

The first word he spoke was directed at me.

With his index finger pointing at me, he boomed;

"You!"

When he had the attention of my trembling body, he added;

"You will be the class monitor."

What a surprise!

What an honor!

I thought to myself, "No person is all bad. There is some good in everyone."

As the class teacher, he taught us all the subjects. He was at his most enthusiastic when he taught us the history of Zanzibar. Our textbook of the history of Zanzibar was written, by Mr. Kanga—in Gujrati. All the textbooks in my grade were in Gujrati. We learned the English alphabet in the sixth grade.

Wow! This teacher is a historian and a published author of a textbook!

With Abbajaan's help, I aced the test on the history of Zanzibar. My satisfaction came not from acing the test but rising in Mr. Kanga's esteem.

During that year, we had a field trip. Mr. Kanga took us to Beit –el - Amman, the museum with Zanzibar's historical artifacts. After the tour, he let us play a while in Mnazi Moja before escorting us back to school. On our way to school, we passed a fruit vendor. Mr. Kanga stopped us and treated the class to bananas! That incident is deeply etched in my mind. As I look back on my student days, Mr. Kanga was the only teacher who bought us a treat. I realize now that Mr. Kanga could not have stopped himself from doing so even if he wanted to. Generosity is in the genes of the Parsees.

Fourth grade seemed much longer than all the other grades. The feeling at the end of that grade was similar to the feeling a speaker has when he has reached the end of his memorized speech and now cannot wait to walk away from the lectern and the intimidating scrutiny of the audience.

My first day as a teacher at the Sir Euan Smith Madrasah was in the fall of 1953. It was also Uncle Munir's first day in grade school. Ammajaan, asked me to accompany Uncle Munir to school "so that he does not get lost".

"Lost?"

Uncle Munir knew his way to anyplace in Zanzibar, better than I did.

Moreover, after I finished grade school, the school had moved into a new building only a stone's throw from our home. You could see it from our home.

I believe, the real reason was that our mother was afraid that Uncle Munir might panic and run back home.

So, together, hand in hand—to make sure that he did not run back home—we walked together, to our first day at school.

I left him in his class after introducing him to his teacher and I walked to the teachers' lounge.

There, after six years, once again, I came face to face with Mr. Kanga.

Mr. Kanga had shrunk!

I could make eye contact with him without hyperextending my neck!

His light green eyes twinkled with a suppressed smile which was searching for an excuse to burst out into a hearty laugh. He radiated confidence in his ability to teach well that day and an invitation to novice teachers to ask him for help. He sat sprawled out in an extra-large easy chair, fanning his flushed face with an *ukindu*[86] hand fan. The picture was that of a happy fat man who was at peace with himself and the world and always took extra helpings of both food and life.

---

[86] Woven dried coconut leaves.

I introduced myself to him, but that was not necessary. He remembered who I was. I asked him some questions about my syllabus and he was extremely helpful. We can all tell a person who is helpful because that is his job. Mr. Kanga came across as a person who was eagerly waiting for someone to ask for his help and his manner left no doubt that the door to him was always open, in case I needed more assistance in the future.

Like two kids who just happened to be seating next to each other on their first day in kindergartner, we became instant best friends.

When the school bell range, signaling start of the first class, I left the teacher's lounge and began walking towards my class. My mind could not reconcile the impression I had of Mr. Kanga as I was walking to school that morning and what I thought of him now. It did not take long for me to arrive at a new opinion.

"Mr. Kanga is no monster".

"He is a pussy cat."

"A huge one? Granted. But a pussy cat all the same."

As I stepped into my class, my train of thought was broken, by the shuffling sound of students standing up and by forty pairs of apprehensive eyes sizing me up in silence.

"Good Morning class"

"Good morning, Sir."

"Please be seated."

Then, I began my first class on my first day as a teacher.

The new Madresah Mr. Kanga and I taught at.

CHAPTER THIRTEEN

The Parsees

I cannot quote with certainty, the number of Parsees in Zanzibar, but I can say with confidence, that they were too few to field a cricket team.

A cricket team is composed of eleven players and at least a couple of reserves. To maintain moral, motivation and survival, a team has to have enough good players to win an occasional match,

The Parses did have a few good players, who played for the "Cosmos'$_1$ a team composed of communities too small to have their own teams. The communal teams had sponsors who made an expensive sport affordable for the players. The Cosmos had none. "Cosmo", of course, is an abbreviation of "cosmopolitan" A Mswahili wit once called the Cosmos, *"Hana mama, Hana baba teamu"*—a team which has no father and no mother" and the nickname stuck.

They call themselves Parsees as they hail from *Pars, a* province in Iran. Cosmopolitan that Zanzibar is, there were others who too claimed to be Iranians. Sheikh Abdullah Saleh el Farsi had a weekly religious question and answer hour on the local radio station, *Sauti ya Unguja,* the voice of Zanzibar. We also had first generation Iranians— who were addressed as *Agha*—embedded in the Ithnashari community. They looked, dressed and did the same communal functions as the Mullahs of Iran that we have watched on American TV news channels. By far, the largest number who claim to be Iranians, are a group of Waswahilis who get offended if they are addressed by any name other than "Washirazee[87]."

The Parsees practice Zoroastrianism. A religion founded in Iran by Prophet Zarathustra. His place of birth, death and even the era he lived in is uncertain to scholars of ancient Iran. A conservative consensus is 1000 BC. A few historians place it in 6000 BC.

Out of ignorance, the Parsees have been referred to as "Fire worshippers."

> *Say not that they worship fire,*
> *They worship God alone, the almighty Sire.*
>
> *Firdausi.*

Firdausi was the nom-de-plume of Abu Qaasim, a Muslim. He is one of the brightest stars in the firmament of Farsi poetry and best known as the author of the epic poem—*Shahnama*—without a copy of which, no Parsee home is complete.

Fire was revered by ancient Iranians for centuries before Zarathustra was born. So was their unusual custom of disposal of their dead. Like all prophets, Zarathustra also chose not to

---

[87] Persons from Shiraz, Iran.

THE PARSEES

rock the boat of a long standing local custom, but to incorporate it into his philosophy.

Just as Prophet Mohamed had chosen the *Kaaba*[88] for Islam, Prophet Zarathustra chose a flame, as a focal point to concentrate on during the worship of the one Supreme Being, *Ahura Mazda*—The Eternal Light. The focal point does not have to be a flame. The sun or the moon will do just as well and like Muslims; they face their *Mihrab*[89] and worship Him, five times a day.

Their scriptures, *Gathas, Yashts* and *Vendidad are* written in *Avestan*, like *Sanskrit*, a dead language today. Their rituals are performed in an *Agiyari*, a "Fire Temple", by priests who are addressed as *Dasturji*. The suffix "ji", like the Japanese "san" is an honorific. In all Indian languages, Mahatma Gandhi, is referred to as "Gandhiji" or "Mahatmaji." Never, just "Gandhi."

Through social contacts with the Parsees in Zanzibar, I am vaguely familiar with their historic background. To get the dates straight, I asked Grandma to get me more details on the internet. To my surprise, came up with dozens of sites on Zoroastrianism. The internet has made a writer's task easier.

I was aware that it is a monotheistic religion. I believe Akhenaton, a pharaoh who lived in 1358 BC, was the first recorded monotheist, but his religion died with him. That makes Zoroastrianism, the oldest monotheistic religion.

---

[88] The cubical building in Mecca covered by a black ornate drape. Muslims pray facing the Kaaba.
[89] A semicircular niche, in a wall of a mosque indicating the Kiblah = the direction of the Kaaba.

I knew that they do not accept converts. The only way to be a Parse is to be born one. I have always regarded such religions as condescending and arrogant. It was the one Zoroastrian tenet that I found offensive.

As I read the following internet downloads, my resentment quickly changed to admiration.

> *"God gave us birth in our respective religions for a good reason.*
> *To convert is to question and rebel against HIM.*
> *All faiths are equal and eventually lead to Him*
> *On judgment day, He will let into heaven,*
> *The righteous among the practitioners of all His religions.*
> *Those who fail the test will be punished.*
> *There is no physical place called "Hell".*
> *The punishment is emotional, not physical.*
> *After the sinners have received appropriate punishment,*
> *They too will join the righteous and live forever in heaven"*

Wow! [90]

What a liberal religion!

Is it any wonder, that of all the religions I am familiar with, I have found Zoroastrians to be the most tolerant of other religions?

---

[90] http://tenets.zoroastianism.com

THE PARSEES

The Parsees gave us one of the great civilizations of the ancient world. Hoshang, the discoverer of fire, founded the first dynasty. His grandson Jemsheed discovered and gave humanity one of the great joys to live for— Wine.

When Ghalib[91] refers to *"Jaam-e-Jemsheed"*, (Jemsheed's goblet), he is referring to this very Jemsheed, who possessed a fabulous goblet. The goblet was always full and after every sip, it spontaneously filled itself to its brim.

The empire reached its peak during the reign of Cyrus the great. Most of us are familiar that the 22K race is called a "Marathon" because a courier ran that distance from Marathon to Athens, where he collapsed and died after delivering his message.

Few are aware of the content of his message which was; "We have sited the approaching fleet of Darius the Great of Iran at Marathon".

Another little known fact is that the "Magi"—the three wise man, who came to adore Jesus in the manger—were Zoroastrians. When Alexander the Great defeated Darius of Iran, at Gaugamela in 331 BC and precipitated the decline of the great Iranian civilization, Zoroastrism was still the religion of the land.

The fall of the Iranian Empire was followed by the rise of another great civilization—Islam. During the expansion of the

---

[91] Mirza Assadullah Khan Ghalib. The most revered Urdu poet and a contemporary of two great Urdu poets: "Daag" and "Zuffer." Zuffer was the last emperor of the Moghul dynasty.

Muslim empire, some of the Iranians fled from the advancing armies, out of fear of being coerced into Islam, a fear that still persists in the Parsee psych.

When a Parsee is pressured into doing something against his will, he is likely to object by saying;

"You are trying to convert me to Islam by beating me into submission!"

The pattern of fleeing from an advancing army is similar throughout history. If an endangered population has a shore line, they hop on ships and find a hospitable shore to practice their religion in. This was the reason for the earliest immigrants to our country.

When I spent a summer in Yorkshire, England, I was surprise to find a preponderance of Catholics in that area. It so happened that when Cromwell was after them, like mountain goats, the Catholics headed for the hills to find a safe haven.

When the Zoroastrians feared religious persecution from the invading Arabs, they did the same. They fled to *Fars*, *Yezd* and *Kerman*, provinces in the mountainous region of northern Iran. The few Zoroastrians left in Iran live in this mountainous area and constitute less than 1% of Zoroastrians in the world.

A few of them did not feel secure even in the mountains and sailed away in a ship in search of a safe haven.

THE PARSEES

In 716 AD, after a long voyage during which they almost perished in a storm, the ship arrived at Sanjan, a port 75 miles south of Daman on the west coast of India.[92]

Dastur Dhaval, along with a few senior Parsees, disembarked and went to the court of Jadi Rana, a liberal Hindu ruler of Sanjan, to ask permission to land and settle in Sanjan.

After a long arduous voyage, the Parsees looked haggard and more like incognito terrorists then refugees. The Rana suspected treachery.

Could this be a Trojan horse? He wondered.

The Rana listened patiently to their plea. He told them that he will let them know of his decision, after meeting with his advisors and told them to go back to their boat

The next day, the Rana's courier came to the boat and delivered a pot filled to the brim with milk. The symbolic message was unambiguous.

"We are over populated. This is no room for immigrants"

The Parsees were devastated.

The message was clear.

"Pull up your anchor and keep on going"

The panicked Parsees wailed;

---

[92] Who are the Parsees? (1958).Author: Sohrab K. H. Katrak. ISBN 0-7661-2959-4

"Oh, *Ahura Mazda!*"

"This is no reply. It is a death sentence"

"We can't just keep on sailing forever."

"We will all die at sea."

"If we resume sailing, where do we go?"

All through this clamor and commotion, Dastur Dhaval, the high priest, maintained a cool head. In the short time he had to give his answer, he came up with a reply, which he hoped would make the Rana reconsider his decision.

He put a spoonful of sugar in the overflowing pot of milk and returned it to the Rana as his response.

When Jedi Rana received the pot of milk with sugar in it, he was impressed with the reply.

He allowed the Parsees to settle in Sanjan; but with some restrictions.

1. They were to leave their weapons on the boat and not rearm after landing.

2. The Parsees were not to speak Farsi any more but learn and speak Gujrati, the local language.

3. They were to hold their weddings after sunset.

4. Their women must wear the Sari.

4. Out of respect for their Hindu hosts, they must not slaughter cows.

THE PARSEES

It is over a millennium since the Parsees landed at Sanjan. To this day, the Parsees have kept their word. They speak Gujrati, their women wear saris, their weddings are held only after sunset and although Zarathustra did not forbid them from eating beef, the Parsees of India, don't eat beef.

Every Idd, Ammajaan placed a pitcher of *"Idd milk"* and a bowl of *"Sev"* –delicacies served only on Idd—in a *Sineea*,[93] a large round metal tray; covered the tray with a small white table cloth and had our servant deliver the treats to the homes of friends.

When the servant returned home, the *sineea*, the plate and the pitcher were returned rinsed and wiped.

When a *Sineea* came back from a Parsee home, it came back rinsed, wiped—and with a spoonful of sugar in it—a Parsee tradition which began on that suspenseful day, on a boat in Sanjan harbor.

Almost all the Parsee families in Zanzibar had immigrated from Mumbai. Some had come to manage branch offices of firms in Mumbai. Others were highly trained professionals. All of them were highly ambitious and industrious and were willing to move from Mumbai to better themselves.

A famous Parsee, born in Zanzibar, was Freddy Mercury. His given name was Farooq Bulsara. (5th September 1946—24th November, 1991.) He is better known in Europe, particularly in the UK. He wrote and sang, "Bohemian Rhapsody" and "We are the champions of the world".

---

[93] A large round metal tray.

Does that ring a bell? If so, you too have known a Parsee from Zanzibar.

His family fled Zanzibar for England in 1964, for the same reason that I could not return to Zanzibar— "Mpinduzi"—the 1964 revolution in Zanzibar.

His fans were hoping to hold a music festival in Zanzibar in 2006 when Freddie would have been sixty years old. I am sure the minister of tourism in Zanzibar rubbed his hands in glee at the prospect of tourist dollars rolling into Zanzibar, not just once but annually after that.

Unfortunately the minister of culture, under immense pressure from the homophobic clerics, gave the thumbs down sign.

Freddie was gay.

The photograph on the right is of a statue of Freddie Mercury, overlooking Lake Geneva in Montreux, Switzerland. Since 2003,

Freddy Mercury

during the first weekend in September, his fans gather here to celebrate "Freddie Mercury Memorial Day"

Before departing Bombay, Parsees visit their sacred flame in *Udwada,* a city about 100 miles from Mumbai, which to the Parsees is what Mecca is to the Muslims. There they light a lamp from the flame in the Agiyari to take along with them wherever fate takes them. The flame in *Udwada* came from Pars, Iran, with the first Parsees who landed at *Sanjan*

Every Parsee home, all over the world, has an oil lamp lit from the sacred fire in the Agiyari in *Udwada*; a flame that is never allowed to extinguish. The lamp is enclosed in an ornate glass cage, which is hung on any wall except the one facing the north. One explanation for not facing the north while praying is that, nothing good came to them from the north while they lived in Iran—specially the winter storms.

Having lived in Wisconsin, I too share with them an aversion for the weather that comes to us from our north.

To a Parsee, fire is sacred. This theological belief created a dilemma for *Dakhma-nashini*—disposal of a corpse. As is the belief in many religions, including Islam, a dead body, particularly the flesh, is considered *Nasu*, impure.

Cremating a dead person, according to the tenets of Zoroastrianism, would be a desecration of fire. Unfortunately, burial in land or at sea is also sacrilegious. Since all the usual options were unacceptable, the Parsees came up with an ingenious method of disposing their dead.

They feed them to the vultures.

Mumbai has the "Tower of silence," a place where the Parsees take their dead for *Dakhma-nashini*. In the center of the "Tower of Silence" is a shallow dry well covered by a metal grill. The dead body is laid on the grill, naked; because that is how the Parsee entered the world and that is how he will leave it.

The vultures do the rest.

I have heard the Parsees in Zanzibar mention that the body is not "really" naked. It is covered with yogurt. I never dared ask them why, for fear of getting a nightmareogenic answer. Also, I love yogurt and hope that nothing will prevent me from enjoying it. So, I remain uncertain about whether or not the custom is to maintain the modesty of the deceased. The story may not even be true.

On second thought, it may be true. Parses love "Korma"—a meat dish. Korma has yogurt in it as a flavor enhancer. Perhaps the vultures share a common taste with the Parsees.

In a matter of hours the bones are picked clean and drop to the bottom of the dry well—a site where democracy is practiced at its strictest. The bones of princes and paupers mingle randomly.

At one time the "Tower of Silence" must have been out of town, but Mumbai, like all cities, grew and engulfed it.

People can be unreasonable.

In the United States, people build or purchase homes next to International Airports—lots and properties are much cheaper there for an obvious reason—and then, they complain incessantly about the noise from arriving and departing airplanes.

The inhabitants of Mumbai are no different.

The new neighborhood started complaining when chunks from "carryout" human flesh, broke off the talons of the departing vultures and splattered on the heads of pedestrians.

To placate the neighbors, the Parsees built a high wall around the burial well.

The wall is a "state of the art" example of the marvels of civil engineering. The architects studied the flight characteristics of vultures and their rate of climb after a full stomach.

In her novel, "The Crow Eaters", a humorous novel about the Parsees, Bapsi Sidhwa, mentions that she has observed that fully satiated vultures "at full throttle" are unable to fly straight out over the wall. To that observation, I dare add, that circling to gain altitude will not help either. The steep bank required, would make them stall.

After the state of the art wall was built, it did not take long for the vultures to learn that after a meal, it is best to rest on a perch and try to depart later later after they have pooped off some pay load.

The decision Jadi Rana made, was the best thing that ever happened to India. The contributions the Parsees have made towards commerce, fine arts, and the sciences is outstanding, their humor unique, their hospitality exemplary and their generosity unmatched.

When we consider that the Parsees makeup less than a fraction of 1% of the population of India, their contributions towards the progress of India are remarkable.

The melting pot is not unique to the U.S.A. It exists wherever there is inter communal mingling, a high standard of living and easy access to university education. Within three generations, an alarming percentage of the Parsees in the United Kingdom have lost their identity and bear no resemblance to the Parsees I knew. God forbid, but the same could happen to the Parsees of India, particularly in Mumbai.

There are only about 140,000 Parsees worldwide. Of late, the attrition rate of the Parsees is disconcerting. In Iran, about two centuries ago there were over a million of them. Now there are hardly 18,000. Today, outside Iran and the subcontinent of India—a mere 4000!

Like good stewards, every generation hopes to leave behind the world; at least as good as we found it and hopefully a little bit better. I am sad and pessimistic about my generation's chances of upholding this tradition.

The Zanzibar I have illustrated now lives only in my memories.

It became extinct in 1964.

Every week a species of fish becomes extinct. Every month I read about a species of a mammal that is not around anymore. Every year the Audubon Society adds a painting to its collection of extinct birds. Every century a people and its unique culture cease to exist.

With every one of these irretrievable losses, the world becomes poorer in diversity.

This book is an endeavor, to preserve for you in words, a world rich in diversity that I was fortunate to live in.

(1.)   http://tenets.zoroastrianism.com

(2.)   Who are the Parsees? (1958). Sohrab. K. H. Katrak.

Pub: Herald Press, Karachi, Pakistan.

Chapter Fourteen

Ramadan

I have looked forwards to Ramadan's with mixed feelings and look back at it with nostalgia.

Ramadan is the holy month of fasting. Life is about the same, most of the year but during Ramadan, the ambience changes overnight. From dawn to dusk, restaurant doors are shut, the deserted streets are astonishingly quiet and the radios blaring music out of homes and shops are silent. Schools are closed for the month. Businesses, if open, do so for short, unpredictable durations.

People are polite, considerate and charitable. Those who do not pray during the rest of the year, pray during this month. Those who consume alcohol daily, abstain from it. Those who use profanity for an adjective for every noun, use unadorned nouns. Smokers stoically suffer withdrawal. Wars, take an intermission.

It is <u>the</u> month for total spiritual immersion.

Almost all religions have some variant of a fast. For a Hindu, a fast is a day to avoid certain foods, like onions and garlic. For some Christians, it is abstaining from a favorite food or a beverage. The purpose, I believe, is spiritual—cleansing, penance and empathizing.

A Christiane colleague of mine whose wife is a minister told me how much he admired the Muslim concept of fasting during Ramadan;

"For a month, you guys choose to walk in the moccasins, of those who cannot afford more than one meal a day, every day of their lives."

I accepted his explanation with a puffed up chest.

This is a memoir, not a thesis.

The Muslim fast begins when the *Muezzin*[94] calls the faithful to the Morning Prayer at dawn and ends with his call for the Evening Prayer at dusk. During that interval <u>nothing</u> can enter the mouth. No water. Not even medicine. You cannot fast, if you must take pills, elixirs or even insulin shots. You cannot smoke or swallow saliva.

You cannot help but pity a manual laborer dripping sweat in the midday sun to eke out a living during Ramadhan.

Children are eased into a full fast. They begin with a "Half a fast" which entails skipping breakfast and no snacking or drinking anything till lunch time. As they get older they progress to a "Three quarter fast" which is extending the "Half a fast" till tea time. Tea time is at four PM. You are a big boy and the pride and joy of your parents when you do a

---

[94] A person who calls Muslims to a prayer from a minaret.

"Full fast" for the whole month. This milestone is reached by age of nine or ten

About thirty minutes before dusk, we gathered in our living room from where we could clearly hear the sounds from our kitchen.

Rat-tat-tat is a knife dicing chilies on a cutting board. An intermittent bang is made by Jaffer, our servant, hacking bony parts of a chicken or a lamb. A high pitched ringing sound is a pastel pounding dried spices inside a brass mortar.

A rhythmic, scratching low pitched sound comes from a maid sitting on a *"mbuzee"* grating fresh coconuts. A *"mbuzee,"* literally a goat, is an interesting kitchen tool which when unfolded does look like a goat. It has four legs, a flat surface for a back and the front has a cylindrical neck, with an oval metal grater for a head.

Our maid sat astride the "back" of the *mbuzee and* placed an empty platter under the "head." With both hands she twirled a coconut split in half over the "head" as shreds of coconuts rained on the platter.

The shreds when mixed with diced chilies, a pinch of salt and a squirt of lemon juice made chutney to go with *bhagias*[95]. Most of the shredded coconuts gets soaked in water and then squeezed to yield "coconut milk"—a "must" ingredient in Swahili cuisine.

These are all "prep" sounds—sounds of ingredients put together for sauces, chutneys and for marinating,

---

[95] A deep fried ball of a bean paste. It is similar to "Falafel"

ZANZIBAR

Dinner will not be served for at least an hour.

One soon learns to maintain patience and ignore these sounds.

About fifteen minutes before dinner is served, is when you hear sounds that make the mouth drool uncontrollably.

The sounds are: "Shoe" and "Chhum."

Soups like "Dal" are made in a pressure cooker. The "Shoe, Shoe. Shoe" is the sound of steam escaping from the cooker, to keep the pressure at a predetermined level. When those sounds stop, the soup is done and dinner will be announced shortly.

So that they are piping hot when dinner is served, hors d'oeuvres, like samosas[96] are cooked last.

We learned very early, that the sound to keep your ear cocked for is—"Chhum." It is heard every time a samosa is dropped in a frying pot. A small pot is capable of only a few "Chhums." A large one is good for a dozen or more "Chhums".

When a cold wet samosa is dropped in boiling oil, water droplets splatter for a few seconds giving the first note, "Chh". Then air trapped in the Samosa, escapes to the surface, out of its three corners, in a stream of hundreds of tiny bubbles giving the note, "Uuu". When all the air in the samosa has escaped, you hear a flat "Mmmm" as the color of the samosa slowly turns from white to yellow and ultimately to a golden brown.

---

[96] A deep fried, triangular filo dough pocket filled with spicy ground meat or vegetables.

As the samosa's are strained out of the frying pan, the 'Mmmm" gets softer and softer. Finally, after the last samosa is strained out of the frying pot, there is silence.

Once again, after a thirty second interval, the melody repeats itself.

With experience, you learn to ignore the notes and pay attention to the duration of the silent intervals. When the silence is prolonged beyond thirty seconds—the silence, announces louder than a thousand dinner bells rung simultaneously—"Dinner,......is served."

Dusk is signaled by an Azaan[1], a drum beat or the report of a canon. In Zanzibar it is a siren. The few minutes before the siren goes off, is an excruciating suspense.

Phupejaan suffered it the most. She helped Ammajaan cook and the aroma of the delicacies worsened her hunger and heightened her suspense. At dusk, when it was almost time for the siren to go off, she would declare;

"The siren must be broken."

The implication was that we might as well go ahead and break the fast.

In all the years we were in Zanzibar, the siren never malfunctioned, but that did not prevent her from repeating the pronouncement every other dusk.

Like the Old Faithful, the siren always came and was always on time, to sighs of relief, and to a stampede to the table.

My nose was the first, to inhale the feast, while I sprinted to the table. Then my eyes opened wide, at the sight of the feast and drank it all in, in a blink.

Impatiently my siblings and I, sat in our chairs. And waited. And waited. And waited.

The last person to straggle to the table was like a ferocious general in full regalia, sitting astride an excited stomping horse. When the last person sat down, it was as though, the tip of the general's sword, which was menacingly pointing at the sky, swished down to point to the heavily laden table, as he thundered; "CHAAARGE"

And we obeyed. Enthusiastically.

No one talked.

I kept eating till the distension of the abdomen made breathing in uncomfortable. I then went to a couch to sprawl out on.

Soon you hear a ringing. Like an intermittent ring of an old fashioned door bell. It is Awaaz, the coffee seller, passing by. We hail him. He comes up the flight of stairs to our balcony. He pours a cup of coffee and hands one to each of us. While waiting to refill our cups, he updates us with local news before we read it in the next day's paper. We sip thick, strong coffee, freshly roasted, ground and brewed from Arabica coffee.

Coffee is indigenous to Arabia and still considered the best in flavor. Pilgrims returning from Hajj are credited for introducing coffee to the rest of the world.

About an hour after tipping the last cup of coffee, a deep breath becomes possible. We get off our couches, head to the mosque for tarawih and walk off our dinner—at a slow pace.

A tarawih is a two hour long prayer performed only in Ramadan, after Isha—the fifth and the last prayer of the day, at around eight PM.

The Imam, a person leading the prayer, is usually a *Hafiz*—a person who can recite the entire Qur'an by heart. During Tarawih, he recites the first chapter on the first evening of Ramadhan and the last one on, *Lailatul Qadr*—the twenty-seventh and the holiest evening of Ramadan. The evening, when the first verses of the Qur'an were revealed to Prophet Muhammad.

After Tarawih is free time.

In Ramadan, the vivacious nights are a striking contrast to the drab days. Till the sun illuminates the city again, it is revelry time. Time, to hang out with friends. Time, to go to the movies. Time to shop in the bustling streets where radios blare out of homes and shops and car horns and bicycle bells are heard continuously.

This is an experience available only in countries with a predominantly Muslim population. As students in Dublin, Ireland, uncles Babu, Makbul, Moin and I shared an apartment and fasted during Ramadan. There, all we experienced during Ramadan was hunger, nothing tempting to look forwards to break the fast with and homesickness.

For school children, the goal is to find any excuse to stay awake as long as possible so that you can sleep away as much of the fast as possible. If you stay up as late as you can, it is possible to sleep till midafternoon, while away the rest of the afternoon at a movie and be home in time for *Iftar*—the breaking of the fast.

Since the fast begins with the Muezzin's call to *Fajr*, the dawn prayer, Muslims have a *suhoor*, a meal, just before dawn. My mother was the first one to wake up and prepare the *suhoor*. I am certain that she used an alarm clock to wake her up but I do not recall ever hearing the alarm clock. What woke me up was my mother shaking and shouting at me to wake up for the third or fourth time.

There is no torture worse than having to wake up after only an hour or two of sleep.

Suhoor is usually a light meal. Usually we had *Khitchdee*, a dish made of rice and beans. Adding *Ghee*, clarified butter, to *Khitchdee* made the morsels smooth. Adding lots of it, keeps you satiated a long time. Fats do that by delaying gastric emptying. After we learned this trick, we drowned the *Khitchdee* in *Ghee*.

Suhoor, has to be consumed before dawn. This created a need for a crier to wake up people for *suhoor*, before the *muezzin* did. At the end of the month, the crier was tipped handsomely for his service.

When the wind up alarm clock was invented, that service became obsolete but it has persisted because of the tip at the end of the month. We had several who "woke us up" for *suhoor*.

Ferjala made his rounds with a hurricane lamp, although we had electric street lights. Carrying that unnecessary burden puzzled me, as it was common knowledge, that Zanzibar was the first city south of the Sahara to have electric street lights.

My guess is that in Indian hamlets without electricity, a hurricane lamp was and is a necessity. The hurricane lamp became associated with a Suhoor crier and over centuries, like a top hat on a chimney sweep, became a trademark of a *suhoor* crier.

As he walked by a Muslim home, "Wake up Muslims, Time for *suhoor*" was his loud high pitched harsh cry.

We also had a duo of Waswahili. One of them, the dancer, wore long feathers in his hat and his skin was painted like a Zulu warrior. They stopped in front of every house. His partner played a drum and the warrior danced to the rapid drum beat with fury while shaking a wooden staff to which several little brass bells were attached. They did not utter a word. I assume they believed that the noise they made served their purpose adequately. The performance lasted only a minute or two. Then they walked to repeat their performance at the next house, to the rhythm of "Teetang tee tang. Teetang tee tang. Teetang tee tang"

The irony is that the appropriate time for that service is at about four AM. These criers came in our neighborhood before we were in bed. What used to be a service has degenerated into an entertainment.

A lunar month has either 29 or 30 days. On the 29th day of Ramadan, we gathered behind a battery of four cannons in Jubilee gardens, an open area large enough to accommodate a few thousand persons.

The garden is bound by the Sultans palace and the Beit-el-Ajaib in the north, the Portuguese fort in the east and what used to be my grade school on the south. A band stand is in the middle of the garden, food stalls line the embankment and the battery faces the ocean in a waist high chain link fenced off area.

Idd was celebrated on the 29th of Ramadan, only if the Sultan personally saw the new moon at dusk on that day. If he did not, than it was celebrated on the 30th, whether or not the moon was observed by anyone, because a lunar month cannot have more than 30 days and it is a sin to fast on Idd.

Children gathered by the battery hoping and praying that the Sultan would see the moon that night. Then, tomorrow will be Idd—no *Tarawih* or waking up for *suhoor* tonight and no fasting tomorrow.

On the possible eve of *Idd*, members of the police department are on duty at the battery. A gunner and his mate, stand at attention behind each of the cannons. A chief inspector stands about 6 ft. behind and in the center of the gunners

At dusk, a crowd gathers between the embankment and the sultan's palace, to scan the sky for the new moon. The crowd consisted mainly of young Muslim children with high hopes of not going through another day of fasting.

If we were fortunate that day, a low murmur starts at some spot in the crowd. Upon turning your head in that direction, you'd see a person excitedly pointing to a spot in the sky to let those around him know where the new moon is. From that person, the murmur gets louder and louder as it ripples away from him and towards the edge of the crowd. Soon the entire crowd is excited and most of them are pointing towards the sky to help locate the spot to the few in the crowd who still haven't seen the crescent.

A few moments later, to the cheers and jumps of joy of an exuberant crowd, a courier arrives from the Sultan's Palace. He proceeds to the embankment where the cannons are and tells the police inspector that the Sultan has seen the moon and has authorized a 21 gun salute to welcome Idd.

This is the message the inspector has been waiting for. He pulls out his pocket watch. Flips open the lid. With the watch in the palm of his right hand, he adjusts the distance of his palm from his eyes till he has established the correct distance for seeing the watch face clearly.

Then he stands, as motionless as a statue.

The gunners remove safety locks. They open the cannon chambers. Next to each cannon is a box of shells. The gunner's mates unlock the box of shells. They pull out the first shell. They hand them to the gunners. The gunners insert the shells into the chamber. Then lock the chamber with a click.

Within ten seconds, the cannons are loaded.

The gunners are still. Their index fingers curled gently over the cannon triggers.

The gunner's mates stand at attention close to the gunners. With both hands they hold the second shell. All shells are held the same way. Firmly. The pointy part, facing the sky.

The inspector is at attention. His baton is tucked under his left arm pit. A breeze sways the fringe of his epaulet. His eyes intently follow the progress of the second hand.

It is time to plug ears with index fingers.

Although there is no possible threat to the eyes, some shut their eyes too. Perhaps, that eliminates the visual cue and heightens the thrill of hearing the first "bang".

All eyes are now focused on the inspector

An eerie silence engulfs the crowd.

You become aware of the breath sounds of the person standing next to you.

Everyone braces for the first "bang".

The crowed is still.

Some are frozen in a hunch.

The very young, adopt a tight fetal position

Breaths are slow and shallow

Hearts beat slower.

The second hand sweeps past numeral X on the dial.

The inspector clears his throat.

The second hand sweeps by numeral XI.

The inspector's chest swells with a deep breath.

The crowds' suspense rises to a crescendo.

A freezing shiver erupts in the center of chests.

As the second hand sweeps over the numeral XII, the inspector roars;

"Number one ……. FIRE".

A flash of light is followed by a puff of smoke from the cannon barrel—then "BOOM" goes the first cannon.

Thousands of birds, who have been roosting in the trees of the Jubilee Gardens, are jolted out of their sleep and take to the sky flapping and screeching and head inland as the evening breeze wafts the first whiff of the acrid smell of burning sulfur over the screaming ecstatic crowd.

The gunner of Cannon #1 opens the chamber with a clang. Takes out the smoking spent shell and puts it in an empty shell box on the ground to the left of the cannon.

His mate hands him a fresh round. The round is inserted in the chamber. The chamber locks with a click.

The gunner's right index finger curls on the trigger.

The mate bends over. Picks up the next round and stands ready to hand it over to the gunner.

The second hand sweeps over the numeral III'

"Number two…….FIRE."

BOOM

(Cheers)

This time only a few birds screech. These are from the stragglers, now over the top of the Portuguese fort.

Another whiff of the smell of a struck match stick wafts over the crowd.

The second hand sweeps over the numeral VI

"Number three.......FIRE."

Boom

(Cheers.)

You do not hear a screech. The birds are too far away to be scared by the boom.

The smoke from the cannons creates a haze over the crowd.

The stink is stronger.

Some cough.

A few rub their eyes.

After the fifth or sixth boom, the bold take their fingers out of their ears. A few of those who had their eyes shut open them and if the sight is not too frightening, gingerly remove their fingers from their ears.

The cheers diminish with each subsequent boom.

After the twenty first boom—there is silence.

The crowd is motionless.

Gradually, it dawns on everyone that the seemingly interminable Ramadan has indeed ended.

You hear sighs of relief. All faces wear a smile. The euphoric crowd heads home— assured that when they wake up the next morning, it will be the day of;

Idd-el-Fitre[97]

---

[97] A major holiday, which celebrates the end of the month of Ramadan.

Chapter Fifteen

Hajj

Performing Hajj is every Muslim's hope; a hope fulfilled by only a fortunate few.

Hajj, one of the five pillars of Islam, is an obligation of making a pilgrimage to Mecca, at least once during a lifetime.

The coveted milestone in a Muslim's life has several prerequisites. The important ones are that the pilgrim be free from <u>all</u> financial debts and must have fulfilled <u>all</u> social and family responsibilities. The few, who are fortunate enough to reach that stage in their lives, are certainly old and infirm and most of them are too poor to afford it.

When I was a child, no one in Kibokoni had done it. The few Zanzibari's who had, were envied, looked up to and respectfully addressed by the title *Hajji—a person who has performed the Hajj.*

Prosperous stores carry the proud prefix of "Hajji"—like "Hajji Abdullah and Sons" and "Hajji Omar Mithaiwalla." The prefix is a subliminal pitch of honesty.

Before the invention of steamships, the only way of getting there was a dhow[98] or a *Kafla*—a caravan of camels. The land route took over a year, through deserts, across rivers and over mountain passes. It was an arduous journey that pushed to the limits, the endurance of even athletic youths. If the travail of the travel did not deter a prospective hajji, there were other factors that did. One of the risks to accept was an attack by tribes along the way whose main source of livelihood was killing pilgrims for their belongings and money.

Many pilgrims succumbed to the stresses of the journey even before reaching Arabia. Many of those who made it there died of heat and disease and were buried in unmarked mass graves. News of their death reached their relatives, by word-of-mouth from the returning pilgrims who had accompanied the deceased and had witnessed the death.

No matter how young or how old you are, it is wise to embark on this pilgrimage with the assumption that the return home is unlikely.

Some sincerely hope to die while in Medina and return home disappointed.

To send off with; "I wish you a death in Medina," is an appropriate sentiment of a loving well-wisher and responded to with "Amen" by the pilgrim.

Death is anticipated fatalistically. "It will come, when it will come". So it might as well come soon after he has made his

---

[98] A ship with a triangular sail. Usually seen in the Indian ocean, the red sea and the Nile.

neeyut—a decision to go to hajj—and spare him the bother of the entire ordeal.

Children are told that throughout our lives, each of us has two angles assigned to us. They sit on our shoulders. The one on your right, records all your good deeds. The bad ones are recorded by the one on your left. The significance of the *neeyut* is that, if death occurs after the *neeyut*, the angel on your right shoulder will give you full credit as though you had performed the hajj, even if you die before taking the first step towards Mecca.

We laugh at jokes about deaths and funerals. Because it frightens us, we avoid thinking, preparing for or discussing it in a serious vein.

Because it is embarrassing to convey our love in our own words, we resort to sending greeting cards with flowery words of a professional greeting card writer.

We avoid awkward situations and are lost if we cannot circumvent it.

What do you say to an elderly loved one about to go to Hajj who may not return?

Most of us would say nothing.

A compulsive talker, may utter something inappropriate, only to regret it later.

We all hold a silly grudge, against someone we love. Over the last five, twenty or even sixty years, we have relived that incident innumerable times and each time we have decided to ignore it, as it was a petty incident undeserving of a confrontation with someone we love and who loves us.

The persons you have the grudge against have long forgotten that incident, but they too have had similar experiences with their parents, and know that some of their words and actions must have caused some unintended pain to those they love.

Fortunately, customs have evolved to facilitate communications during such social occasions. They are a distillation of cultural wisdom gained through centuries of trial and error.

The customs associated with a sendoff to a hajj are necessary and wise.

They require that all parties confront their reluctance and say now, what they will wish they had, when it is too late.

The perspective Hajje has tied all the loose ends of his temporal liabilities. He must now redress probable grievances nursed by his loved ones.

He begins the dialogue by begging for forgiveness. He individually asks everyone in his life, to forgive "any and all, intentional and unintentional" pain he has caused them.

It is an emotionally charged moment.

When my mother asked my forgiveness before performing her Hajj, I burst into tears.

I was too choked up to say;

"What shall I forgive? You have done nothing for me to forgive."

I hugged her tightly and nodded affirmatively—while my head was behind her eyes. Somehow, my body language conveyed my response to her and she acknowledged my forgiveness by tightening her hug.

With that final duty accomplished, the pilgrim is free to leave home with a clear conscious. Free from financial responsibilities. Free from social obligations. Free to devote to his long neglected soul. Free to be a guest in Allah's house. Free to sing all the way to Mecca—with gusto and in chorus with fellow pilgrims;

"Lubbek, Allahuma lubbek"[99]

During one of our visits to India in the 1950s, my grandfather told us of his *"Neeyut"*, to do the hajj.

He was the first of my relatives to do so and we were all happy for him. Before leaving India for Mecca, my grandfather went through the customary ritual of asking for, and receiving forgiveness. I was too young to even appreciate the significance of the exchanges. I just hugged him, and wished him a pleasant journey. He was still young, in his mid or late sixties, and I fully expected to see him again during our next visit to India.

The days of the caravan were over and mass air travel had yet to begin. Pilgrims from Gujarat took a train to *Mumbai*, ("Bombay" in those days) and a steamship from there to *Jidda*—the port of entry, for ships and planes.

---

[99] "Here I come, my Allah, here I come."

Long distance calls were a convenience of the future. There was a steamship mail service between Saudi Arabia and the rest of the world, but the service was overwhelmed by the sheer number of pilgrims during the Hajj and could not be relied upon to get a letter home, before the pilgrim's return. The accepted norm was not to expect any communication from a pilgrim who went to hajj. You just waited to "hear all about it" when the pilgrim came back.

From the moment you land at Jidda, your preconceived ideas of Islam and the world, undergo multiple revisions in a rapid succession.

One out of every four humans on the face of the Earth is a Muslim. A slice of the entire human race representing every race, color and country is here, united by the adhesive of Islam. In one place, you will see all national costumes, hear every language and taste all the cuisines of the world.

Your nose will be exposed to new smells.

Of the five prayers of the day, the noon prayer on Fridays carries the most weight. Most Muslims will make every effort to make at least that one. It is the largest gathering of the week in any mosque.

It is customary to bathe and put on your best clean clothes for that prayer, but even that is usually not enough. Imagine being in a packed Mosque in Saudi Arabia at noon during summer. Now imagine being there before air conditioning was invented. There will be an unpleasant consequence.

To mask it, wearing perfume before going to a mosque is a *sunnah*[100] for women—and men.

Fragrances have dimensions and notes that are unique not only to each Muslim country but also to the cities within them. Just a whiff has the power to transport you back to the site where you first experienced it and overwhelm you with nostalgia.

My first preconceived impression that was revised was that Zanzibar is not the home of the Muslims. The world is.

The Hajj begins in Mecca. A bus takes you there. When a prominent road sign tells you "Muslims only beyond this point" you are at the periphery of Mecca.

When pilgrims arrive at Mecca to begin the Hajj, they shed all external hints of wealth and status. In the house of Allah, a prince dresses indistinguishably from a pauper; for in the eyes of the host, the prince is no better or worse than a pauper.

Ihram is the word for the dress code. Men dress in two sheets of unhemmed, white cloth. One of the sheets is draped over the torso and the other, secured by a belt, is wrapped around the waist.

Women dress modestly but <u>may not be segregated or cover their faces or hands.</u>

A pair of plain sandals completes the wardrobe.

Over the last 14 centuries and particularly during the pinnacle of the Muslim civilization, the hajj provided the hub to the advancement of knowledge. It provided a common meeting

---

[100] What the prophet did.

place for scholars, poets, artists and inventors. In between the rituals, they discussed, exchanged and challenged new information. New advancements in the arts and sciences came to Arabia during the hajj and from there was disseminated to the rest of the world.

During the Dark Age when European civilization was at its lowest ebb, Islamic culture was at its zenith and was the impetus for the renaissance in Europe.

A gathering of millions from all over the world has a negative aspect to it as well. The hajj has been a well-documented source of endemics and also a few of the past major pandemics. The epidemic of Ebola, which rekindled in West Africa during the Hajj of 2014, did not spread to Arabia.

To their credit, the Saudi's have implemented exemplary preventive measures and the Hajj does not pose the threat of spreading epidemics any more.

Billions have been poured into making the pilgrimage comfortable. The infra-structure at Mecca and Medina has surpassed the best in the world in one generation.

The Hajj begins at the *Ka'aba*

The *Ka'aba* is a cubical granite structure in the center of the Grand mosque—*Haram el Sharif*—in Mecca. It was built, over four thousand years ago, by prophet *Ibrahim*, better known in the Judeo-Christian circles as Abraham.

In the pre Islamic era, the *Ka'aba* housed idols and Arabs from all over Arabia made a pilgrimage to the *Ka'aba* to worship them.

The *Ka'aba* is draped in black silk with Quranic verses embroidered in gold thread by premenarch girls in Pakistan. The drape is renewed annually and pieces of the old, a prized souvenir, are proudly displayed in homes.

Walk into any home in the Islamic world and you are bound to see religious symbols. When it comes to calligraphy, there is no equal to Arabic calligraphy. The words "Allah" and "Muhammad" and verses from the Qur'an, in exquisite calligraphy, adorn Muslim walls.

I have been able to identify the Ka'aba since my infancy. Every Muslim home has it displayed prominently. I had cast a thousand cursory glances at it— glances devoid of emotion.

Now, I was about to see it.

I was full of eagerness as I entered the Grand Mosque in Mecca for the first time. My steps had a spring in them; my heart was thumping and deep inside my chest, I had a cold continuous shiver. I climbed the steps to the mosque two at a time and when I entered the Abdulaziz gate, I saw the *Ka'aba* for the first time.

I froze in a trance, gazing at the *Ka'aba*.

I inhaled serenity and my blood carried it to every cell in my body. I had never experienced such utter tranquility before nor have I felt it again since then.

I remained in that status for an eternity.

A cry of *"Allahuakber*[101]*,"* broke the spell. I looked to my left at the source of the cry and saw a handsome, fair skinned, bearded

---
[101] God is great.

Arab in his thirties; his right hand above his head clenched into a fist, his eyes full of sparkle and his face shining with joy. He too had just seen the *Ka'aba* for the first time.

As I turned my gaze back to the *Ka'aba*, the sweep was stopped by the look of a Pakistani girl in her twenties. She was weeping quietly. My initial thought was that she was lost. It is easy to get separated, in a crowd of several millions. Just when I had decided that she was crying because she was lost, I saw another Pakistani girl next to her, with enough facial similarities to be her sister. She too had tears rolling down her cheeks while staring in a trance at the *Ka'aba*.

After I saw the expression on the second sister, I realized that these sisters were not lost.

They had just found something.

A sob made me look below and to my right. Uncle Munir was in an embrace with mother, his face buried in her bosom—sobbing and weeping in ecstasy.

The joy around me was so intense and so contagious that it made the joy, somewhere deep within me, swell to a point where I was convinced that it could swell no more without bursting me. But, it kept on swelling well past that limit. And it kept on increasing exponentially, the way the speed of space rocket increases, when it is past the pull of gravity and is in its unhindered climb towards the heavens.

Then I made a mistake I shall always regret.

I continued my sweep towards the Ka'aba for a second look.

HAJJ

The second look snatched me back to reality. The magic was gone. Now, the *Ka'aba* looked like what it is—a cubicle structure made of granite and draped with black silk with embroidered Quranic verses.

I was warned of this experience.

I had read an article in "The minaret", written by the Imam of the mosque in Washington DC. I read that article with interest as I recognized the author as the Imam who married Grandma and I. The article was written for those getting ready for their first Hajj. In the article, he mentioned that the first time a *hajji* sees the Ka'aba is a unique experience, never evoked in subsequent viewing. He asked his readers to write down immediately what they felt, lest they forget it.

I agree with experience he mentioned. I disagree with his advice. There is no need to write it down. The experience is unforgettable—in my mind, it is as vivid today, as it was on that day, twenty five years ago.

The Hajj begins with *Tawaaf*—counterclockwise circumambulation of the Ka'aba seven times.

It is a solemn ceremony where I witnessed humanity at its best—and also at its worst.

I have witnessed up lifting sights of religious fervor, generosity and consideration. I have also seen professional panhandling. Aunty Rukia fell for the sad story of a con artist during a tawaaf and gave him all the money she had on her—a few hundred dollars.

In a country where pickpocketing is punished by getting the right hand chopped off, I saw pick pockets at work, doing the *tawaaf* in *Ihram* and chanting in chorus;

"Lubek, allahuma Labeck"

The *tawaaf* is continuous. Even in the early hours of the morning, there are always thousands doing the tawaaf. As a child I was told that there is a quorum for the tawaaf. If the number of humans drops below that, angels eagerly fill in to make up the difference.

The tawaaf is interrupted only for the five daily prayers—a demonstration of democracy at its best.

There is a protocol. It has only one requirement—that the *Imam*, stand alone in front of the congregation.

Women with bare faces and hands, children and men, stand at random in concentric rows around the Ka'aba.

For several seconds, persons in the back row scurry ahead filling up spaces in the rows ahead. A person in the last row could zig zag his way to the front row. With the exception of the last row, all rows are filled so tightly that the congregation is literally rubbing shoulders. This scurrying and tight rows is to make efficient use of the space and leave room in the back for the late comers.

Soon the rows are filled and motionless.

Ek he saf me Khade rahgaye, Mehmood aur Ayaaz,

In the same row, stood a servant next to a sultan,

Fir na raha koi bunda ya koi bandenawaz.

For in this row, no one is a servant or a sultan.

Allama Iqbal.[102]

The Imam, while facing the Ka'aba, raises his hands to touch his ear lobes, and says;

"*Allahuakber,*"

Then lowers and folds them at his waist.

The congregation does the same

Then the *Imam* begins the prayer with;

"*Bismillah*…in the name of Allah…"

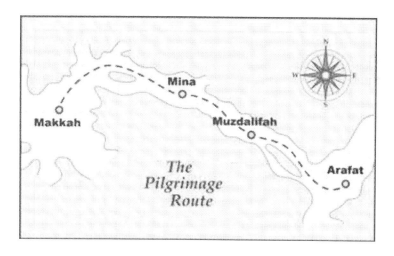

---

[102] The Bard of Pakistan.

Hajj is a ritual that reenacts a segment of Ibrahim's life.

Ibrahim's wife Sarah was unable to conceive and at Sarah's insistence Ibrahim married Hager, their female servant, who gave birth to Ismail. One day, God told Ibrahim to leave Hagar and his son alone in the desert.

Ibrahim complied.

Soon, they were thirsty. Hager ran between the hills of *Safa* and *Marwa* seven times in search of water.

After the first *Tawaaf*, *Hajis* do *Sa'I*, the ceremony of walking and running seven times between the hills of *Safa* and *Marwa*, reenacting Hager's desperate search for water for her thirsty child.

Exhausted after her seventh search for water, Hager laid Ismail on the desert sand to pray to God for help. Separated from his mother, Ismail began crying and thrashing and at the spot where his heel hit the hot parched desert sand, the spring of *Zum Zum* erupted.

Zum Zum is astonishing. It is a mighty river that surges out of a hole in a desert. The water is pure, chilled, well aerated and a joy to drink.

Hajis take home tiny bottles of Zum Zum water for gifts. It is a Muslim's "Holy water."

After *Sa'I*, pilgrims have a refreshing drink from *Zum Zum*, before returning to their hotels for the night.

The next morning a caravan of buses takes you to *Mina* for an evening of prayer and reflection. *Mina* is a much photographed sight. Every square yard of the huge valley, is covered with pitched white tents—like a nursery in Holland when the white tulips are in boom.

The Hajj we did was in 1989—in June. It was hot. I wish I could tell you what the temperature was that day, but I cannot. Local TV and radio stations quit reporting current temperatures when it rises above one hundred and ten degrees Fahrenheit. Perhaps, it is because temperatures above that are meaningless. Knowing that it is 120 and not 130 is not comforting. Some facts are just not worth knowing

At age thirteen, Aunty Sharifah was the youngest in our group. We kept watching her and wondering when the heat will get to her and make her throws in the towel and take refuge in an air conditioned room.

She did not.

Instead of wilting into a wet whiner, the heat energized her and made her chirpier while a steady stream of sweat flowed from the bottoms of her ear lobes and the tip of her nose.

That sight made me realized that this daughter is gifted with wanderlust. If this extreme weather is her idea of fun, nothing can stop her from backpacking the world— nothing has.

The third day, everyone board buses again to spend an afternoon at Mt. *Arafat*—where the prophet gave his last sermon.

At sunset, the pilgrims leave Mt *Arafat to* spend a night on the ground at *Muzdalifah*. I recall that night well. I slept on a thin blanket spread over levelled rocks. I stretched out on it, certain of a sleepless night. But I slept. Like a baby. I woke up refreshed and with a Gujrati proverb;

"Sleep cares not about beddings.

Hunger rejects not, cold rice."

The next morning you gather pebbles for the next ritual of "stoning the Satan" at *Mina*.

When Ibrahim agreed to sacrifice his son, the devil made three unsuccessful attempts to dissuade him. A pillar marks each site. At each pillar, pilgrims throw seven pebbles to reenact Ibrahim's steadfastness and rejection of the Satan.

Just when Ibrahim was about to sacrifice his son, God commanded;

"Stop."

And replaced Ismail with a lamb and an amazed Ibrahim saw the carcass of a slaughtered lamb where his sacrificed son should have been.

After the twenty first pebble is cast, pilgrims slaughter a lamb to commemorate God's testing of Ibrahim and Ismail.

All over the world, Muslims do the same and celebrate it with a four day holiday of Idd-el-Hajj. In Zanzibar, a lamb or a goat is sacrificed on behalf of a single hajji. In countries where camels are available, it fulfills the requirement of seven hajjis.

The sacrificial meat is divided into three equal portions and divided among, the poor, the neighbors and the family that sacrificed it

My parents were there before the days of refrigeration. In those days, hajjis performed the slaughter themselves. My mother recalls seeing trenches filled with tons of unconsumed meat.

Now you don't slaughter yourself. The Saudis have built huge abattoirs and factories to do that for you. The meat is canned or frozen and donated to poor countries.

After the sacrifice, Hajjes return to Mecca to perform *Tawaaf* and spend the tenth evening of the Hajj in a tent in Mina. The next day the stone throwing ceremony is repeated.

The last part of the ritual is *Tawaf-el-Wida*—the farewell *Tawaaf*.

You have reached your goal.

You are now a full-fledged hajji.

You may go home.

Very few do. Almost all hajjis spend some time in *Medina* before heading home.

Just because you performed the hajj, you cannot assume that it was valid. After the *neeyut* a glance at your ledger will show millions of sins recorded in the wrong column of your ledger, which began with a balance of zero, on the day you were born. After the *neeyut*, any deviation from the Hajj ritual or an uncharitable though, word or act, voids the Hajj. So strict are the requirements that out of the millions of pilgrims who perform a Hajj, only one does it right.

The Almighty validates that one perfect hajj and that of everyone else who performed it, with that person. A group prayer or a pilgrimage has this advantage over a solo one.

When your hajj is accepted, faster than you can click a mouse, all the figures in the debit column of your lodger get deleted, the recycle bin gets emptied, and your bottom line is better than the day you were born—it has an impressive positive balance.

Now, is the best time to die.

It can be improved upon only by postponing it till you get to Medina

Medina is the second holiest site in Islam. *Masjid el nabwe,* the mosque where the prophet of Islam is buried, is in Medina.

The city is rich in historic sites

I love historical sites—all historical sites. They are a tangible evidence of an event. I was fortunate enough to see *Masjidul Qiblahtain*, the masjid with two qiblas. A *qiblah* is the direction to the *Ka'aba*. During prayers, Muslims all over the world face the *qiblah*. A mosque is easy to identify from the outside. In the middle of the wall facing Mecca, it has a semicircular projection. On the inside of the projection is a niche—an alcove—called a *Mihrab*. The congregation stands in rows behind the Imam and face the *Mihrab*.

Masjidul Kiblatain was built when Islam had just begun and its *qibla* faced Jerusalem. Once Islam was well established, the prophet decided that the *qibla* should be changed towards the Kaaba. His rational was that, Islam, the new kid on the block, should have a unique focal point of its own, rather than share Jerusalem with the older boys, the Jews and the Christians. So, Masjidul Qiblatain added a new *mihrab* that faced Mecca, while retaining its obsolete one, thus becoming unique—a mosque with two *qiblas*—a beautiful reminder of a transition.

There were other sites I wished to see but could not. I wanted to see the moat that was built under the prophet's guidance to fend off an attack by the Qureshi of Mecca. The Qureshi went there to kill the prophet and Islam. Islam was a threat to their business of catering to the idolaters, who for centuries, had been coming to Mecca for pilgrimage. I could not see the moat. It has been levelled by bulldozers

A taxi driver pointed out to me, the site of a well in Medina that the prophet used to get his drinking water from. There was no point in getting a closer look at it. The well has been filled up with dirt and smoothed over so that you cannot even guess where it could have been.

Date trees that the prophet planted have been chopped down.

Every historical site associated with prophet Mohamed has been destroyed lest Muslims start praying to it.

In Islam, pictures, paintings and statues of the prophet are forbidden. This ban is intentional. It is to prevent Muslims from worshipping the likeness of Mohammad and slipping back into idolatry. Mohamed was a messenger. He wanted his followers to focus on his message—not the messenger.

I understand this concern.

However, I part company with those who destroy historical sites associated with the prophet. I have confidence in the monotheistic faith of the Muslims. Lack of old idols will not dissuade those who wish to revert to idolatry.

They can always make new ones.

Next to performing a Hajj, death is an event a Muslim ponders over a lot; infrequently, when young. Frequently, when old.

For a Muslim, the perfect death, is a death in Medina.

It bestows upon that person, the honor of sharing the soil of Medina with the prophet of Islam—till the day Gabriel blows his horn.

When that sound is heard, all the souls resting in Medina will rise and follow the prophet. At heaven's gate, immigration formality is waved for Allah's VIP.

The prophet is the first to enter heaven triumphantly, to the ecstatic cheering of angels. Then by his coat tails, follow those who once rested with him in Medina.

To understand trans-cultural customs and communications, a person has to be familiar with the cultures involved. Not only are the subtle meanings of words lost but even facial expressions and gestures become inscrutable to those who are versed in just one.

Let us consider the words "hot" and "cold".

In Oriental culture, everything has to be categorized into "hot" or "cold". A food or a beverage has to be either "hot" or "cold". It can never be "tepid" or "Chilled." When they call a food "hot", they do not mean the temperature or even the spices in the food. When an Indian refers to ice cream as "hot", he is aware that ice cream feels cold while it is in his mouth. What he means by "hot" is what the ice cream does to him after it has left his stomach. It heats his body.

Tears too are either "hot" or "cold".

I have my doubts about the classification of foods into "hot" and "cold" but the classification of tears into "hot" and "cold" is bang on and physiologically accurate. When a person is happy, first the eyes get chilled. Then the tears flow. These tears feel "cold."

Tears which flow in sorrow, are "hot".

Whenever I could, I used to drop off my children and later my grandchildren at school. In grade school they hugged me and kissed me before getting out of the car. In middle school, after getting out of the car, they looked both ways and if none of their classmates were watching, they pecked me on my cheek before walking to school. When in high school, they just opened the door and ran to school.

In all instances, I watched them till they were safely inside the school. The sight always chilled my eyes.

Because of Hajj both Mecca and Medina have rental properties. Their rental contract is unique. The price for renting it for the ten days of Hajj is the same as renting it for an entire year. How long you occupy the premises is up to you. Those who wish to linger after the Hajj is over, have a free accommodation till the eve of the next Hajj and some do—at least for a week or two. Sooner or later, however, they all go home.

I am sure that there is some sort of a schedule for their return journey, but all modes of transportation in India ran on a highly flexible schedule. You see the returning pilgrims when you see them. You don't get uptight, because your loved one is not among the earliest returnees.

My grandmother waited eagerly for my Grandfather's return. When over half of the pilgrims were back home and he had not shown up, my grandmother's anticipation gave way to apprehension.

Among the stragglers of the returning pilgrims were the ones who had accompanied my grandfather. The entire *Kafila*, the group that travelled together, stopped by at my grandmother's home first—a bad omen.

Without going through the usual pleasantries, they came straight to the point and told her that her husband had passed away <u>in</u> Medina, <u>after</u> he had completed his Hajj.

mind could not accept what she had just heard. In disbelief, her eyes scanned the silent somber faces she had known all her life. They would never lie to her. Not all of them. It must have happened. Her constant companion since the day she got married will never return to her. She will have to continue her life—alone.

While shaking her head from side to side in a denial, she moaned and tears streamed down her cheeks.

The pilgrims sat quietly letting her bereave. Some of them, who were close to the deceased, shed tears in silence.

In a few minutes her sobbing and weeping stopped abruptly.

Her pretty round face stared at the floor. Her mind was deep in thought. She had accepted the death of her husband, now she was processing where and when he died.

After a couple of shallow breaths, a faint smile flickered across her face.

Her eyes chilled.

She changed her gaze from the floor to the visitors

Her proud face was lit up with a smile.

Her eyes glistened with joy.

Then, a torrent of cold tears washed away, the caked hot tears on her cheeks.

Chapter Sixteen

Sikuku[103]

Births and weddings are celebrated in Zanzibar. Just once.

When the occasion is over, the date of the occasion is deleted from communal memory. The occasion may be recalled incidentally, but never celebrated again.

My birth days came and went unnoticed by everyone. Even my mother did not wish me a happy birthday or cook my favorite food on that day. She too never remembered my date of birth, although she could recall that day and the days before and after that, in minute details.

Zanzibari's vaguely understand, doing something special on a wedding anniversary—if you still love your spouse. But they cannot understand, burning a sack full of money on a 50th wedding anniversary party, when the couple has spent their entire married life, hating each other more everyday than the day before.

I see no reason to wake up on my birthday bursting with joy. A year ago today, was just like any other day. As for my day of birth, I recall nothing. But I am certain that on that day I caused

---

[103] Siku = day. Ku = Big.

my mother agony and inconvenienced a lot of good people—not a day to relive. It is a day to live down. I have no good reason to celebrate that day. Why should anyone else? Especially, the ones who have begun having the aches and pains of ageing and actually wish they were younger.

In my culture, the benefits of reaching a birthday of an impressive figure are wisdom and reverence. My six years of practice of solely Geriatrics, has not verified the former but I subscribe heartily to the later.

I did not know, nor did I ever miss, not knowing the date of my birth, till it was time to go to college in Dublin, Ireland. That was when I first learned that the values of foreigners are at variance with ours. To foreigners, my date of birth defines me and identifies me better than my DNA.

Institutions like colleges and travel agencies and utility companies and banks and rental apartments, cannot take the next step in any direction, till they have your date of birth. They are obsessed with the day you were born and do not give a hoot to whether or not the birth was legitimate.

Where I come from, legitimacy of birth or lack of it has profound legal, social and commercial ramifications. It is a hinge, which opens wide a bank door or slams it shut in your face.

My advice to Zanzibari's' going abroad, is this; When in Rome, do as the Romans do and for your sanity's sake, do so without attempting to understand, why they do what they do.

You must wonder, if children in Zanzibar lead a dull life.

They do not.

We have more holidays than any other country that I have been to. We celebrated all Muslim holidays as we were a Sultanate and all English holidays as we were a protectorate of the British Empire. We celebrated the Sultan's birthday and also Queen Elizabeth's birthday and unscheduled birthdays like the day Prince Charles was born.

The difference between celebrations of Zanzibari children and my grandchildren is that my grandchildren's celebrations are anchored around an individual. Ours were all communal.

Our major social events are weddings.

A procession of friends and family of the groom lead by a brass band playing Bollywood hit songs, starts at the grooms door and winds through the streets to the bride's door. Several servants interspersed in the procession carry trays laden with gifts for the bride. Children, who are not related to the groom or the bride, join the procession for the music and the cheerful ambience.

The groom in a turban and a *sherwani* and *Jodhpurs* rides a decorated horse. Like a prince riding through a town he is strategically placed in the middle of the procession and defended by a van and rear guard of the procession.

Literally and figuratively a red carpet is laid out for the groom and his entourage. They walk on a runner with sprinkled rose petals, as members from the bride's family spray rose water on the guests to welcome them

In Muslim homes you do not walk into a home with your shoes on. A groom is no exception. But since he is a groom, he sits on a chair and his best man unties his shoe laces, slips the shoes of and places them in a shoe rack next to the entrance door. The groom is escorted to his chair on a decorated platform. The assembly is all males. Women gather in a different room.

A Mullah performs the ceremony of *Nikah*. A couple of close male relatives of the bride are sent by the Mullah to get the brides consent for the wedding. The persons meet the bride, get her consent and report it to the Mullah. If affirmative, the ceremony commences and ends within thirty minutes, with a prayer for the newlywed. Then we have a sumptuous dinner followed by a music party.

The minor events were engagements and circumcisions.

An engagement is a hen party at the bride's home. Token gifts are exchanged by the engaging couple. The girl usually gets a ring. Men never get rings, even at weddings. The wearing of gold by males is frowned upon. If they wear anything at all, it is silver. I remember discussing this custom with a Mullah and did not get a satisfactory explanation.

There is no party or feasting associated with engagements which like weddings are arranged. An engagement is announced in a communal paper or posted in a mosque bulletin board to spare the remaining foot dragging suitors from an embarrassing snub.

Circumcisions are a major minor event.

The only time in my life I wished I was a girl was when my circumcision was imminent. I remember Abbajaan taking Uncle

Baboo and I to the outpatient department of our hospital. Then there is a gap in my memory. I do not recall the circumcision. The next sequence I can visualize is uncle Baboo and I sharing a rickshaw on our way home.

Ammajaan was anxiously waiting at the door, for her battle ravaged heroes return. We were promptly put on complete bed rest with only bathroom privileges and fed soups and foods appropriate for patients recovering from surgery.

The bed rest lasted a few days, during which a stream of friends and neighbors, visited us. They sympathized with the ordeal we went through and were impressed by the dismissive manner in which we described our surgery. Before leaving, they wished us a speedy recovery while slipping money under our blankets.

Our *Jamatkhana was* used for large gatherings. Men gather on the first floor, which also has a large kitchen for professional cooks to prepare a feast. Women had a separate entrance to a flight of stairs that took them to the second floor. Lunch is the largest meal of the day and feasts are held at that time. Then groggy from satiety and the mid-day heat, everyone heads home for a siesta.

The interval between *Maghreb* and *Isha* prayers is too short—less than two hours—for a social event. *"Baad el Isha",* after *Isha* prayer, is the time for social events. This interval lasts till *fijr* and is the longest segment of the evening, uninterrupted by a prayer. Zanzibari's have a long night life. Even on working days, they don't go to bed till at least midnight. Indian movies do not end till 1AM.

For festive occasions, we went back to the Jamatkhana, for a music party— 'Baad el isha," of course.

Once again, men and women gathered in their segregated areas. The women listen to the music on the first floor through speakers. Light refreshments are served

Usually, we have local amateur singers. The singer, almost always a male, usually accompanies himself on a harmonium. The second important instrument is a tabla, which sets the rhythm. Occasionally there is a string instrument like a s*arangee* or a violin. Any music party which ends before midnight is considered a flop. A successful one goes on into the wee hours.

We have two Idds. The first one, Idd-*el-fitr* follows the end of Ramadan. The second festival is, *Idd-el-Haj* which falls on the last day of Hajj.

Muslims follow the lunar calendar, which is shorter than the Gregorian calendar by at least one day each month. Because of that, *Idds'* fall during different day of the week, different months and even during different seasons.

On Idd, we got up early, took a shower, got into new cloths and went for prayers at a mosque between the *Beit-el-Ajaib* and the sultan's palace.

In retrospect, the choice of that mosque was odd. We went to that mosque only twice a year and only for Idd prayers. The rest of the year we went to the Sunni Masjid close to our home where the Imam and most of the *Jamaat*, (congregation,) were

Sunni *Hanafi*[104] Indians. The Imam and most of the worshipers in the mosque that we went to for Idd prayers were Arabs and probably *ibadhi*[105]

I remember my father telling me about his first Idd in Zanzibar. This was before my mother and I joined him in Zanzibar. A neighbor took him to that mosque, for Idd prayers. Somehow, they got separated before the prayers began. At the end of the prayers, my father stood outside the mosque waiting for the neighbor to take him home.

For an Indian who had just came to Zanzibar, all Arabs looked alike and every person that walked by him looked like the neighbor. Panic must have seized him. The city of Zanzibar is the world's largest maze. It is impossible for a person, not born in Zanzibar, to get home from any point in the city. He must have felt relieved when he figured out that he was talking to the right Arab, when an Arab smiled at him and told him, "Let's go home!"

My father was a person who liked a routine and since he celebrated his first Idd at that mosque, he went back to the same mosque for every Idd after that.

After Idd prayers, it was time to visit friends and neighbors and enjoy treats served only on Idd. In our circle of friends, *Idd milk* was king. It is a beverage served hot, made out of evaporated milk with pistachios, raisins, almonds, and a pinch of saffron.

---

[104] A subsect of Sunni.
[105] The other Sunni subsect.

Yum! *Idd milk* was always served with *"Thambee,"* hair thin vermicelli browned in butter and sprinkled with nuts.

After lunch it is always nap time.

Idd is no exception. My father was a napper. To make certain that he napped undisturbed, he made us take a nap at the same time. We learned very quickly that it was either that or a punishment, so we trained ourselves to nap during my father's nap. A habit forced upon us but not regretted.

Since my childhood, I have always had a short nap after lunch. Even a 15 minute nap refreshes me and waking up from it, is like starting a new day. The nap made it possible for me to put in twelve to fourteen hour days often demanded of a physician.

The only time I have semi regretted taking a nap was a week before I retired from VPA—Visiting Physicians Association. The firm does only house calls. We had cars provided by VPA and a medical assistant. The assistant drove the car and helped the physicians provide care to patients in their homes. In between patients, I sat in the back seat doing paper work while my assistant drove to the next patient. When convenient, we took a break for lunch. While my assistant went into a fast food place for lunch, I ate my "Brown paper bag" lunch and took a ten to fifteen minute nap in the driver's seat, as it has more leg room.

I was awakened by an ambulance driver tapping on the window of the door on the driver's side. His ambulance was parked by my car. I heard sirens which stopped as soon as the police car pulled up and stopped behind me and then I heard the clanging of a fire engine which screeched to a stop behind the ambulance. The emergency vehicles arrival blocked the traffic in both directions on the two way street.

Traffic backed up in both directions.

Cars honked out of frustration.

Windows flung open, on both sides of the street.

Heads popped out of windows.

Dozens of nosy eyes peered.

I rolled down my window and the ambulance driver anxiously asked;

"Are you alright?"

In annoyance and with a partially suppressed yawn, I answered; "I am fine. Why do you ask?"

"A lady in the fifth floor on your right reported an unconconcious driver in a stationary car"

4:00 p.m. is Tea Time in Zanzibar. A custom the English picked up from us. At teatime a substantial snack is served to tide you over till dinner which is around 8 PM. Unlike the English, we boiled tea leaves for about three minutes then let it steep a while. Some families added a tea masala and/or sugar. We added only cardamom peels.

Tea time is also an exploratory social invitation to a new acquaintance. It is also a cheap way of fulfilling a social obligation to a large group of people you do not particularly care to spend much face to face time with.

On both Idds and on the next three days after that, a fair takes place at *Mnazimoja*. When one thinks of Typhoons, one correctly associates it with South East Asia. In 1872, the only recorded typhoon hit Zanzibar. It uprooted all but one coconut tree and gave the area its name, *Mnazimoja*—a Kiswahili word for "a lone coconut tree". Today, there is no coconut tree in *Mnazimoja*. The one that survived the hurricane was chopped down to create a, half a mile square level area with two cricket and one soccer field. A ground for field hockey was just north of Mnazimoja, and south of the tower of The Cable and Wireless Company. Kikwajuni Road separated the two fields.

Mention the word *"Mnazimoja"* to any Zanzibari and his eyes will get misty. Every one of us harbors a moment of triumph on this field that we have recalled with joy innumerable times. The kick, that scored the winning goal. The perfectly timed swing of a bat that sent a cricket ball out of Mnazimoja and in to the fairway of the English golf club. The thrill of a catch at the slips, off the bat of the star batsman of your rival team. Mnazimoja, created such moments for Zanzibaris' to treasure and recall with nostalgia.

If you ask uncle Baboo, his moment has to be the day Abbajaan hugged him in front of a jubilant crowd at cricket pavilion #1, as he was walking back from the pitch, waving his bat that had scored eighty two runs, to give victory to the Sunni Cricket Club.

You will have to ask the younger uncles their moment in the sun at *Mnazimoja*. I left home for college before that.

For four days, *Mnazimoja* is converted into a fair ground. The concept is similar to the agricultural fairs we have in the Mid-West, except it has nothing to do with agriculture and everything to do with fun.

The field is lined with temporary stalls. As children, our first stop, of course, was the toy stalls. Then we sought out the entertainment stalls. Our favorite was the *"Karagosi"* tent. For ten cents, we were entertained for fifteen minutes by the puppets *Karagosi* and *Fatuma* with their skits in squeaky Kiswahili.

There were also tents for belly dancers, magicians and freaks

The human mind finds fright entertaining and no fair is complete without amusements that induce it. The more fright they can generate, the more popular they get. We got our share of it on a Ferris wheel. It had four benches. Each could sit two (small) children. The contraption was hammered together by a local carpenter who chose to remain anonymous. It did not have a brake or a motor. Those functions were performed by three burly Waswahilis.

As I look back, the memory of those rides frighten me more now, than they did then. Those rides were not inspected or licensed. That I survived those and other childhood adventures is a miracle I believe in.

Food tents did a brisk business. Since we are multi ethnic we had a wide variety of foods to choose from.

As we got older, our choices of entertainment evolved. First to get skipped were the toy shops, then the puppet shows and finally the rides. At puberty the only reason to go there was girl watching. After marriage, even that is not much of an incentive and we skip the fair till the first child is a few years old.

Then the child and his Dad sitting next to him laugh at the antics of *Karagosi* and *Fatuma*.

Then the child goes through the phases his Dad did.

The last day of Idd is like the last day of any holiday. You go to bed with a heavy heart. However in Zanzibar, you fall asleep to the cheering anticipation of the next Holliday—which is always, just around the corner.

Chapter Seventeen

A Ride to Die for.

Ammajaan's funeral was the first American funeral in the Qureshi family. Like most funeral parlors in the US, her parlor also was palatial with extravagant interior decor. We were escorted by somber ushers in designer suits wearing Rolex watches to a "private" room, where Ammajaan lay in an open casket..

Her teeth appeared clenched her expression that of a daunting fighter. She had died of status epilepticus[106]. I thought that after death the facial muscles relaxed but they hadn't. It was not an expression of the mother I knew.

In sorrow, I gazed at her for a while.

The tide of values she had taught me was in a flow and each advice was a wave crashing emphatically on the embankment at the Forodhani of Zanzibar.

Here lay a person who admonished me against getting into debt and if absolutely unavoidable, to repay it as quickly as possible and she left suddenly, while I was still holding a fistful of IOU's to her. She drilled into me never to be in debt and then left me suddenly and indebted to her. I had not done enough for her. I was

---

[106] A prolonged epileptic seizure without a break

too busy making a living. Retirement was just around the corner and that is when I had planned to set aside time, to look after her.

Now, that was not possible.

I was thwarted, then frustrated and finally angry.

Retirement will soon be here and those extra free hours assigned to her care, will be spent in sorrow and in guilt.

Even though I did not turn around to look, I sensed impatience in those in the row behind me. I raised my hands, palms up, and said *"Surat el fatiha*[107]*"*, then swept my hands across my face.

I took one last look at her, leaned over and kissed her right cheek, left the casket and walked over to sit on an empty chair.

As I sat down, I realized that I had just kissed a dead person.

It felt strange.

It was like kissing an ice cube.

She was in a funeral home refrigerator for several days to allow time for all her children to make it to her funeral.

My mind went back to a time, when we were alone in our family room in Monroe when she had wondered about this day.

"Before me," she said, "no one in my family had been out of even Gujrat and here I am a world traveler. Who knows how much more I shall travel and which country's dirt, I shall mingle with."[108]

---

[107] Islamic equivalent of the Lord's prayer.
[108] "Where I will get buried."

Of course, neither of us could have guess that. But, if we were still in Zanzibar, her funeral would have been predictable.

Funerals in Zanzibar are an impromptu communal responsibility. We have no funeral homes, hearses or even a refrigerator large enough to accommodate a human body. Embalming and cremation is forbidden. Most villages do not have illuminated roads and cemeteries. Almost all Islamic countries are in hot climates and burial in the few hours before sunset, a necessity.

Even the children of the deceased who live in Dar-es-salaam or Pemba miss the funeral. A son or daughter who went on an errand to a *chhamba*[109] could return home in the evening and get stunned by the news of a parent's death—and miss the burial.

Within minutes of the last breath, a crier is out announcing the death and a few young volunteers skip work and go to *Chungani*[110] cemetery, to dig a grave. Within an hour, the body undergoes *Gusul*[111] by the deceased's child of the same sex, wrapped in a *Kafan*[112] and sent to a mosque for a funeral prayer and then the body is placed in a bier.

The bier is a simple wooden stretcher with four handles. The body is covered by a lid which is covered by a rug inscribed with verses from the Qur'an.

---

[109] A farm.
[110] The cemetery for the Sunni Muslims.
[111] Bathing
[112] A white muslin cloth.

The all-male funeral procession begins at the mosque and proceeds to *Chungani,* which is about a mile from the southern edge of stone town.

A lead person chants;

"La illaha illalah wa Muhammadun rasulullah[113]"

And the procession repeats the same chant in a chorus;

Each handle of the bier rests on the shoulder of a mourner. The burden and the privilege of carrying the deceased are shared equally by the procession.

After walking about a dozen steps, the two carriers in the front are relieved by two fresh mourners. The ones, who were just relieved from the front two handles, slow down and relieve the two mourners carrying the rear two handles, who walk briskly to get ahead of the bier and wait in one of the two lines to get their turn to carry the front two handles.

The deceased who are fortunate, end their life's journey with a ride on the shoulders of all their sons. For days, a stagnant cloud of disbelief and sorrow, hangs over a neighborhood, after a funeral, in which, it is the father's shoulder which, gave a ride to his son or daughter.

Unfortunately, we were not in Zanzibar. We were at the Green Hills Funeral home, in Palos Verdes, California.

I accepted a different funeral ritual with a shrug of my shoulders as I thought;

---

[113] There is no God but Allah and Muhammad is his prophet.

"*Desh tewo ves*[114]"

The murmur of small talk in the gathering stopped suddenly. My peripheral vision noticed uncle Mac standing up from his chair. I shifted my gaze to bring him in my central vision.

I believe he was about to give an eulogy, but barley a couple of words left his lips when the room, as though on a cue, burst into a wail and hugged the nearest person.

Aunty Zarina was nearest me. We hugged each other tightly and let our tears roll down on our partners back. When everyone had cried out their hearts, there was a decrescendo in the crying as everyone began to regain their composure and wiping their wet cheeks.

Soon, the last person's wailing trailed off into a silence.

For two breaths, the room was still and silent.

Then the murmur of small talk resumed.

Soon it was time for the funeral prayer. As the eldest son, it was my privilege to be the *Imam*[115] at Ammajaan's funeral prayer. I stood alone in the first row. Behind me were rows of male mourners. The last rows were formed by females

The prayer began without a preceding *azaan*[116].

That was correct, but did not feel right.

---

[114] A Gujrati proverb ;"You dress the way people dress in the country you are in"
[115] Leader.
[116] A Muezzin's call to prayer.

Soon after a child is born, it is made *pak* with a bath, then wrapped in a blanket and the midwife exclaiming; "*Mubarak Ho*". '*Mubarak Ho.*[117]" presents the child to the proud father. Beaming with joy, the father cradles the child in his left arm. Then, he whispers in the child's left ear, the first words the newborn hears—the Azaan[118].

This *azaan* is not followed by a prayer. The unused *azaan* is carried forwards untill death and cashed in at that child's funeral prayer, to mark the end of his temporal life and the beginning of a new one.

I looked back to see if everyone was ready. They were.

I raised both my hands and as my thumbs touched my ear lobes, I said out loud,

"*Allahu akber*[119]"

Then folded my hands at my waist.

"*Allahu akber.*" Responded the crowd, touched their ears with their thumbs and folded their hands in front of them as I started reciting "*Surat-el-fatiha*"

Spoken Arabic is harsh on the ears. Like German, it has grating and guttural sounds and sounds that I associate with clearing of the throat and choking on a hunk of steak.

---

[117] Congratulatins.Congratulations.
[118] The Muezzin's call to a prayer
[119] God is great

This was the first time I was an Imam of a large gathering. There was no PA system. And I had to recite loudly. Although I did not understand a word of what I was reciting, the sounds were as soothing to me as a mother's lullaby is to her cranky baby.

A language that tortures ears can also sooth them with music.

Omar ibn Khatab, a sworn enemy of nascent Islam, was bent on nipping Islam in the bud. One day as he was walking by his sister's house, he overheard his sister reading the *Qu'ran*. Normally, the short fused Omar would have killed her on the spot but instead, he was charmed into standing still. He froze in his steps and just stood and listened. The more he listened, the more he became convinced that only God can compose verses with such meaning and music.

It was at this moment, that he became a champion of Islam and went on to become the founder of Cairo, Egypt and a Caliph of Islam.

I used to be skeptical of such stories. Now, they are credible.

The rest of that *namaaz*[120] is a blur . I believe the casket was carried in a hearse which parked by the closest curb to the gravesite. Plaques marking graves are level with the ground and almost concealed by grass. There are no crosses or monuments jutting out of the lawn, which gently slopes down to a highway like a golf course fairway. Beyond the highway, is an unobstructed view, of the calming Pacific Ocean.

---

[120] Prayere.

A plain pine coffin was transferred out of the hearse and onto a bier which was then carried to the gravesite, the way it is done in Zanzibar

I took several turns at carrying the bier and got relieved by Californians I did not know but were obviously friends of my three siblings in California.

In a funeral procession, conversation is considered disrespectful of the deceased. To prevent the congregation from distracting to their pressing temporal problems, a lead chanter recites;

La illaha illallah wa Muhammadun rasullah"[121]

And the procession occupies its mind by echoing the same phrase.

I took another turn at carrying the bier and my thoughts went back to the times when what I was doing at that very moment, almost happened several times.

I relived her acute asthmatic attacks. As the oldest child, it was my job to fetch the doctor when Ammajaan had one of her attacks in the wee hours of the night.

We did not have a telephone and most doctors didn't have one either. I walked to the doctor's home, rang his door bell and had him follow me on foot to our home while I carried his doctor's bag.

Ammajaan sat in bed holding on to a bed post, unable to speak and drenched in perspiration. Every breath was an immense

---

[121] There is no God but Allah and Muhammad is his prophet.

physical effort. Every labored inspiration caused a wheeze that could be heard across the home.

The doctor's demeanor was always calm and reassuring. After a history and a listen with a stethoscope, he usually gave her a shot. Under his breath, the doctor always whispered *"Bismillah*[122]*"*, and then slowly squirted the medicine in her vein. He always hung around to make sure that the attack was well controlled before leaving her bedside.

Then, her lips turned blue—a sign I associated with the end of her attack. Her breathing would slow down; her muscles relaxed and she would mercifully collapse into a long deprived sleep. I witnessed dozens of those spells.

Her holding on to the bed post was to recruit her accessory muscles of respiration, an ominous sign that I have observed only twice in my thirty years of the practice of Pulmonary Medicine. The sweating was due to the onset of respiratory acidosis. I learned that from an anesthesiologist during my surgical rotation at Baggot Street Hospital in Dublin. The poor anesthesiologist, in 1961 Ireland, did not have an O2 Sat.[123] He made a living guided only by clinical signs of the patients he had put to sleep.

---

[122] "In the name of Allah". Perfectly credible, if the doctor was a Muslim. But Ammajaan was convinced that Dr. Dinanath said that too. Dr. Dinanath was a Hindu from the Punjab. Smart doctor, he was. When all you can offer as a doctor is a prayer, why not do it in that patient's religion?

[123] An equipment to measure the oxygen saturation of blood.

The blue lips were due to a low level of oxygen saturation. Curing blue lips was easy. Just turn up the oxygen flow. Somnolence was due to the onset of muscle fatigue, CO_2 retention and impending CO_2 narcosis. Sweating meant alveolar hypoventilation and respiratory acidosis and it called for more rapid and deeper breaths with the Ambu bag[124].

What I considered to be signs of improvement, were clinical signs of a patient knocking on death's door.

She made it through all of them through sheer will power.

The reason?

She had little children to take care of.

Even as a ten year old boy, I understood what fueled those valiant fights.

My mind then flashed forwards to her spell in Medina, Saudi Arabia.

To make her life complete her final wish was a "Family Hajj". She wanted all her "babies" with her for a Hajj and for us to do *Umra*[125] for Abbajaan.

We agreed.

From then on, Ammajaan lived on cloud nine. Every time she had company, before the visit was over, she always managed to maneuver the conversations to her upcoming Hajj.

---

[124] A bellows like gadget to force in more air during inspiration.
[125] A mini Hajj that can be performed on behalf of a deceased person. An "Umra" bestows upon a deceased grace, after his death.

The anticipated response, of course, was;

"Amen. May Allah fulfill your wish! And with all your children too! How wonderful! What a……….. !" "Wow!"

But that response was not enough. Ammajaan did not drop the topic till she heard;

"I know of no one else who has done that."

Only then, she would allow the flow of conversation to divert to another topic.

Unfortunately, the "perfect" Hajj that Ammajaan sang and danced about ,did not happen.

Uncle Mac had his first heart attack just a month before our departure.

In those days, the recommended period of recuperation was six months. No work, no stresses, no driving and no travelling till your six month stress EKG cleared you.

The family had two choices.

Postpone the "Family Hajj" till next year or go without Uncle Mac.

We had already sent in a large nonrefundable deposit on our all-inclusive trip, arranged by a mosque in Los Angeles. We decided to go without Uncle Mac. We expected to do it again within a year or two anyway. Uncle Mac could join us then.

During the Hajj, Ammajaan was euphoric. She had done her first hajj with Abbajaan in the 1950's. The wealth from oil drilling had yet to trickle down to the infrastructure. She told us about how the Saudi's looked forwards to hajj. For centuries, the hajj was the main source of Saudi Arabia's economy and hajjis were welcome with open arms..

Our first steps on the soil of Saudi Arabia were in Jeddah. I was impressed with Jeddah airport. It is an ultramodern airport with a unique architecture. From air, it looks like an oasis with dozens of tents pitched in a desert. The airport has all the modern amenities that money can buy.

We missed our connection to Medina, and had to spend over 24 hours in that airport before we could board a plane to Medina. It was the most comfortable layover I have ever had at any airport. We shopped. I remember buying aunty Sharifah her first wrist watch during the layover. We ate breakfast of pancakes stuffed with fried eggs and ground beef made to order while we waited. Five times daily, the PA system blared out the *azaans* and there was a spacious opulent mosque in the airport which made you look forwards to the prayers.

Ammajaan was there before all this was built and pointed out to us a place that held a real tent where a couple of officers with a rubber stamp sat behind an orange crate, stamping away passports of arriving Hajjes and *Mualims*[126] fiercely competed to offer their services.

While we were in medina Ammajaan got an asthma attack.

I still remember a young Arab-American medical student on our chartered bus who was sniffling, sneezing and coughing in

---

[126] Locals who guided you through the Hajj ritual for a living.

our air conditioned bus, with recirculated air. Naturally, most of us caught his flu and had a miserable time. To Ammajaan, it caused pneumonia and an extreme exacerbation of her asthma. It was the worst attack of her life.

During the peak of the crisis and with thirty years of pulmonary medicine under my belt, I pronounced to myself, "This is it."

It was a moment of "Sweet sorrow."

I will be sad and will miss her

The end of life is inevitable. Almost all of us have no choice over where that will occur. Ammajaan had the choice of departing from Medina[127]. Not any old Medina but from THE Medina—Al Medina al Munawwarah.

Miraculously, she fought her way out of it, and made me feel guilty at what I had thought and hoped would happen.

By the next morning, Ammajaan had improved so much that I accepted that the crisis was over.

I thought to myself,

"Well, it will not happen this time. *Insha allah*[128], it will happen next time, when all of us, including Uncle Mac, are here."

The next day, although still very weak, she decided to accompany us to a mosque. When we left the mosque, I held her left

---

[127] Several countries have cities named Medina. Literally, Medina is a city.
[128] God willing.

hand in my left hand and with my right arm wrapped around her waist, we walked a few steps to a waiting taxi.

It was hot and I was tired, sleep derived and irritable. As we were walking, in between her breaths, she wedged in a word or two. When strung together, the words said, "Excuse me if I do not talk to you while we walk."

No matter how hard her breathing was, she believed it is impolite not to engage those around you in a conversation

My head imploded and I thought to myself,

"Ya Allah ! Why can't you stop being polite when you are not up to it? Save your breath for the walk. Why is a negative evaluation of your social etiquette by anyone—including your son—so important? Why do you care about what anyone thinks or says about anything?"

When I calmed down that thought made my guilt worse.

Yelling in my head at my mother, when she just got through an almost fatal attack?

Not nice.

"*La ilahaillalah wa Muhammaden rasulullah*" said the lead chanter, and the procession responded to the chant in a chorus.

Now, my mother's bier was about half way down to the open grave.

Each of my leg weighed a ton. I sighed more then I breathed. My thinking was slow, labored and obsessed by a single reverberating word.

"Why? Why? Why?"

Why now?

Why not when we were in Medina?

She deserved it.

I cannot think of a better mother then her.

"Why? Why? Why?"

I was carrying the right front handle of the bier. While shaking my head from side ti side in disbelief, I kept asking over and over again

"Why? Why? Why?" while the lead chanter kept chanting;

La illaha illallah wa Muhammadun rasullulah"

And the procession chorused back;

La illaha illallah wa Muhamadun rasullulah"

I took several turns at carrying the bier. Several Californians who I did not know did the same. I also handed over the bier handle to uncles Baboo, Moin and Munir and the hand overs felt right.

Why? Why? Why? My obsessed mind continued.

I took another turn at carrying the bier. Uncle Mac approached me to take over the handle. I handed it over to him and waited a few steps to relieve the person holding up the rear handle behind me. As I waited, I saw the back of uncle Mac carrying the front handle.

In a flash, the answer to my; "Why?" "Why?" "Why?" shuddered through me, like a bolt of lightning.

It was as though, my mind had taken a video of my tossing up into the air, pieces of a jigsaw puzzle from its open box and while I was staring at the puzzling pieces on the floor, my mind reversed the tape. Pieces flew off the floor to their correct place in the box and in my hand was a pictorial answer to my question, "Why?" "Why?" "Why?"

"That's it!" "That's it" "That's it!"

It was <u>because</u>, uncle Mac was not with us in Medina.

I answered my own question, as I relieved the man carrying the right rear handle behind me.

As a man, I had projected onto my mother, what I would have chosen for myself—a death in Medina. An error I have made over and over again because I have evaluated both heaven and earth from a man's perspective. Her super human fight to cheat death once again, – and in of all places, Medina—now made perfect sense.

As a child, my mother taught me everything I know about Islam. One of the *hadiths*[129] she mentioned was;

"Heaven lies beneath your mother's feet".

---

[129] Sayings of Prophet Muhammad. These sayings are his opinions as a person, not as a messenger of Allah. Hadiths carry wisdom but not the weight that Qu'ranic verses do. Qur'anic verses are the words spoken by Allah.

She knew that once she became a mother, she had transcended into a world that men do not comprehend and even if they do, cannot aspire to enter it.

It is a circle where members are irrevocably guaranteed a place in *Jannatul Firdous*—the First class section of heaven, reserved for angels—and mothers.

A mother knows where her ultimate home is and with absolute impunity, chooses her penultimate home.

Ammajaan turned down a funeral in Medina in favor of a funeral in California so that all her sons could carry her bier to her grave.

Ammajaan entered Green Hills Cemetery as spectacularly as Cleopatra had entered Rome. Of the two, Ammajaan's entry exuded absolute authority. Cleopatra had no say in who carried her. Ammajaan did.

The engulfing somber fog lifted like an untethered helium balloon. My eyes sprinkled ice cold tears. My skin pores squirted joy. My right hand shot up and groped for the handle of an open umbrella, my feet tap danced and my heart belted out for the whole world to hear;

"Oh when the saints, go marching in.

Oh when the saints go marching in.

I wanna be, in that number,

When the saints go marching in."

ZANZIBAR

A New Orleans Funeral

CHAPTER EIGHTEEN

A Gift From The Gods.

In 1999, I signed up for a week of a Cardiology "Mini residency" at the University of Florida in Miami. I flew to Melbourne three days before the course started, to visit Champak, a friend I met, during my years at college in Nairobi. We were meeting again, after forty two years.

The last time we met was when I was on my way to Dublin to begin my medical studies and we met in my cabin in the Breamer Castle while she had docked in Mombasa .When he returned to Nairobi, he had to cremate his mother in law who had passed away during the hour he spent with me in Mombasa.

We lost all contact during the subsequent four decades. After a career of teaching in England, he decided to enjoy his retirement in Florida. He invited me to visit him after he acquired my phone number from a mutual friend.

Since the last time we met, I often wondered if the reason we had not met earlier was a superstitious compulsion to avert another disaster like the one after visiting me in Mombasa.

During my flight to Florida, I wondered if the four decades had changed his appearance. It hadn't. Apart from thinning hair through which you could see his scalp and graying hair on his temples he looked the same. He even weighed the same as he did when we were in college. I recalled his secret. He always stopped eating when almost satiated. Sometime during the past forty years he had taken up smoking and enjoying Scotch before supper. Apart from that he was still the same good old Champak.

We talked in Gujrati, as we used to when we shared a college dorm in Nairobi and the forty year interval vanished and I felt like we were continuing an unfinished discussion which was interrupted yesterday.

He lived in Gujarat and active in Mahatma Gandhi's *Sutyagraha* movement. He was at a high risk of injuries from the *lathis*[130] of the police and spending years in jail as an agitator. I suspect that his parents feared for his safety and coerced him into moving to Kisumu to work in his uncle's pharmacy.

Overnight, that small town on the shores of Lake Victoria became a tourist destination attracting hordes of tourists.

Kisumu is the ancestral home of President Barack Obama. The president's father, a Lou,[131] was born near Kisumu and his grandmother, aunts, uncles and nephews still live here.

Champak worked for his uncle for a couple of years, had a falling out with him and decided to go to a college to become a teacher.

That's where we shared a dorm and did homework together.

---

[130] A staff, that Indian police use instead of truncheons.
[131] A tribe in Kenya..

He was a *vanya*.₂ Sound business principles were ingrained in his genes. Because of his business background, the college put him in charge of our canteen—really, a locked closet with soft drinks and snacks.

No matter when a student wanted a bottle of Pepsi or a chocolate bar, Champak would walk from the dorm, across a soccer field sized lawn and into the main building, to open the closet and make a sell.

His "business" was open 24/7/365.

This is the business ethic that brought the *Vaniyas*[132] commercial prosperity in East, Central and South Africa during the first half of the twentieth century and has made gas stations and the Ma & Pa motels all over the USA, a successful venture during the second half.

While in Kisumu, one night, he woke up from a sound sleep overwhelmed by an unexplainable grief and he cried himself to sleep. The next morning, the problem son, received a telegram stating that his father had passed away. I believe he lost his mother after he finished college.

My mother had passed away several years ago but I was still in bereavement. Her untimely death had cheated me out of an opportunity to take care of her in her old age. My goal was to work to see my children through college and then retire and take care of her. When she passed away, I had achieved almost all my goals, except the last one.

---

[132] The merchant cast.

When I met him in Melbourne, his mind had had forty years to adapt to a life without parents. He listened to my regret with the faint indulgent smile of a person who has been there and has the answers up his sleeve.

"Don't believe the TV commercials. There is nothing glamorous about the 'Golden years.'

To wish that your parents had lived longer is to wish to prolong life's ugly rear end. Parents who trained for a profession do not start a family till they are in their thirties. By the time their children retire those parents are in their eighties or nineties

Most of them suffer the unrelenting pain of osteoarthritis, the constant fear of becoming physically dependent on others after an unexpected stroke, the fear of losing their mind from Alzheimer and worse of all, surrendering their dignity in the presence of their loved ones;

Is that 'living'?"

I turned my head from side to side in agreement.

During the last weeks of her life, my mother was a bedridden quadriplegic with a tracheostomy and a feeding tube. I did not wish to prolong that. I was for "Do not resuscitate" and against any extra ordinary measures to keep her alive.

"But, we do know friends who had a chance to do *sewa* [133] for their parents," I persisted.

"Yes. Those parents were married in their late teens.

---

[133] A Hindu word for serving parents with overtones of duty and honor.

Don't envy them.

They too feel the way you do."

With his head, he traced several lazy eights in the air in front of him. Indians convey better with their heads then with their tongues. That gyration when translated, is close to;

"I swear upon my mother's ashes that what I am saying is true."

Unconvinced, I asked;

"They do? Why? If I had their good fortune, I would not complain."

Champak went into a deep thought. His mind was sifting through several possible answers. His eyes were focused somewhere between him and I. After a few moments, he focused on my face and said;

"Suppose I have the ability to turn the clock of time back."

"Okay."

"You are retired and your parents are self-reliant, in good health and without dementia. You have ten years, free from all encumbrances, to do your *sewa* your way."

"Great"

He let me ponder till he felt I had lived through those years.

"Your ten years are up and you have had your wish. Now how do you feel?"

"Better."

"Just better? Do you need another ten years?"

"No."

I sensed what he was driving at. Another ten or even twenty years will not make me feel that I had paid off my debt in full. I will still feel that I had not done enough. The debt Is unrepayable.

"Your guilt is due to the misuse of the word "debt." It is a commercial concept which my cast and I worship and live by. A bank profits from interest it charges on loans, which never exceed the ability of the debtor to repay in time or the collateral banks demand. Commercial words and principles have no place in family affairs. What your parents did for you is not a 'debt.' As long as you think of it as a "debt" you will feel miserable. Start thinking that you owe them nothing."

"I owe my parents nothing?"

With his eyes fixed on my puzzled face, he threw his knockout punch.

"*Maat, Peeta, Guru Devum.*[134]

It was a gift from the gods."

"A gift?'

He started nodding his head up and down rhythmically while his point sunk in. When he thought it had, he continued;

"Yes, a gift—an unconditional one. Like your life and their love"

---

[134] Your mother, your father and your teachers are gods"

He did not wait for my response and gave me the cure for my guilt;

"Just accept the gift. And do your best to emulate them".

The human mind needs time to adapt to the finality of death. That is a good thing. It allows a mind to remain clear and functional to take care of the funeral and the unexpected and important legal and financial decisions that need immediate attention.

The best time for emotional support from friends, is after the funeral and when the mind is going through the phase of depression.

Death was a taboo subject even among healthcare workers till Elizabeth Kubler-Ross dissected and teased out, the phases a bereaved mind goes through, in her classic text book "On death and dying."

If there are no psychological obstacles, after a variable amount of time, most persons who had a healthy childhood accept their parents death as an inevitable end of every life.

My father's was the first death in our family when I was in my fifties. We had his 8 by 10 portrait on a book shelf in our home in Monroe. For years, with averted eyes, I walked by it quickly to avoid sadness and tears

In our current home, we have a portrait of both my parents on a wall in grandma's sewing room. Occasionally, I go in that room to look out of the front window to check on how much snow has built up on our driveway or to determine if the front lawn needs mowing.

Now, on my way out, I linger at that portrait.

I do so, because memories of the joyous events we shared, flood my mind.

I leave the room happy and as I do so, I look at them and say;

"Thank you for your gifts."

The picture in the sewing room.

CHAPTER NINETEEN

The Staircase

We lived in a two story house in Kibokoni. The main entrance on the first floor faces north towards Christ Church Cathedral. Like all the houses in Zanzibar, there is no name or a number on the door—or anywhere else. That information is redundant. Everyone in Zanzibar knows who lives in which house.

To the left of the main entrance, was *Majuri's* one room "studio" apartment. To the right was a two room apartment that Mr. and Mrs. Boyd lived in. There were three more two room apartments south of the stairs.

"*Majuri*"—I never knew his real name—was from the *Punjab*[135]. "Punjab" literally means "the land of the five rivers." The rivers: Beas, Sutlaj, Ravi, Chenab and Jhelum, like the fingers on a hand, are almost equidistant from each other and nourish well, one of the five great wheat growing regions of the world.

He could speak Punjabi[136] but there was no one in Kibokoni that he could converse with in that language. Like all Punjabis he also spoke Urdu and through his trade, fluent Kiswahili.

---
[135] A state in northern India.
[136] The language of Punjab. A resident of Punjab.

He dressed in, a *sulwar*[137], a waistcoat over his *kamiz*[138] and a turban with a tail. The Sikh, another community from the Punjab, wears turbans without a tail. Unlike the *Rajasthani's*[139] who wear dazzling colored turbans, the Punjabi turbans are of a subdued color.

On his right shoulder he carried a small suit case with multiple small compartments containing tiny perfume bottles. Perfume, even in the half ounce size, is too expensive for the average inhabitant of *Ng'ambo*[140]. *Majuri* bought the largest size he could get, and transferred them into tiny affordable bottles.

He crisscrossed *Ng'ambo* hawking;

"*Mafuta Majuri*"[141]

When he first started hawking perfume and did not know Kiswahili well, he cried *"Majuri"* instead of the tongue twisting; *"Mzuri."* The sharp eared Waswahilis noticed the mispronunciation.

In Kiswahili culture, it is kinder to mispronounce a word in a conversation rather than embarrass a stranger with the correct pronunciation. If they were interested in his wares, they responded with;

---

[137] Loose trousers.
[138] A shirt.
[139] From the state of Rajasthan.
[140] The area east of the stone town with huts.
[141] Perfume.

THE STAIRCASE

'*Kariba, Bwana Majuri*"[142]

That is the reason he became better known as *Bwana*[143] *Majuri*.

He was a kind, considerate and a polite gentleman who was equally at ease with men, women and children.

Our daily newspapers were only in Gujrati and English. He did not subscribe to either as he could not read or speak those languages. He was not an intellectual. He had a wife and a child in Punjab that he hoped to bring over as soon as he could afford a larger apartment.

When we were children, Hamisi, a Mswahili friend, and I often visited him and discussed local gossip. In his company, we felt like grownups.

By late afternoon, he returned home. We had a well in our backyard where he drew water and bathed. He used to smear yogurt on his head to shampoo it. I asked my mother if she had observed that in Gujrat. She had not. Probably, it is a Punjabi custom and the benefits from a yogurt shampoo, known only to the Punjabis.

He then cooked for himself. I can see why in *Punjabi*[144] the word "*roti*" is synonymous with dinner. They are huge. They certainly comprise most of a Punjabi's caloric intake. The *rotis* Gujratis eat are paper thin. Punjabi *roti* is at least half an inch thick, made out of whole wheat flour and sautéed slowly over a small

---

[142] Welcome, Mr. Majuri."
[143] 143 An honorific. Like "Sir," Strangers and elders are addressed as "Bwana"
[144] The language of Punjab

flame from a Kerosene burner. The size of this *roti*—called *parathas*--is the hallmark of the staple diet of Punjab.

He did not eat rice. Rice does not grow in Punjab. He did not eat fish. Punjab is landlocked. I have never seen him cook chicken or red meat. He ate only *roti*, vegetables and *dal*[145]. His diet said eloquently, that he was from the Punjab and a Hindu.

Muslim Punjabis rarely eat vegetables or dal. They eat meat—all kinds of meats—and lots of it.

Every Hindu home I have been in has a portrait or a statue of a Hindu god. *Majuri* had neither. He was not a practicing Hindu.

When *Majuri* was done with his meal and cleaning up his kitchen, he discarded any leftover dal and vegetables. He always had a little left over *roti* even if it entailed ending his meal not fully satiated.

He broke up left over *roti* into little bits. He then walked to his open door with a bowl of bits of roti in his left hand and with his right; he tossed the bits into the air yelling;

"*Injo khunguru yangu.*" [146]

And the squawking, circling *khungurus* caught the pieces in midair.

The ritual was a familiar entertainment in Kibokoni.

After he fed his *khungurus*, he played records on his gramophone. I do not recall it, but my mother tells me that as soon

---

[145] A bean soup.
[146] Come, my crows"

THE STAIRCASE

as I heard *Majuri* play the gramophone, I ran down and listened to the records with him and ignored her pleas to come up for dinner—the reason, my parents purchased their first gramophone.

After my nap, the day before I left Zanzibar for Dublin, I heard *Majuri* yell ;

"Injo khunguru yangu".

I put on my *champals* [147] and went down to let an old friend know that I was about to leave for Ircland. All Zanzibari's are familiar with England, not so with Ireland. To skip an explanation between England and Ireland, I used the word "England" or *"Ulaya*[148]*"* instead of Ireland.

When I met him at his door, he still had a crumb to toss. He gave me an acknowledging smile and I waited for him to toss the last crumb with an;

"Injo khunguru yangu".

I told him of my trip to "England" and like a true friend he was sincerely happy for me.

His parting advice was;

"Study hard. Play a little, but not too much. Make your parents proud. Come home soon with an English diploma—and without an English wife."

---

[147] Sandals.
[148] Literally, Europe. "Ulaya ingressa" is the correct word for England. However, "Ulaya" is used synonymously with England.

We both chuckled at the humor coated admonishment in the last clause. A son retuning home, with a foreign bride, is a universal parental dread.

To get to the second story, you entered the house by the main door on the first floor, walked about ten paces south, then turned left towards the bottom of the flight of stairs and climbed up northwards for about 15 steps to get to the second story.

The stairs was made of inch thick solid boards of teak. Teak is durable. Insects avoid it as it has a natural insecticide in it. Even when exposed to sun and rain, teak can last for over four centuries.

The reason we do not have ancient Hindu palaces and temples in India is because they were made of teak. Those structures are now part of Indian dust. The only place I have seen teak temples is in Nepal. These were built less than a couple of centuries ago.

Vaghjee Pragjee, a rich *bhatia*[149], built the house as an investment. He did not scrimp on quality and chose teak for the doors and the stairs. Abbajaan bought the house from Vaghjee Pragjee in the mid 1940's and converted, three two room apartments, into a large family room, a kitchen, a dining room and two bedrooms. The rest was rented out.

From the time I was three and till I reached my sixth birthday, monsters lived under that flight of stairs. I never discussed their presence even with my closest friend. It was a highly personal relationship. A papa and a mama monster lived under that stair

---

[149] Hindu merchants from the state of Kutch.

case. I do not remember ever seeing them during day time, but soon after the Muezzin called the faithful to the sunset prayer, and darkness enveloped the area, the two of them moved in there unobtrusively.

Like all monsters, these too had little ones. The little ones did not live under that staircase. They lived under my bed and of course only after dark.

The little ones under my bed were not an insurmountable challenge. Yes, they were little but there were lots of them, so there were more and faster claws to contend with. The advantage I had over the little cannibals was that I was the one in charge of my environment. If I wanted to get in or out of bed after dark, all I had to do was to flick a switch to turn the lights on. Monsters, like all nocturnal predators, are photophobic. After returning to bed and before turning the lights off, the only precaution I had to take was not dangle any of my few limbs by the side of the bed and to make certain that they are all safely within my tucked bed sheets. This was in the days before night lights were invented. In those days, survival depended on maintaining sharp wits

Maneuverings the stairs was more of a challenge. While the sun was up, I climbed and descended those stairs with impunity. But once darkness fell—the stairs were unlit—climbing the stairs took a lot of forethought and innovation to distract the monsters long enough, so that I could sprint past their reach. I knew I was safe when I felt an artificial breeze that disturbed my balance for a moment and shoved me off my trajectory, the way a Volkswagen beetle is when an eight wheeler overtakes it on an interstate highway. The shove I felt was the wind escaping from his fist as his open hand just missed grasping me.

About the time I started grade school, I could not sense their presence anymore and I haven't been aware of them since then. The entire family of those monsters must have moved out to haunt some other three year old boy's home.

I assume that as a child I was no different from other children. Mother was always there as far back as I could remember. She fed me when I was hungry and nursed me when I was sick and even though she had servants to help her, she did not delegate the vital tasks to them. Feeding her family was one of those tasks. The servants did the prep work but she did the actual cooking.

My mother was often incapacitated by asthma. During one of her acute attacks she was unable to make dinner. Abbajaan decided that we should get a carry out and sent me to Abdullah Muslim's restaurant for a carry out [150]*paya* and *tandoori*[151] *naan*[152].

Mr. Muslim, I found out years later, was not born a Muslim. He was a Hindu of the *Luhar*[153] cast. While in his early twenties, he fell head over heels in love with a gorgeous Arab girl. Zanzibar had a rerun of the feud between the Capulet's and the Montague's.

---

[150] A soup made out of goat feet.
[151] Oven
[152] Bread.
[153] A blacksmith.

Sunny Zanzibar, unlike cloudy Stratford-upon- Avon, does not enjoy tragedies. The boy converted to Islam, called himself Abdullah and to drive home the point that he was not a Hindu any longer, he chose the unusual surname "Muslim".

He sat in front of his restaurant where he could greet customers coming in and also to keep an eye on the till. He was short, pudgy from all that good Arab cooking and wore a *khanzu*[154] and a *koffeeya*[155], His upper lip was clean shaved and his chin was obscured in a huge cumulonimbus beard. He was a Muslim and he wanted his facial hair to proclaim it "loud and clear."

The clean upper lip was not in fashion in the early days of Islam. Massive beards and mustaches were. The clean upper lip evolved because some *Munafiks*[156] abused the venerated mustache.

A couple of strokes of a hair brush towards the forehead, two pokes of the pinky for peepholes, a few sweeps of a hair spray over the upswept mustache and—presto !— the *Munafik*'s mustache became a mask and incognito, he could have a fun filled evening at a *Muykhana*.[157]

When the secret was a secret no more, true Muslims—Muslims with both, the tongue and the heart of a Muslim—began the bother of the daily shaving of only their upper lips.

---

[154] A garment similar to a night shirt.
[155] A cap
[156] A person whose tongue says that he is a Muslim, but his heart does not.
[157] A bar.

True Muslims always emphasize that they have the tongue and the heart of a Muslim to generate awe in their listeners. They converse in Kiswahili but do not heed the wisdom in Kiswahili proverbs;

"The tongue has no bone; the heart has no eyes"

I still hope, but have yet to hear, a true Muslim concede that the brain is the essential organ of a Muslim's anatomy.

Perhaps, it is because it is easier to convince the heart of a dogma. Then, the head is likely to follow.

In my early teens I was impressed by the moral of a movie. Accompanied by celestial music, a couplet faded in and faded out, before the screen announced; "The End."

"For those who believe, no explanation is necessary,

For those who do not, no explanation is possible"

The word "bar" is so abhorrent to true Muslims that just before I left Zanzibar, they launched a campaign to delete the letters "bar" from Zanzibar and change the name to a more Arabic sounding "Zanzibeer".

The irony is obvious to Europeans but escapes the true Muslim. He has only one word for the prohibited beverage—"*Sharabu.*" His vocabulary does not have the specific words "Merlot" "Mead" "Brandy" "Beer" "Whiskey" or even "Champagne."

The campaign must have fizzled out, as the island is still known as Zanzibar with its offensive suffix still firmly attached to it.

While in grade school, collecting and trading "coupons" was a fad. They were rare and found only in expensive newspapers and magazines. We cut them out, filled in our name and address, put a five cent stamp on it and mailed it. Several months later we received interesting color brochures. I remember showing off my brochure of pretty girls on water skies inviting me to visit Florida to water ski with them the following winter.

Ibrahim Patel explained to Mr. Muslim what the new fad of couponing was all about. Mr. Muslim went through a stack of newspapers that he used to wrap the carry outs in, cut out several coupons and handed them to Ibrahim.

Mr. Muslim was a nice man.

I went to the kitchen at the back of the restaurant and ordered our evening meal. It was ready and wrapped in newspapers within a few minutes.

The strange thing about the wrapping was that they were printed in Afrikaans—a language of the descendants of Dutch South Africans. There were none of them in or near Zanzibar.

As I approached to pay Mr. Muslim, the cook yelled from the kitchen, the items I had ordered. In most restaurants, the cooks and the waiters are illiterate. The only way the cashier can determine what to charge, is by this long distance vocal communication across the crowded restaurant.

When I arrived home with paya and crisp tandoori naan, Ammajaan got out of bed and went to the kitchen. In a frying pan she put some Ghee[158] and masala[159]. When the masala was done, she dumped the *paya* in it to transform the insipid *paya* into an edible dish.

Then she went to bed without eating a bite of the carry out.

I was not aware of or even cared about her appearance. The first difference I recall noticing between the anatomy of my father and my mother was that my mother had a crack in front of her chest. This was most noticeable when she carried me. To confirm my hypothesis, I checked out the anterior thorax of my Mswahili nurse maid while she carried me.

She too had it.

I made my first deduction of the difference between boys and girls. Boys have a butt crack.

Girls have two.

They have one in the back, where we boys have and an extra one on the front of their chests.

Q.E.D.

The first time I realized how important my mother was to me was when I was old enough to drive a car. I distinctly remember hanging out at Mnazi Moja with my friends when I heard of a tragic car accident. An Arab boy we knew had just got a license and took his mother for a ride. He rolled over the car and his mother died in that accident.

---

[158] Clarified butter.
[159] Spices

For the first time in my life, I wondered how I would feel if I had done that to my mother. The thought hit me like a lightning bolt and made my muscles shudder from the jolt. I did not believe I could live with that guilt. For the first time in my life, I realized how much I loved my mother. From then on I was considerate of her.

I sensed that she was uncomfortable when we left home without her knowledge. I got in the habit of letting her know that I was leaving, where I was going and when to expect me back home. I believe that reduced her fretting, but not enough to let her fall into a sound sleep, till she heard my stealthy footsteps climbing the stairs, much later then promised.

I was the first to leave home to go to college in Nairobi in 1951.

That is when Ammajaan's insomnia began. It kept getting progressively worse and reached its peak when the last child left home.

Next to leave was uncle Baboo.

Everyone has always called him "Baboo". The nickname has always seemed odd to me, but not important enough to research it.

About three years ago, Faisal asked his father why we called him by that name. Uncle Moin knew the answer. Of all your uncles, uncle Moin has the best past memory. I too listened with interest.

The word "Baboo" is used by Indians to refer to a baby boy.

"Congratulations! Is it a "Baboo?" or a "Baby?" This is the usual inquiry when one hears of the birth of a child. "Baby," ofcourse, refers to a girl.

In Gujarat, the privilege of naming a child belongs to a *Phupejaan*[160]. Each time Ammajaan was pregnant with one of us, Abbajaan wrote to Khairoon, his only sister, and got her choice of a name for a girl and a boy. This was BU—before ultrasound. The names we have were determined by our *Phupejaan*.

It was also before we had airmail. Mail came by steamships. It usually took weeks to deliver letters. Delivering mail is not the reason steamships are built. Carrying cargo is. Delivering mail is a cherry on the top of a sundae. Cargo ships went from one port to another, unloaded the cargo and headed for the next port determined by the cargo they just loaded on the ship.

My Phupejaan's letter, with her choice of a boy and a girl's name, did not arrive for several weeks after uncle Baboo was born. My parents did not know what to call him, so they called him by the generic name "Baboo" while waiting for his name to come by sea mail. Having called him Baboo for several weeks, out of habit, they kept on calling him Baboo. The first time, Mehmood, his real name, was used was when he registered for grade school.

In 1952, a technical college for Muslims was inaugurated with a lot of fanfare in Mombasa. Uncle Baboo, Ibrahim, one of the

---

[160] Father's sister.

Patel boys and some of Baboo's friends were among the first class to attend the school and got certified to repair radios. Then, uncle Baboo and a few of his classmates went to London, England to study and get certified in repairing televisions.

Uncle Baboo was the first in our family to go to Europe. Going to glamorous England was so unusual that only a lucky few did it and were envied by those left behind.

Indians believe the name a child carries, determines his future. Hindus consult an astrologer to choose a child's name. Muslims name their child after a successful person. After uncle Baboo left for England, Mohammed Shah. M.D., named his new born son Mehmood, after Uncle Baboo—the lucky one to be the first kid in Kibokoni to go to England to study.

Dr. Shah's family lived in the second story, in a house across the street from us. The distance between our homes was barely six feet. Because he was a physician he had a phone. We did not. We talked to each other from our windows.

Dr. Shah was a *Sayyid*[161], the highest "cast" among the Muslims. His father made a living as an *imam*.[162] Raised in a strict Muslim environment, he was well versed in Islam and deferred to with religious inquiries. He was a bright student and the Nawab[163] of his state gave him a scholarship to go to Aligarh University—the most prestigious Muslim University in India.

---
[161] A descendant of the prophet's daughter, Fatima.
[162] A person employed by a mosque. He leads the prayers in that mosque. He is as poor as a church mouse.
[163] Literally .a governor and usually the largest land owner in the state.

In the mornings we woke up to Dr. Shah's recitation of a chapter of the Qur'an in his home. At the end of the chapter, he shut the Qur'an, kissed the cover and placed it reverently in a Qur'an holder on a bookshelf.

Then he got in his Mini Morris to make home visits

He spent the rest of the mornings, at the Ithnashari[164] Clinic in the ornate building facing the ocean, that Sir Tharia Topan built and his afternoons in an office on the first floor of the building he lived in.

He was thin and of average height. He parted his luxuriant curly hair in the middle. His teeth were dark brown and his lips chronically red from decades of chewing pan[165]. His torso hinted of a bend towards the right from a surgery for the removal of a lobe for Tuberculosis.

He was a competent physician.

For a professional man, he dressed casually—too casually. About the time Dr. Shah came to town, Raj Kapoor's hit movies *"Awara"* [166]was released. The protagonist in that movie—Raj Kapoor—is a homeless person and dresses like one. An Ithnashari wit spotted the similiarity between Raj Kapoor's and Dr. Shah's ward robe. From then on, behind his back, he was better known as "Dr. Awara"

---

[164] Muslims of the Shia sect.
[165] Tobacco, chalk and beetle nuts wrapped in a leaf.
[166] Home less. A tramp.

His wife was a physician as well. When she delivered her first child, the couple was at a loss. They lacked the basic skills needed to take care of a new born infant. My mother, among other skills, instructed them in the art of diaper changing.

I recall saying *"Kwahere"*[167] to him before going to Medical school.

We lost touch with each other after that.

Thirty five years later, Dr. Shah called me from New Jersey. His family had immigrated to the USA.

He informed me that his son Mehmood had changed his name to Mahender—a Hindu name. That he was not Muhammad any longer. He was Manohar—another Hindu name. His daughter Amina too had changed her name to a Hindu name, which I cannot recall. His wife did not have to change her name. She was a Hindu and we knew her by her Hindu name.

Since the last time we met, I thought, life must have been unkind to this family.

When a newborn goes through a string of illnesses or brings bad luck to his family, the obvious reason is that he was given an inauspicious name. The cure is renaming that child.

I understood why people changed names. As I wondered why the family did not switch to more auspicious Muslim names, he added;

"And we have converted to Hinduism"

---

[167] Goodbye

The cordless phone slipped in my hand. Just in time, I grasped it by its upper third and readjusted it with my left hand.

I do not recall anything from the remaining conversation that followed.

I quit teaching and went to Dublin, Ireland in 1957 to study Medicine. Soon after that Safiyun, your Phupejaan, left for New Delhi for college. In our family albums we all have a photo of Safiyun with Pundit Jawaharlal Nehru, the prime minister of India. It was taken at the gathering of "foreign" students in New Delhi. Safiyun was considered a foreign student as she was born and raised in Zanzibar and carried a British passport. Safiyun then went to Glasgow, Scotland to become a dietician.

Two years after I started Medical school, uncle Mac joined the same college. Since Mac and I were in Dublin, Baboo left England to work in Dublin so that we three could live cheaper by sharing an apartment.

Two years before I graduated from Medical school uncle Moy came to Dublin to go to school and now there were four brothers in Dublin sharing an apartment. Your family album has a picture of the four of us in tuxedos, taken before a college prom in Dublin. When that picture reached home, uncle Munir was incapacitated with jealousy. He wished he too was in that picture. That never happened. The five brothers were never together in Dublin or in London.

After Uncle Mac and I came to the USA, uncle Moin finished his training in Dublin and took a job with Scotland Yard in London.

THE STAIRCASE

Uncle Munir, the baby of the family was still in High school—the only sibling living with our parents. He was in Zanzibar during the *Mpinduzi*[168] in 1964. His recollection of the event is not horrifying. He remembers spending his non curfew hours at The Euan Smith Madrasah which was now converted into a temporary shelter for refuge *Mangas*.

The Mangas were the Arab shopkeepers and farmers in the distant villages. Unlike most of the Arabs in town, who were descendents of Arabs who had married Africans, the *Mangas,* were of a pure Omani stock. They were fair skinned and spoke Arabic at home. Somehow the Swahili's in the remote areas of Zanzibar sensed anarchy and took out their pent up hatred of the Arabs on the *Mangas*. Men and boys were killed brutally, their women raped and mutilated. I am not sure how the survivors got to town but when they did, they were sheltered at the Madrasah. Teachers cooked for them and students served them the meals and did whatever else they needed help with.

Suddenly, there were Chinese and Russians in Zanzibar, who spoke fluent Kiswahili without an accent. Several times, all the students in all the school were told to leave their classes, line up the streets linking Zanzibar to its airport and wave a Chinese or a Russian flag at a dignitary coming into town in a motorcade.

High school kids suddenly thought it was cool to go to college in Moscow, Russia. Abbajaan got wind of the latest trend

---

[168] The revolution of 1963.

among high school kids and became alarmed. He gave Munir about an hour's notice and smuggled him on to a ship going to Bombay in 1964

Ammajaan's nest became empty.

When she was a young mother and her fretting over the safety of her baby became unbearable, she would seek reassurance by unobtrusively peeking into her baby's crib and watch intently till it took a breath, then she would return to bed hoping to catch some sleep.

Later, when her babies had grown up, it was the unique sequence of notes from of the stair case that brought recognition and reassurance to her, while she waited in bed for their return home.

When Grandma and I were in Arlington, Virginia, every Thursday I attended an evening Cardiology teaching session at George Washington University.

This was before we had the echocardiogram, an innovation that rendered obsolete, the skill of evaluating murmurs with a stethoscope.

Dr. Proctor Harvey was a brilliant cardiologist, with remarkable ears. He could imitate murmurs in a perfect pitch and cadence and could remember patients better by their characteristic murmurs then by their faces.

My mother could do the same.

She could identify who was coming home by the pitch and the rhythm of the footsteps which caused the stairs to vibrate in a unique fashion. When the last child came home the unique melody by that child, lulled her into a restful sleep.

Now, her nest was empty.

The stair became mute.

The last melody in the stairs repertoire left the stairs with uncle Munir.

So did its soul.

Munir ran into communal rioting and massacres in Ahmedabad. Ahmedabad was not a safe a place either so he was sent to London, England where he shared an apartment with Uncle Moy in 1967

When Abed Karume the first president of Zanzibar, declared that no Indian woman could refuse a proposal of marriage from a Mswahili male, most Indians who could, smuggled their wives and daughters out of Zanzibar. This was when Ammajaan too left to live in Ahmedabad, India.

Abbajaan decided to weather the storm till he could sell our home—a significant asset. Everyone with authority in Zanzibar, including Aboud Jumbe the Vice President of Zanzibar, was his students when they were in High School. He sought the help of everyone who could help him cut the red tape and allow him to sell our home.

After three frustrating years, he gave up, donated our home to *Welezo*, a mental hospital, and left for India with a load of cloves.

ZANZIBAR

After graduating from Medical school, I came to the USA in the summer of 1963 to do my Internship at St. Luke's Hospital in Newburgh, NY. Two years later, uncle Mac came here to do his Internship at the same hospital.

I met Grandma at Doctors Hospital in Washington DC. I was a second year resident in Internal Medicine and Grandma was a nurse on the medical floor. We got married on January 26, 1966.

Uncle Bachoo was born on June 13, 1967 at the George Washington University Hospital in Washington DC. Aunty Bai was born on July 8, 1968 in Wilmington, Delaware while I was a staff physician at the Emily P. Bissell Hospital.

I joined The Monroe Clinic in Monroe, Wisconsin in the fall of 1969.

Uncle Baboo left Dublin for Zanzibar before I graduated from medical school. He married Aunty Sabiha in Ahmedabad in 1964 on the day India's Prime Minister, Pundit Jawaharlal Nehru died. A planned boisterous wedding had to be toned down out of respect for the Prime Minister's death.

After their wedding, the couple settled in Nairobi. Economic and political turmoil followed Kenya's independence on December the twelfth, 1963. Uncle Baboo—and thousands of other Indians--decided to leave Kenya. He sent Shaheena and Masood with aunty Sabiha to live with my mother in Shah Alam, Ahmedabad and he came over in 1971 to stay with us in "The brick house" on 17th street, Monroe and work for Walt

THE STAIRCASE

Ruffner's TV repair shop. Uncle Baboo liked his prospects here and decided to stay in the USA.

This was before 9/11. It was easier for immigrants with Muslim names to immigrate to the USA. Grandma and I knew Joe Trigoning, a Republican state senator from Schulsberg, Wisconsin. We asked for his help. Within a couple of months he called me and informed me that Aunty Sabiha and your cousins Shaheena and Masood will join us before Christmas which was only a few weeks away.

It was winter when we drove to pick them up at O'Hare. Usually Grandma or I drove. This time, Uncle Baboo asked if he could drive and we let him. That was a mistake. He was so full of adrenalin that he drove as fast as the station wagon could go on Highways with patches of snow and ice.

I was relieved to get out of the car at O'Hare and decided that I will drive back to Monroe.

We walked to the gate where passengers disembark. We could do that before 9/11. The pesky security check and the intimidating presence of armed guards everywhere, is an aftermath of 9/11. As was often the case, passengers disembarked on the apron and walked to the gate.

Among the early ones to walk down the planes stairway, was Uncle Baboo's family. Aunty Sabiha's Sari was fluttering in a breeze as she hurriedly walked while blowing kisses to uncle Baboo. Masood and Shaheena were skipping, waving and shouting with joy.

Standing behind the transparent glass wall we could not hear them. Uncle Baboo stood next to me. His right foot resting on a floor heating board, his hands holding on to a railing, his body leaning forwards, his face in a serene smile, his eyes streaming tears.

Grandma and I got married in Washington, D.C. on January 26, 1966. Phupejaan Safiyun spent the summer of 1966 with us in D.C. She then returned to Glasgow to finish her training and went to Shah Alam to live with *Dada Abba* [169] and *Dadee amma.* [170]

In 1972, while we lived in "The yellow house" at 807, 21st Avenue in Monroe, Phupejaan Safiyun came to live with us. Within a year, Uncle Munir left England to live with us in the "Yellow house,"—the house where aunty Sameena was born on April 27, 1973.

For two years, uncle Munir and Phupejaan drove together to Beloit to study at the Blackhawk Technical College. Phoopeejaan got a certificate in medical record keeping and worked at St. Clair Hospital in the medical record department.

I saw my medical colleagues from a different perspective through Phupejaan's eyes. We used to dictate all our history and physical examinations.

The bulk of the medical record staff spent most of their days typing our dictations. One of my colleagues had a deserved

---

[169] My father.
[170] My mother

reputation for having the lengthiest dictations. To even out the work load, the girls drew straws to decide who will be the one assigned that day to do only Dr. Kneubuhler's dictations.

Uncle Munir finished his two year course in aircraft avionics. Dr. Fencil, my partner at the Monroe Clinic, was the chairman of the Board of Directors of Blackhawk Technical College. At the graduation ceremony he awarded diplomas to all the graduating students –except uncle Munir. The incident was reported prominently in the Beloit newspaper.

The next day, a red faced Wayne Fencil came to my office and apologized to me on behalf of Blackhawk Technical College.

To get a diploma in aircraft avionics, students have to pass an FAA administered written and a practical examination and a security check. A security check is essential as these technicians have excess to passenger airplanes. One of the security requirements is that the graduate must be a citizen of the USA.

Till graduation day, Blackhawk Technical College was unaware that uncle Munir was not a US citizen and hence was disqualified from receiving a diploma.

After passing his examinations but with no diploma, he could not get employment in the field he trained in. The father of a classmate and a good friend of Uncle Munir worked at the General Motors auto plant at Janesville, Wisconsin. He pulled strings and got uncle Munir a job with a good pay and great benefits at that GM plant.

Uncle Munir worked at GM for only a few years and in the fall of 1976 moved to Inglewood, California, to live with my parents and work with uncle Moin.

Aunty Rukia and uncle Moin got married July29, 1972 in England. Grandma and I went to that wedding. Phupejaan stayed in the "Yellow house' to babysit Bachoo and Bai. My parents flew from India to attend that wedding and came to live with us in the "Yellow house" in August of that year.

The next month uncle Mac and Aunty Fatu came to visit us and my father performed *Nikah*[171] that married the couple in the "Yellow house" in September of 1972. One more wedding took place in that house. In the fall of 1973, my father performed the Nikah at Phupejaan's wedding. It was probably the first Muslim wedding in Monroe. The Monroe evening times gave it a detailed coverage.

Uncle Moin and aunty Rukia came from London, England for Phupejaan's wedding. They both had good jobs with a promising future and had purchased a house in Surrey.

While here, they considered relocating to the USA so that all of the Qureshi's could see each other more often. After they returned to England they took a leave of absence. Their old jobs were held open for two year— a good insurance, in case they did not like the USA. They liked the USA. In April of 1976, they came to the USA, stayed with Phupejaan for a few weeks and then settled in Los Angeles.

---

[171] The Islamic wedding ceremony.

Shahdia was born in England. She is the only cousin, who has dual citizenships and carries a valid USA and a British passport. That gives her flexibility. Whenever she is in a foreign country hostile to the USA, she can always fall back on her British passport or vice versa.

My parents moved to California in late 1976 just in time to escape from another Wisconsin winter. After they left Wisconsin, they visited us only during summers. Like most retired Muslims, they lived in an apartment next to a mosque. It makes going to a mosque five times a day convenient.

Phupejaan's wedding, was the first time since 1953, that Ammajaan had all her babies with her under one roof. An occasion that was sweet with a touch of sour.

She would have preferred if we were all together under her roof in Kibokoni.

Our home had an unfinished third floor. Since we were toddlers, in her mind, she had finished constructing apartments on the third floor of our home, designed to satisfy the taste of each of her children. Three and even four generations of a family living together in a huge home is common in Zanzibar. Ammajaan too hoped to spend her last years in such a home.

The last time we were in Zanzibar,we went to Kibokoni, so that grandma, Sharifah, Shahdia and Feisal could see the home we were raised in. After a tour of the Cathedral Church of Christ, we walked south towards our home.

Zanzibar

To our right was Abdullah Muslim's Restaurant, shut and boarded. On both sides of a once busy street, stores and homes were shut and boarded. The ambience was uncanny.

We walked towards our home. To our left was Rulmul's garage. Shut and boarded.

Mr. Rulmul, in his mid-sixties, was an auto mechanic and a driving instructor. He taught Abbajaan and I to drive.. He was an instructor from the old school who twisted your ear and / or slapped the back of your head every time you did something wrong while driving. He did that to me and said he did that to all his students including Abbajaan.

Mr. Rulmul had a gentler side as well.

At age ten, on my way home from the market on a hot day, I stopped at Hamisi Machungwa's fruit juice stand. To the west of the Church Cathedral of Christ in Africa is a UMCA book store and across the street and south of the book store is an open area where Hamisi had a fruit juice stand.

Most Waswahili first names are the days of the week or the month they were born in. Thursday evenings and Fridays mornings are the auspicious segments of a week. Those born on a Thursday are named *"Hamisi"* and *"Juma"* is the name for a child born on a Friday. The three auspicious months of the year are Ramadhan, Rajab and Shabaan. Three common Kiswahili names are, *"Ramadhani,"* *"Rajabu"* and *"Shabanee."* If a Mswahili is born on Idd, he proudly calls himself by the uncommon name of "Iddi."

"Machungwa" is not a surname. It is the Kiswahili word for an orange. He sold mainly orange juice. Hamisi Machungwa is a person who was born on a Thursday and sells orange juice for a living.

The "Last name" resembles English surnames like Smith, Taylor and Carpenter but unlike the English, Hamisi's children will not carry "Machungwa" as their last name. They will be known by whatever trade they will choose to engage in.

Hamisi sold two kinds of juices. Orange was the most expensive and cost twenty cents per glass. *Mkwaju,* tamarind juice, at ten cents per glass was the cheapest. Of course, he sold half a glass of either, at half the price of a full one.

I had a five cent coin left in my pocket and decided to quench my thirst with half a glass of *"Mkwaju"*[172] *and ordered it.*

To my surprise, Hamisi placed a full glass and a half a glass of *Mkwaju* in front of me.

I told Hamisi that he had made a mistake. I ordered only half a glass of *Mkwaju.*

Hamisi got irritated and told me loudly;

"You said; *'Glassee unusu'* not *'Nusu glassi'* and *'Glassi unusu'* is what I put in front of you."

He taught me the unforgettable difference between the two phrases, but would not take back the full glass.

---

[172] Tamarand "

ZANZIBAR

I checked my pockets one more time.

I still had only a five cent coin.

Mr. Rulmul was also there, drinking his last swallow from a glass of orange juice. He had a hearty laugh at my predicament, told me that Hamisi was right and tossed a ten cent coin on the table as he left the stand.

I placed my five cent coin next to it and drank the *Glassee unusu* of *Mkwaju*.

We had kind neighbors in Kibokoni.

To our right we could see the second story of the home where Sharifah Patel was raised. The Patel's were from Surat, India where Patel (Literally a farmer.) is a common surname among Hindus and Muslims. There were dozens of Patel families in Zanzibar but this family was the only Patel family in Zanzibar who were Muslims. Now, all of that family lives in England.

Our family was closest to the Patel's and we grew up together. We even took vacations together. One of those was on Prison Island. There was only one huge house on the island and we were the only occupants of the house the beach and the island. We also had a natural swimming pool in our backyard. It was an irregular swimming pool size hole that tunneled to the ocean

The island is a sanctuary for tortoises. I recall seeing only one tortoise in Zanzibar Island. It was in Chwaka. When I asked the natives how old the tortoise was I did not get a precise answer. The best guess was; "It was there when my great grandfather was around".

THE STAIRCASE

The best documented tortoise is the one in a Zoo in Calcutta (Now, renamed Kolkata.) A few years ago the Zoo celebrated the two hundred and fiftieth birthday of the tortoise which was donated to the Zoo by "Clive of India." Baron Clive of Plassey was a habitual suicider. After plenty of practice he performed a perfect one in 1774.

Prison Island is literally crawling with tortoises. I asked Faisal, Shahdia and Sharifah to ride them. As soon as they sat on them, the tortoises retracted their feet and head and the three looked like they were resting on a rock after a long hike.

"What do we do now?" one of them asked.

I took a stone and rubbed the shells of the tortoises with it and three of them were off, like jockeys from the starting gate at Ascot.

From the beach of Prison Island, we could see the stone town and could identify the cars that drove in front of the Palace. The beach looks like it is covered by fresh untrodden snow. The water is clear. Bluish green close to the shore where the sea weeds are and sky blue further out where it is deep and devoid of weeds. The water is inviting—and treacherous.

Phupejaan and Zarina Patel swam out to the sky blue water and the undercurrent in that deep part swept them out towards Zanzibar. Sharifah Patel was the first to notice that the two girls were in trouble and started screaming and pointing at them.

Uncle Baboo and I were in the greenish blue water and looked in the direction Sharifah was pointing at and saw the girls frantically trying to swim back to the shore. We tried to swim to where they were but the current pushed us back faster than we could swim ahead. We decided to swam back to the beach, and then ran across the beach to a point further north of where the girls were. I pointed at Phupejaan and asked Uncle Baboo to swim towards her and I swam towards Zarina. The current pushed us towards the girls. When we reached them we were able to pull them back towards the beach. The first few yards were hard swimming but as soon as we reached the shelf where the water was greenish, there was no current and the two girls made it to the beach on their own.

Sharifah Patel still relives this incident in her nightmares.

We walked by the Bapu soap factory. The front door that used to be open during business hours was closed. There was no grinding sound or the smell of coconut oil from the factory; a clear sign that the factory is closed.

That factory had several machines that squeezed oil out of copra[173] to get coconut oil which was used to make soap for washing clothes. They were sold in blue, foot long rectangular bars. The soap was too harsh for bathing. The blue in it was to brighten white clothes.

As a child I heard rumors about the night shift at that factory. You could hear the machines squeezing oil out of copra in the middle of the night although no human was present. The correct Zanzibari explanation is that ghosts were the night shift.

Zanzibar, like all ancient towns, is rich in ghost stories.

---

[173] Sun dried coconut meat.

THE STAIRCASE

Every neighborhood has several of them.

Aunty Sharifah is convinced that Hotel Tembo, the Hotel we stayed in while we were in Zanzibar, is haunted. In her words, the encounter is convincing. Ask her about it.

To our left we passed the home where aunty Fatu[174] was born and raised in. A cyclist rode by us and all I saw was his back. Uncle Moin was a few steps ahead of me and saw his face. He recognized Hassan Maldaar who lived about three blocks away.

Uncle Moin shouted, "Hey! Hassan."

Hassan was my student at the Madresah. I braced for the sight of a middle aged face with a few wrinkles and some gray hairs.

Hassan, applied his brakes, got of his cycle, turned around and a middle aged face with a few wrinkles and some gray hairs, looked at us in surprise.

We walked on by Dr. Shah's office. The door was closed. The windows on the second story were shut. We knew that they now live in New Jersey. The place appeared unoccupied

To our left was an old familiar sight which warmed my heart.

On a wall in the homes of all my siblings, hangs a professional family portrait of the Qureshi family taken in Zanzibar, before uncle Munir was born.

That picture was taken on the flat roof of our home with a back drop of the top of a huge bread fruit tree. It was of mature

---

[174] Uncle Mac's wife

height when I was a toddler. It is still there. Not any taller but certainly much wider then before and as always as majestic as a statue of Queen Victoria.

Since I left home, the sight of a breadfruit tree always makes me homesick.

We were now facing the front of our home. The main entrance was shut and locked. *Majuri's* apartment door too was shut and locked. Mr. and Mrs. Boyd's apartment was lifeless. We knew that Mrs. Boyd moved out of their apartment after Mr. Boyd expired. She was taken in by a *Kokanee*[175] family who took care of her for the rest of her days.

We stood facing our home. The main door was locked, the home was vacant and under renovation. My mind flashed back to the days when I used to listen to Ammajaan's plans for the third floor.

Has Ammajaan gone behind our backs and contracted to get that floor finished to her specifications? I wondered,

Right away, I dismissed that farfetched thought. Besides, there was no heavy equipment on the flat roof to suggest an imminent construction there. All the ladders, wheel barrows and empty paint cans were only on the first and second floor.

A lady from one of the adjacent homes gave us startling information. Our home was sold and the buyer was planning to move in as soon as the renovation was completed.

Our home was sold?

---

[175] People from Kokan ,on the west coast of India

Zanzibar, as in all Muslim countries, has a *waqaf* department. Owners can donate a property in perpetuity to that department, with the understanding that the *waqaf* department will maintain it and use income from the donated property for a specified purpose.

In most instances the income supports a mosque or an orphanage. In our case, the income was to support a charitable Mental Hospital. All my siblings have been under that impression.

Well, anything is possible in the anarchy that ruled Zanzibar after Abbajaan's departure.

I was disappointed that I could not enter and climb the stairs of my home

I so wanted to see and touch the stairs.

Now, I am too old. I do not have the stamina for a long plane flight or the strength to climb those stairs.

But you can.

Yes, it will still be there and will be there three centuries from now.It was made of teak.

You have a lot of time left to do it.

When you do, like climbing any other wooden stairs, you will hear; "Thud, Thud, Thud." as you climb it.

But, it will not sing for you.

It is functional but dead.

You see, it's soul left with uncle Munir.

The Qureshi siblings

at

Aunty Sameena's wedding.

Mehmood. Munir. Makbul.
Mehboob. Safiyun. Mohiyudin.

Chapter Twenty

Mombasa

Mombasa, what a catchy name!

In most minds, the word arouses a longing to experience an exotic striptease of sights, sounds, and smells.

Mine does not.

I was less than five years old when my family and I were in S.S. Karagola, returning to Zanzibar after our first visit to India, when I became irritable and developed a fever. Since we were in the middle of the Indian Ocean, the ship's doctor took care of me. He isolated me on the ship with the diagnosis of Typhoid Fever. Zanzibar was only another 10 hours away, but the ship's Captain, would not let me stay aboard and made me get admitted into a hospital at the next port of call—Mombasa.

My mother and siblings continued the voyage to Zanzibar. Till that day, I was never separated from my mother. When sick, the one person a sick child needs the most is his mother and I was separated from my mother for the first time when I had my first serious sickness. I could not understand why I was in a strange place and why my mother and my siblings were not with me.

ZANZIBAR

Fortunately, Abbajaan[176] got off the boat to stay with me and his presence was partially reassuring.

The window of my classroom in grade school faced the Indian Ocean. Often—especially when bored—I glanced at the ocean, Several times a day I saw just a puff of smoke resting on the horizon. Then a mast, with flags on it, would poke through the ocean. Even before the funnel of a ship was visible, I could tell if the ship had a person with an infectious disease aboard. The ship flew a solid yellow flag, just like the one, S.S. Karagolla flew, when she abandoned me in Mombasa. The absence of a yellow flag on the mast always made me sigh in relief. Some unfortunate little boy did not have to go through, what Mombasa made me go through.

.

The next time I was in Mombasa was after a summer vacation in Zanzibar. Three Zanzibari students at the teachers college in Nairobi: Ibrahim Jaffer, Hashim Esmail and I flew to Mombasa. We had several hours to kill before boarding the evening train to Nairobi.

Bollywood hit movie "Aan" was playing in Mombasa.

The premier of a Bollywood film, with the usual fanfare, is held in Bombay. Immediately after that, a stack of about a dozen circular metal cans about a foot in diameter, containing thirty two millimeter films of the movie, is flown to Nairobi; the city with the largest Indian population. When the attendance at

---

[176] My father.

the Nairobi cinema starts dwindling, the stack of cans is sent to cities in East Africa in a descending order of the population of Indians.

A film playing in Mombasa has already been in Nairobi. All our classmates in Nairobi had seen it. If we did not see it while we were in Mombasa, we will never see it. The stack of cans will move on to other cities and finally to Zanzibar and then sent back to Bombay.

We will be the only students at the Teacher's College who had not seen the film. The Nairobi students will be discussing the movie and the only ones unable to participate will be the three Zanzibari students. That will be terrible. It will only reinforce their view that we were bumpkins from Zanzibar. We could not let that happen. The honor of Zanzibar was at stake.

Fortunately, there was a matinee show that day. We calculated that we had enough time to see the movie and have ample time to catch the Five PM Train to Nairobi.

Unfortunately, the movie was longer than usual and none of us wanted to leave without seeing the dramatic end to the movie.

We ran out of the cinema just as the screen displayed "The End", hailed a taxi and told the Indian driver to fly to the railway station.

He did.

When he screeched to a stop at the Mombasa Train station, the platform was visible from our taxi.

ZANZIBAR

Three jaws dropped and three pairs of terror filled eyes popped out, as they saw the back of the caboose of our train pulling out of Mombasa Train Station and getting smaller and smaller and the clickety clack from its wheels getting softer and softer.

Damn. Damn. **DAMN.**

I did not utter that word three times. The three of us said it once, almost simultaneously.

Not arriving at Nairobi the next morning had unpleasant consequences. We shall face the music from three directions—the College, The Education department of Zanzibar which was paying for our education and our parents.

The heartless taxi driver had a hearty laugh at our predicament.

When he had exhausted his laughter, while wiping tears, he suggested that he could try and get us on the train—for an exorbitant fare. The fare, of course, will be gladly accepted in advance with no guarantee of catching the train.

Like a Phoenix, hope rekindled. We could still extricate ourselves from the mess.

We did not haggle. That would have been a stupid waste of the precious little time we had. Besides, had he asked, we would have readily given him the pants off our butts.

We looked at each other and then simultaneously looked at him, and nodded acceptance of his terms.

He put the gear in reverse, roared backwards and spun the taxi a hundred and eighty degrees and while still in a spin, put it in a forward gear and sped forwards leaving smoke and dust swirling behind us. For about a quarter of a mile he was on a paved road. Then he swerved into a field, following vaguely visible ruts, while tossing us in every direction in our beltless seats. He bounced through pot holes, splashed through streams, skidded through mud and scythed his way through tall weeds.

Suddenly, he stopped.

Our torsos were thrown forwards and through the wind shield our bulging eyes saw a serene dream—our train stationary at a tiny train station with its engine hissing off steam like an impatient person tapping his foot.

A few years after we graduated, Champak Shah, met me in Mombasa. As always it was joyous visit.

We did not meet again for over four decades. I missed not seeing him. He did not attempt to contact me and I hesitated to do so as I was certain that he was superstitious enough not to invite another catastrophe while visiting me. After the last time we met, when he returned home to Nairobi, he was shocked to hear that his mother –in –law had passed away suddenly, during the hour he spent visiting me—in Mombasa.

I have not been in Mombasa since then and hope never to be there

While I was at The Monroe clinic, the word of mouth that spread our reputation was;

"If there is something wrong with you, The Monroe Clinic will find it."

Our secret was the time we spent with each patient. We blocked off an hour for a new patient. Our competition hardly spent fifteen minutes.

I had a patient who was a CEO of a large, well known company. To achieve and especially to maintain that position, must require scientific deductions before making a business decision.

He used to come to see me with his wife annually

An executive checkup involved documenting all pertinent past medical history, family history, travel history, inquiry into all the systems, a head to toe physical examination and finally a panel of tests.

Towards the end of the day we met the patients and reviewed with them the results of the evaluation, diagnosis if any and treatment if indicated.

The first year, all the studies were boringly normal. But in passing, I mentioned that I was uneasy about a spot on his face. With some hesitation, I advised him to have the spot biopsied to put my mind at ease.

The following year he reported that his dermatologist too was equivocal about doing the biopsy but was glad he did. It was cancer.

The following year, again everything was negative. My index finger did not like the feel of a spot in his prostate. I reassured him that I was being overcautious but he better have a Urologist feel it too. The Urologist did a radical prostectomy to remove a prostate cancer.

The third year, the only abnormality that concerned me was a subtle change in his Electrocardiogram. The CEO was an avid asymptomatic jogger. I did not think he had a heart problem. Subtle EKG changes can be due to a cup of coffee before the test. Rarely, it can be due to something sinister. I chose not to ignore the change and recommended that he have a stress EKG done by a cardiologist in his community.

I never saw that patient again.

His wife showed up for her annual checkup the following year and informed me that her husband had undergone a triple coronary bypass surgery.

The CEO and the three specialists I referred him to, apparently thought highly of me. The CEO continued to recommend me. He even sent his wife to me for annual follow ups.

But, he did not wish to see me anymore.

The calm and collected CEO had succumbed to superstition.

So would all of us

To other ears, "Mombasa" is a caress that elicits an exotic strip tease of sights, sounds and smells. To my ears, it is a pain in the ear.

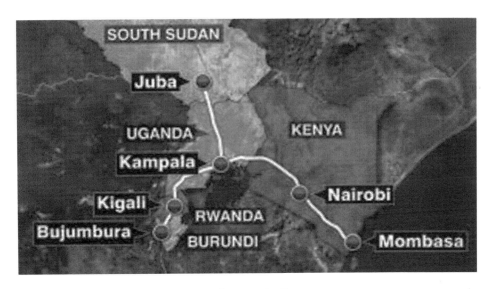

East African Railways.

CHAPTER TWENTY ONE

Burning Bridges Behind You.

During my years in Zanzibar, I often wondered what turmoil Abbajaan[177] went through when he boldly announced a voluntary exile into the Dark Continent. As I approached my senior year in high school, I too wondered what it would be like to get uprooted from Zanzibar and get transplanted in a strange land.

While I was a junior in High school, several graduating seniors, relocated to Dar-es salaam; a prosperous, bustling metropolis with plenty of unfilled jobs with impressive wages and rapid advancements.

That option left me cold.

Dar-es salaam was for the devotees of *"Laxmi"*—the goddess of wealth. Laxmi did bestow wealth but only on the devotees who could keep up on her faster paced path.

Zanzibar, was for the devotees of *"Shanti"*—the goddess of tranquility. Shanti's path was less lucrative but had a leisurely

---
[177] My father.

pace; I have been a devotee of "Shanti." Till the day I retired, money was never a decisive incentive. Since I retired, I have had doubts about my allegiance to *Shanti*.

To a tourist, the ambience of Dar-es salaam appears identical to Zanzibar's and superficially, it is. A Zanzibari's eyes notice the similarities between the two, but do not equate Dar-es-salaam with Zanzibar.

Only Zanzibar is Zanzibar.

Only Zanzibar is home.

Since the first day I considered what I would like to do for a living, I had decided on a career in medicine. Zanzibar had lawyers, architects dentists, and all other professions well represented and meeting them socially or seeing them on the street never aroused in me a desire to be in their shoes and do what they did for a living.

However, meeting any of the doctors in town always excited me. Before their office hours, it was a thrill to watch them on their way making house calls with their black doctor's bag. The ones, who just started a practice, did so on a bicycle with their black bags on the rear seat. Those who were well established did it in a chauffeured car. Just watching them go by doing their daily routine would cheer me up.

Imagine you are a star struck teenager who dreams of but never expects to meet your idol. Now imagine that you are in your home town shopping mall. A film shoot is going on and you get a glimpse of your idol.

What you are feeling now, is what I felt each time I saw a physician.

There were two occasions when I had the full attention of a physician. Seeing them at their dispensaries for an ailment was one of them. Quite often, I had to go to their homes and ask them to accompany me to our home to treat one of my mother's acute asthma attacks in the middle of the night. The time it took to walk with the physician to our home, was another one.

I eagerly took advantage of those opportunities to pump the physicians for information about the best medical schools, what it took to go through the schools and the pros and cons of a physician's life,

None of them flicked me off like a bug that landed on their sleeves. They were flattered by my interest in their career and answered my inquiries seriously.

By the English Golf Club, there was a little clubhouse where some of the professionals would meet after a swim in the ocean and chat a while. Aboud Jumbe, my biology teacher, Dr. Kingwaba, the first Mswahili to become a physician, Dr. Fowzy the first Zanzibari ophthalmologist and several other doctors from the hospital hung out there. During the years when I taught in Zanzibar, I too was there whenever one of the doctors was there, and hung on to every word they exchanged, particularly when they were discussing medical topics.

High school was the highest level of education Zanzibar offered. For anything higher, we had to leave the island. The only University in East Africa was Makerere, in Kampala, Uganda;

an excellent University, but with all the seniors from all of East African High schools vying for admission, the odds of getting admitted there, particularly in Medicine, were discouragingly low.

Our choices were India or the Middle East. The choice between the two was made by our mother tongues. Arabs went to the Middle East, particularly Cairo, Beirut and Baghdad. Indians went to India or Pakistan.

We were a British Protectorate and upon our return to Zanzibar, the qualifications with the highest prestige and remuneration were the British ones. Six decades after the dissolution of the British Empire, the financial superiority of a British degree has levelled off but the prestige remains.

Even now, in what used to be the British Empire, you are perceived as a full-fledged surgeon, only when after your name and M.D., you can add FRCS. (Fellow of the Royal College of Surgeons.) The FRCS is usually followed by the letter "E" for England, "S" for Scotland and "I" for Ireland depending on which of the three colleges certified the surgeon.

The cost of hanging a British medical diploma in a waiting room was prohibitive. Only those who had won a scholarship or had wealthy parents could consider it. My parents were not wealthy.

In my senior year in High school, Abbajaan and I discussed my future. It was not about which career I wished to pursue. He was well aware of that. It was about how to finance it. He had spent a few hours calculating the cost of a medical education.

"I can comfortably afford to send you to a medical school—if you choose a school in India."

I demurred. I did not wish to aim low and settle for the second best. It had to be the best.

"If that is your decision, you will have to work for the shortfall."

I nodded acceptance.

He suggested that I work in Zanzibar, live at home and save every schilling of my salary, to fund my British education.

I agreed.

Qualifying with a better credential was worth the wait and the extra expense.

Students from my graduating class, who did not want to or could not afford further education, met with Mr. Phillips, the head of the personnel department for the Protectorate of Zanzibar.

He told us of the openings, their job descriptions and the starting salaries. We were familiar with those details from talking to students who had graduated the year before. We listened politely and in mild boredom.

Suddenly, we reacted with surprise which soon turned to horror, when Mr. Phillips mentioned that some of us will have to fill posts in Pemba.

Pemba?

Pemba, the sister island of Zanzibar, was a choice worse than Dar-es-salaam. Pemba had fewer amenities then Zanzibar. It was a little better than a desert island but not by much. None of the three largest towns in Pemba, Mkoane, Wete, and Chake Chake had a cinema or a cricket pitch. Commuting to Pemba was impossible. The only transportation between the two islands was by a ship that anchored in Pemba once a week.

In my case, paying for board and lodge in Pemba would defeat the purpose of working. If I turned down a position in Pemba, I would automatically disqualify for any post in Zanzibar, now or in the future. The only option then will be working in Dar-es-salaam, which also could not circumvent the expenses of board and lodge.

The odds of getting posted in Zanzibar were discouragingly low. So were the odds of going to school in Britain. I began to wonder if fate was conspiring against me by placing obstacles on my desired path. Perhaps I was destined to study in India.

I applied. The flame of hope for a position in Zanzibar was not bright. It was but a flicker but a flicker never the less.

Abbajaan was on the Board of Directors that assimilated the privately run Sir Euan Smith Madresah, a grade school for Indian students, and all the teachers in that school into the Education Department of His Highnesses Government. The teachers of the Madresah[178] were elated. They now had job security, an increase in pay and a retirement plan. Abbajaan was

---

[178] "School" in Farsi.

their hero. I sensed that as I went through grade school. I was treated with deference by some of the teachers.

Abbajaan learned that one of his students, Saifudin Hassujee, started teaching at the Sir Euan Smith Madresah. Hassujee had trained at the Teachers Training College in Nairobi. Another of Abbajaan's student, Hashim Esmail was a senior at that college and Ibrahim Jaffer who graduated with me from High School, had just left for that college. I believe Saifudin's addition to the staff of the Madresah aroused Abbajaan's curiosity and he looked into the college.

He found out that Zanzibar offered two scholarships a year for Zanzibari's to attend the Teachers Training College. For the year 1951, Ibrahim Jaffer was the sole applicant.

Abbajaan, a math teacher, figured out that if I went to Nairobi for two years, lived at home and worked four years at a much better teacher's salary, by the summer of 1957, I shall have the savings to fund a medical education—in Britain.

A lucky break!

No need to fret about a posting in Pemba. Two years in a college in glamorous Nairobi followed by four years of a challenging job at home in Zanzibar was better than six years of a boring desk job in Zanzibar.

It took me less the five seconds to make up my mind and in less than a week, I was on my way to Nairobi to begin my first semester—three weeks late.

When the day came for me to leave for Dublin to start my medical school, it seemed like I had waited an entire lifetime.

My parents and siblings were on the boat, Breamer Castle, to see me off. My father did not say a word. My mother was unusually quiet. She wanted to avoid the embarrassment of sounding choked up. She was fighting back tears. My siblings were having a great time inspecting my cabin and with excitement explored the luxurious amenities of a top rated passenger ship.

The ships fog horn sounded twice in quick succession. This was a signal for visitors to leave the ship.

As she gave me a departing hug my mother's advice was;

"Conduct yourself in Ireland, the way, you have in Zanzibar."

I was taken aback and thought;

"Thank God. She really does not know of any of the mischiefs I am famous for all over Zanzibar"

She then kissed me on my cheek. That surprised me. Abbajaan gave me a somber hug and said nothing. The envious siblings were light hearted in their goodbyes and hugs. Then my family headed for the gangplank, descended it and stepped into a motorboat, which took them to the wharf.

Every so often, one of them would look back and wave to me and I would wave back to them. As I was doing so, it occurred to me that this was the first time that I can remember my mother kissing me. She kissed all my siblings profusely while they were babies but that gesture of affection stopped when they started walking.

I kept waving and hoping that my mother would turn around and wave at me at least once.

She didn't.

I went to the highest deck of the ship and reclined in a chair as the waves lapped on and gently rocked the anchored ship. There was a breeze blowing from the island. Occasionally, I got a whiff of cloves. Ah! The smell of home. Not due to an early case of homesickness, but because there is a factory next to the wharf which distills clove oil and some of the residual oil leaves the factory's chimney along with smoke and goes where the wind is going.

The Breamer Castle gave its customary departure hoot and pulled up her rattling anchor. Then the engines began rumbling "Thump. Thump. Thump." which made the propellers churn up a wake at the stern and the bow to plough ahead.

The island of Zanzibar is encircled by a coral reef; the way a pearl necklace encircles and shows off a beautiful woman's neck. The water above the reef is quite shallow; in some spots less than 12 inches deep—a great place for snorkeling. Sharks prefer to stay in deep waters, so they remain beyond the reef and away from the shores of Zanzibar. This is why Zanzibari's can swim in the waters around the island without the fear of these predators—a natural safety net that does not exist on the beaches of neighboring Tanganyika and Kenya.

ZANZIBAR

When the Breamer Castle approached that reef, she clanged back her throttle to "Slow." A motorboat which was following us steered to the side of the ship where a rope ladder was thrown overboard. A pilot got off the motor boat and climbed up the ladder. The Breamer Castle then picked up speed and meandered till she was safely out of the coral reef and in the deep unobstructed Indian Ocean.

The ship slowed down once again. The pilot descended the rope ladder and stepped into the following motorboat, which turned around and sped towards Zanzibar, while the Breamer Castle accelerated to a cruise speed and proceeded on course.

A thing of beauty is a joy from every angle. I wanted drink in Zanzibar city's waterfront—perhaps for the last time—from the deck of the departing Breamer Castle.

As I gazed at her, ever so slowly, Zanzibar started sinking into the Indian Ocean. The first to disappear was the Jubilee Garden. This was followed by the Portuguese fort. Then the Sultan's palace and finally my old grade school, the Sir Euan Smith Madrasah. It was surreal. The upper parts of the buildings were clearly discernible but the horizon was slowly rising above the vanishing vista. Even the colossal Bait –el-Ajaib could not fend off the unrelenting onslaught of the steadily rising horizon. That too got swallowed up. Finally, all I could see was the solid red flag of Zanzibar, fluttering away proudly, atop the clock tower of the Beit-el-Ajaib.

The sun was setting as my glistening eyes watched that last symbol of home sink.

I am among those whose cheerful disposition is directly related to sunshine. I enjoy watching sunsets but I experience transient sadness as soon as the sun has set. This sunset, caused a profound sadness as though my grief laden heart had followed the flag to the ocean floor.

It was dusk. The horizon was blank and boring. My mind wandered to the challenges ahead.

Most of those who did not succeed were brilliant enough to win scholarships, but succumbed to homesickness. I empathized with their terror of leaving home and the humiliation of returning a failure.

In a few cases the reason was obvious—lack of motivation and discipline. They were mediocre students at home and worse when abroad. These were children of wealthy parents who went to Europe for a long vacation under the pretext of further education. Several were coerced into medical schools by their parents to follow in their footsteps and to take over their practices upon their return.

Most students who left home for further studies were in their late teens and had never spent a night away from home. Overnight, they woke up in a confusing culture, climate and cuisine.

These students succumbed to the agony of homesickness—the greatest challenge and often the last straw which caused the highest dropout rate in the first semester. The odds of survival improved with each subsequent semester but homesickness never abated.

I heard that College hours kept their minds occupied but the rest of the lonely waking hours were obsessed by thoughts of home. Even the comfort of hearing the voices of family was not available. Long distance calls was a miracle of the future.

Communicating across even a short twenty mile hop between Zanzibar and Dar-es-salaam was by mail only. From Dublin to Zanzibar, the turnaround time was about three weeks. Every semester, a foreign student received a letter with the news of a parent's funeral—which had occurred three weeks before the letter arrived.

About three weeks after responding to a letter from home, students eagerly watched the mailman deliver mail on their streets. He delivered it before students left for college and again in the late afternoon, after they were back from college. The nuisance "junk mail" was not thought of yet. Every letter in the mailbox was worth reading. Most of them were reread several times and with pleasure.

Hearing the door bell and hearing mail drop through the mail slot of the front door was a thrill tinged with apprehension. The apprehension evaporated after reading the following, after the formal salutation;

"By the grace of Allah, we are all well here and hope that you too…………………………."

The desire to spend a summer at home was always there but the cost was exorbitant and the time spent at home disruptive of studies.

BURNING BRIDGES BEHIND YOU.

For medical students, the best opportunity was during the third summer which provided a hiatus between the preclinical and clinical years. Subsequent summers were taken up by stays in hospitals for rotations in Medicine, Surgery and obstetrics.

Those who passed all the exams at first try could hope to go home during the third summer. Those who did not, had to spent that summer studying and repeating those exams and were not able to go home till after they received their Medical degree—a six and a half year wait.

A wait during which engagements, weddings, births and deaths among those close to you will happen and the student abroad will have to celebrate or mourn those events belatedly and in solitude.

One striking segment in the narration of all the premature returnees was that every one of them had a reliable route of retreat. Those who succeeded in achieving their goal did not.

A full-fledged Hindu doctor, who returned home holding his heads high in triumph, put it best;

"The first day in England was hell. It was as though the night before I had died in my bed at home in Zanzibar, walked across the bridge between the here and the hereafter and was reincarnated in a terrifying alien planet. When I turned around for a last look, I saw my funeral pyre engulf the bridge I had just crossed, collapse it with a crash and everything I loved in the world I had left behind was obscured by leaping flames and swirling smoke.

My first impulse was panic and an urge to run back home before it was too late.

But, it was too late.

I had only one choice— keep going. There was no other option. With sadness and reluctance, I kept going.

I engrossed myself in studying and found it to be a great escape from homesickness.

Given enough time, the mind can adapt to any environment—if it has to."

My trend of thought was interrupted by a shiver.

The sun had set and the air turned chilly. My toes and finger tips felt cold. Then, I felt another little shiver.

I was not alarmed.

Even in tropical Zanzibar, this was not an unusual sensation when at sea at dusk. I had experienced it multiple times before while fishing.

I had nothing with me to cover myself with for warmth.

I felt another shiver and then another. I decided to go to my cabin to warm up.

I sat on my bed and waited to get warm.

I felt another shiver.

It does take a while to warm up.

I sat patiently for warmth to return to my body.

A few more minutes went by and my body still felt as though it was just pulled out of an icy pond.

Another shiver shook my body.

I kicked off my shoes, pulled aside the blanket and the top sheet, got into bed and pulled the sheet and the blanket up to my chin.

In about a minute the shiver stopped and I felt my body warming up

A smile of relief crossed my face.

I decided to enjoy the warmth another minute or two.

Then panic struck me.

My skin was flushing, I felt nauseous and feverish. Every muscle in my skeleton ached. Then my head felt as though it was in a band vise that was getting tighter with each heartbeat.

"What the hell?

What a good time to come down with Malaria?"

A Zanzibari is familiar with malaria. It is so common that we do not bother the doctor with it and every home has a bottle of non-prescription quinine to take for it.

I reassured myself with the thought; "I will have a few rotten days but I will be just fine after that."

I decided to skip dinner take two aspirins and go to bed.

Just as I was about to doze off to sleep, I was jolted into sitting up in bed and hyperventilating in panic. It just dawned on me that in the morning, the Breamer Castle will be docking at Mombasa.

MOMBASA?

I will be sick in Mombasa?

Again?

If I am sick in Mombasa, it will not be from just stupid Malaria.

It will be Tuberculosis or something worse.

The ship's doctor will not even hesitate before sticking me in a Mombasa Tuberculosis Sanatorium to spend boring months or perhaps years and then return ignominiously to Zanzibar—vanquished in a war before it was declared.

I am not returning to Zanzibar.

I will not set foot in Zanzibar until I have an MD., after my name.

While in Mombasa, I will act normally. Not even the cabin steward must suspect that I am sick.

If I absolutely have to see the ship's doctor it will be when the ship is in British territorial waters.

Mombasa is just the first siren on my voyage.

There will be more.

I will defeat them as and when they challenge me.

BURNING BRIDGES BEHIND YOU.

But first, I have to defeat Mombasa'

This time I will cheat Mombasa.

Mombasa will not stop me.

Nothing will stop me now.

Nothing.

Nothing.

Nothing.

Epilogue

Descendants of Mustafa Kureshi

Generation 1

1. **MUSTAFA₁ KURESHI** . He married (1) **SUGRA MALIK**.

Mustafa Kureshi and Sugra Malik had the following children:

1.1. MEHBOOB₂ QURESHI. He married (1) DIANE MILLER.

1.2. MEHMOOD KURESHI. He married (1) SABIHA KURESHI.

1.3. MAKBUL KURESHI. He married (1) FATIMA MUKADDUM.

1.4. SAFIA KURESHI. She married (1) SATTAR SHAIKH.

1.5. MOHIYUDIN KURESHI. He married (1) RUKIYA SHAIKH.

1.6. MUNIR QURESHI. He married (1) ZARINA AHMED.

Generation 2

1.1. **MEHBOOB₂ QURESHI** (Mustafa₁ Kureshi). He married (1) **DIANE MILLER**.

Mehboob Qureshi and Diane Miller had the following children:

1.1.1. MUSTAFA₃ QURESHI.

1.1.2. SAFIYUN QURESHI. She married (1) CHRIS MILLER.

1.1.3. SAMEENA QURESHI. She married (1) TIM QUINN.

1.1.4. SHARIFAH QURESHI. She married (1) SAM ENGLISH.

1.2. **MEHMOOD2 KURESHI** (Mustafa1). He married (1) **SABIHA KURESHI**.

Mehmood Kureshi and Sabiha Kureshi had the following children:

1.2.1. SHAHINA3 KURESHI. She married (1) JAWAD WARIS.

1.2.2. MASSOD KURESHI. He married (1) NAZ KURESHI.

1.3. **MAKBUL2 KURESHI** (Mustafa1). He married (1) **FATIMA MUKADDUM**.

Makbul Kureshi and Fatima Mukaddum had the following children:

1.3.1. SAFINA3 KURESHI. She married (1) JOEY SMITH.

1.3.2. MURAD KURESHI.

1.3.3. SORAYA KURESHI. She married (1) MARUF HIDER.

1.3.4. SHEHNAZ KURESHI. She married (1) ROBERT YATES.

1.3.5. MAJID KURESHI. She married (1) KHUSHBU PATEL.

1.4. **SAFIA2 KURESHI** (Mustafa1). She married (1) **SATTAR SHAIKH**.

Sattar Shaikh and Safia Kureshi had the following children:

1.4.1. ASIF3 SHAIKH. He married (1) KAUTHER KAZI.

1.4.2. ARIF SHAIKH. He married (1) FATIMA WAHAB.

1.5. **MOHIYUDIN2 KURESHI** (Mustafa1). He married (1) **RUKIYA SHAIKH**.

EPILOGUE

Mohiyudin Kureshi and Rukiya Shaikh had the following children:

1.5.1. SHAHDIYA$_3$ KURESHI.

1.5.2. FAISAL KURESHI. He married (1) JESSICA NGUYEN.

1.6. **MUNIR$_2$ QURESHI** (Mustafa$_1$ Kureshi). He married (1) **ZARINA AHMED**.

Munir Qureshi and Zarina Ahmed had the following children:

1.6.1. SHEHZAANA$_3$ QURESHI. She married (1) MICHAEL SHRADER.

1.6.2. MUSTAFA QURESHI. He married (1) AMNA KHALID.

Generation 3

1.1.2. **SAFIYUN$_3$ QURESHI** (Mehboob$_2$, Mustafa$_1$ Kureshi). She married (1) **CHRIS MILLER**.

Chris Miller and Safiyun Qureshi had the following children:

1.1.2.1. JAKE$_4$ MILLER.

1.1.2.2. SAM MILLER.

1.1.2.3. MIA QURESHI MILLER.

1.1.3. **SAMEENA$_3$ QURESHI** (Mehboob$_2$, Mustafa$_1$ Kureshi). She married (1) **TIM QUINN**.

Tim Quinn and Sameena Qureshi had the following children:

1.1.3.1. MORGAN$_4$ QUINN.

1.1.3.2. NICK QUINN.

1.1.3.3. LUKE QUINN.

1.2.1. **SHAHINA**$_3$ **KURESHI** (Mehmood$_2$, Mustafa$_1$). She married (1) **JAWAD WARIS**.

Jawad Waris and Shahina Kureshi had the following children:

1.2.1.1. ALEEM$_4$ WARIS.

1.2.1.2. ANISA WARIS.

1.2.1.3. AZIZ WARIS.

1.2.2. **MASSOD**$_3$ **KURESHI** (Mehmood$_2$, Mustafa$_1$). He married (1) **NAZ KURESHI**.

Massod Kureshi and Naz Kureshi had the following children:

1.2.2.1. RIAZ$_4$ KURESHI.

1.2.2.2. RIZWAN KURESHI.

1.2.2.3. ARMAN KURESHI.

1.3.1. **SAFINA**$_3$ **KURESHI** (Makbul$_2$, Mustafa$_1$). She married (1) **JOEY SMITH**.

Joey Smith and Safina Kureshi had the following child:

1.3.1.1. ZAIN$_4$ SMITH.

1.3.4. **SHEHNAZ**$_3$ **KURESHI** (Makbul$_2$, Mustafa$_1$). She married (1) **ROBERT YATES**.

EPILOGUE

Robert Yates and Shehnaz Kureshi had the following child:

1.3.4.1. JACOB$_4$ YATES.

1.5.2. **FAISAL$_3$ KURESHI** (Mohiyudin$_2$, Mustafa$_1$). He married (1) **JESSICA NGUYEN**.

Faisal Kureshi and Jessica Nguyen had the following children:

1.5.2.1. HASSAN$_4$ KURESHI.

1.5.2.2. ZAKARIYA KURESHI.

1.6.1. **SHEHZAANA$_3$ QURESHI** (Munir$_2$, Mustafa$_1$ Kureshi). She married (1) **MICHAEL SHRADER**.

Michael Shrader and Shehzaana Qureshi had the following children:

1.6.1.1. SAMAH$_4$ SHRADER was born in 1950.

1.6.1.2. DEEN SHRADER.

1.6.1.3. ADAM SHRADER.

1.6.1.4. LAITH SHRADER.

1.6.2. **MUSTAFA$_3$ QURESHI** (Munir$_2$, Mustafa$_1$ Kureshi). He married (1) **AMNA KHALID**.

Mustafa Qureshi and Amna Khalid had the following child:

1.6.2.1. KHADIJAH$_4$ QURESHI.

Prepared By:

UNCLE VERNON MILLER . vjmiller15@gmail.com

Made in the USA
Charleston, SC
08 January 2015